I0120576

*Emergent Genders*

*PERVERSE MODERNITIES*
A Series Edited by Jack Halberstam and Lisa Lowe

# EMERGENT GENDERS

Living Otherwise
in Tokyo's Pink Economies

*Michelle H. S. Ho*

DUKE UNIVERSITY PRESS
*Durham and London*
2025

© 2025 DUKE UNIVERSITY PRESS
*All rights reserved*

Project Editor: Bird Williams
Designed by A. Mattson Gallagher
Typeset in Minion Pro by Westchester Publishing Services

Library of Congress Cataloging-in-Publication Data
Names: Ho, Michelle H. S., 1984-[date] author.
Title: Emergent genders : living otherwise in Tokyo's pink
economies / Michelle H. S. Ho.
Other titles: Perverse modernities.
Description: Durham : Duke University Press, 2025. | Series:
Perverse modernities | Includes bibliographical references and
index.
Identifiers: LCCN 2024017838 (print)
LCCN 2024017839 (ebook)
ISBN 9781478031376 (paperback)
ISBN 9781478028123 (hardcover)
ISBN 9781478060338 (ebook)
Subjects: LCSH: Gender identity—Political aspects—Japan.
| Gender identity—Economic aspects—Japan. | Gender
expression—Japan—Tokyo. | Popular culture—Japan—Tokyo.|
Cross-dressing—Japan—Tokyo. | Popular culture and
globalization—Japan. | BISAC: SOCIAL SCIENCE / Ethnic
Studies / Asian Studies | POLITICAL SCIENCE / Globalization
Classification: LCCN HQ1075.5.J3 H57 2025 (print)
LCC HQ1075.5.J3 (ebook)
DCC 305.30952/135—dc23/eng/20240922
LC record available at https://lccn.loc.gov/2024017838
LC ebook record available at https://lccn.loc.gov/2024017839

Cover art: Xavier Portela, *Tokyo Glow—Reality is a manga.*
Photograph courtesy of the artist.

*For those who are living otherwise.*
*This one's for you.*

# CONTENTS

## ACKNOWLEDGMENTS

This book could not have taken form without the voices, insights, and feelings of multiple individuals I have been fortunate to encounter over the past decade or so. I think of this endeavor as a collective one even though only one name will appear on the cover. You have all helped me to write this book as I journeyed through this arduous and wondrous process.

My interlocutors, who appear anonymously throughout this book, are ever present in the stories and in my thoughts as I penned them. Patrons at my field sites, Paradise and Garçon (pseudonyms), have taken me under their wing with an open heart, offering their experiences, connections, and, most of all, friendship. The employees and management of these same establishments have patiently put up with my inquisitive—and at times intrusive—questions alongside their workload, not to mention my scrutiny and regular presence at their workplace. They showed me how living otherwise is vital to their survival. I am honored by the trust they placed in me.

I deeply indebted to Victoria Hesford, who during and since my graduate studies at Stony Brook University (State University of New York) has been a constant source of encouragement for this project as I figured out how to turn it into a book. It was Vicky's unwavering support and belief in me and my work that propelled me to the finish line. My intellectual mentors, Kadji Amin, Anne Allison, Martin F. Manalansan IV, Jack Halberstam, and Kazumi Nagaike, have pushed me to think about the relationship between capital and queer and trans lives in exciting new ways. Kadji's brilliance shaped my thinking around the category of transgender, trans lives, and material inequalities. Anne, Martin, Jack, and Kazumi have been extremely generous with their time during a book manuscript workshop and provided extensive feedback that sharpened the ideas and contribution of this project.

Funding from the Japan Foundation through a Japanese Studies Fellowship afforded me the resources to be based in Tokyo and conduct long-term fieldwork for this project in 2016–17. I thank Shion Fujita in the Japan Foundation's Japanese Studies and Intellectual Exchange Department, who thoughtfully gave me assistance as a fellow. Jason G. Karlin hosted me as a visiting research fellow in the Graduate School of Interdisciplinary Information Studies (GSII), University of Tokyo, which furnished me with institutional resources during my fieldwork year. Since my graduate studies at the University of Tokyo GSII, Jason has shown me the ropes of how to be a scholar. At Wakō University, Ikuko Sugiura kindly allowed me access to precious archival materials collected by the Society of Social History of Transgenderism in Postwar Japan (Sengo nihon "toransujendā" shakaishi kenkyūkai), which I have drawn on to understand the historical context of gender crossing.

A Diversity Predoctoral Fellowship from the School of Humanities, Arts and Social Sciences (SHASS) at the Massachusetts Institute of Technology (MIT) in 2017–18 gave me the uninterrupted time and space I needed to do analysis and writing. While at MIT, Ian Condry and Paul Roquet hosted me as a visiting scholar and predoctoral fellow in Global Studies and Languages. Ian and Paul were wonderful mentors who extended their time and expertise to engage with me and my work.

A dissertation workshop titled "Gender and Sexuality in Japan," organized by the Center for Japanese Studies at the University of California, Berkeley, in 2018, put me into contact with a wonderful community of scholars who provided productive criticisms on my project, particularly Keiko Aiba and Jennifer Prough. An Association for Queer Anthropology (AQA) Diversity Mentoring Workshop in 2018 introduced me to Mary L. Gray, Miranda Joseph, and Tom Boellstorff, who graciously offered guidance on my project.

At the National University of Singapore (NUS), I received funding that supported the project in various ways. A Faculty of Arts and Social Sciences (FASS) Start-Up Grant enabled me to work closely with line and developmental editor Candida Hadley, whose careful reading and thorough editing have led to a more polished manuscript. A FASS-ARI (Asia Research Institute) Book Manuscript Workshop Grant provided the opportunity to be in conversation with experts whose works I have long admired, Anne Allison, Jack Halberstam, Martin F. Manalansan IV, and Kazumi Nagaike. I thank ARI's capable administrators, Sharlene Anthony, Sharon Ong, Minghua Tay, and Valerie Yeo, who aided me in hosting and budgeting for a physical workshop, though we had to shift online due to the pandemic. A FASS Book Grant Scheme furnished the funds for indexing and production costs. A postdoctoral fellowship in the Department of Communications and New Media (CNM) gave me an institutional home to work in while seeking a more permanent position. Colleagues in CNM lent their help when I was struggling with the demands of book writing alongside other roles of service, teaching, and research: Weiyu Zhang, Hichang Cho, and Alicia Kong Wai Cheng. I am especially grateful to Michael J. Basaldella for addressing my pleas each semester to reschedule all my classes to later in the day so I would be able to work on my manuscript every morning.

I have been privileged to be surrounded by an intellectual community of scholars across NUS who are similarly committed to gender and sexuality issues in Asia: Tracey Skelton, Mie Hiramoto, Rebecca Lurie Starr, and Shu Min Yuen. In 2020 the five of us, led by Tracey, cofounded the first Gender and Sexuality Research Cluster (GSRC) at NUS; our FASS-supported seminars and discussions gave my ideas a home to grow from. My writing group, especially Padma Chirumamilla and Renyi Hong, read drafts of early chapters and gave invaluable suggestions for the book to develop. My friends Shobha Avadhani and Jaime Hsu Fang-Tze have mentally and emotionally nourished me with dinners, conversations, and positive energy when things were looking bleak; they have also been among the first to celebrate my accomplishments. This chosen family has shaped this project and my life in profound ways.

Aspects of this book at different stages of the project have been presented at numerous conferences and invited talks and seminars at universities around the world. I would like to thank the following scholars for inviting me to speak, serving as discussants, co-organizing panels with me, offering their friendship, doling out advice on the book process, helping to shape this project, or supporting my work in other ways over the years (my apologies if I missed anyone): Thomas Baudinette, Annisa R. Beta, Evelyn Blackwood, Amy Borovoy, S. P. F. Dale, Chris A. Eng, Patrick W. Galbraith, Sabine Frühstück, Gavin Furukawa, Alexandra Hambleton, Benjamin Hegarty, Yuko Itatsu, Lucetta Y. L. Kam, Thiam Huat Kam, Francisca Yuenki Lai, Heidi K. Lam, Helen Hok-Sze Leung, Eva Cheuk-Yin Li, Wesley Lim, Wen Liu, Ayumi Miyazaki, Yuki Nakayama, Keiko Nishimura, Shunsuke Nozawa,

Tricia Okada, Jahyon Park, Amanda S. Robinson, Ayako Saito, Vivian Shaw, David H. Slater, Carolyn S. Stevens, Kyoko Takeuchi, Akiko Takeyama, E. K. Tan, Jia Tan, Hiromi Tanaka, Denise Tse-Shang Tang, Grace En-Yi Ting, Mattias van Ommen, James Welker, Alvin K. Wong, Tomiko Yoda, Claire Dan-ju Yu, Ting-Fai Yu, and Charlie Yi Zhang.

At Duke University Press (DUP), Elizabeth Ault has been instrumental in shepherding this project and nudging me along as I worked to feel more confident as a writer. I am grateful to her and the team at DUP—Malai Escamilla, A. Mattson Gallagher, Benjamin Kossak, Jes Malitoris, Kim Miller, Chris Robinson, Chad Royal, Olivia Schmitz, Laura Sell, Bird Williams, and H. Lee Willoughby-Harris—for tirelessly working behind the scenes in the publishing process. Elizabeth and her editorial assistant, Benjamin, recruited four perspicacious anonymous reviewers for the manuscript, who have thoroughly engaged with the project and extended generative suggestions to strengthen my arguments and contributions and refine the overall flow and structure of the book, which I believe is now much improved.

This project was sustained by my family in Singapore, who have kept me going across the years. They have weathered many challenges while I pursued an academic career in Japan and the United States. As I worked on this book, our beloved fourteen-year-old furry family member passed away from cancer at the height of the pandemic, leaving us in utter devastation. One of my siblings came out as trans, and as we moved them to Australia to begin a new chapter in their life, I reflected on what publishing this book might mean to them. My partner deserves special gratitude for many years of sacrifices, unconditional love, and an enduring faith in my ability to write this.

# Introduction

*Tracing Emergent Genders*

"I wanted to promote *josō/otoko no ko,*" Hayashi said simply, referring to the phenomenon of male-to-female cross-dressing.[1] I had asked how they had founded Paradise, one of the first *josō/otoko no ko* café-and-bars established in the 2000s in Akihabara, an area in Tokyo renowned among Japanese and non-Japanese people alike for the fandom and consumption of anime, manga, and video games.[2] Hayashi, who was in their late twenties and was tall and lithe, with alabaster skin, delicate features, and long, straight hair—traits often considered the ideal of feminine beauty in Japan—was asexual and practiced *josō* (male-to-female cross-dressing). Together with Miho, Hayashi's business partner, an attractive cisgender bisexual *josō* individual in his early thirties, they had built Paradise from scratch, making ends meet by personally serving customers in the early days.

They were ahead of their time. As entrepreneurs who practiced *josō* in their everyday lives and in this sense had a personal stake in the business, Miho and Hayashi proudly proclaimed to me how they had played a major role in promoting *otoko no ko* (boy/male daughter) over the years. At its nascence, *otoko no ko* was a slang originating in internet culture in the 2000s to refer to two-dimensional *josō* characters in Japanese manga and games.[3] However, its eventual adoption in real life by transgender women and cis heterosexual men alike to designate their *josō* practices complicates how we might understand such categories. Miho and Hayashi, who knew the establishment they owned was driven by profit, leveraged consumers' growing interests in *josō/otoko no ko* to drum up business. In turn, Paradise also inspired young amateurs doing *josō* to market themselves as *otoko no ko*, eventually shaping, as the following chapters show, the same culture that had informed their practices in the first place.

Come nightfall, around the time it opened, the gray five-story building housing Paradise would become shrouded in darkness and, from the outside, was indistinguishable from other bars, cafés, and restaurants (figure I.1). Inside, amid the warm lighting, *otoko no ko* were a feast for the eyes. Mostly in their twenties, they were beautifully made up, with stylish long black, blonde, and brown hair and checkered dresses in various colors and designs. Stefanie, a gorgeous, tanned, full-figured twenty-year-old with long dyed-brown hair, introduced herself using feminine speech and *watashi*, a feminine or gender-neutral first-person pronoun. From the moment I met her, her carefree manner made me feel at ease and comfortable enough to ask her questions about herself—something I realized I could never do at maid cafés, establishments staffed by cis women in costume. I learned that Stefanie identified as *toransujendā* (transgender) and was romantically attracted to cis men. She was also a college student who worked part-time at the café-and-bar. We were deep in conversation when her colleagues joined us and introduced themselves. They wore similar uniforms and, like Stephanie, adopted feminine speech and first-person pronouns and paid special attention to their hair and makeup. Half of Paradise's employees were cis straight men. The other half, like Stefanie, were non-cis and/or nonheterosexual.

Only a few blocks from Paradise was Garçon, a themed establishment staffed by *dansō* (female-to-male cross-dressing) employees. Housed in a nondescript building, one small storefront in a vast sea of maid cafés, high school girl cafés, and shops selling merchandise related to idols, anime, manga, and video games, Garçon was easy for most passersby to miss.[4]

I.1　An alley in Akihabara close to where Paradise and Garçon were located. Courtesy of Xavier Portela, xavierportela.com.

From the outside Garçon could have easily been mistaken for a regular bar. But inside it offered something different. Garçon was narrow in the way many bars in Tokyo are, only slightly more spacious than the tiny bars in the district of Golden Gai.[5] However, its minimalist, windowless interior, lit by subdued orange lights and sheltered in gray curtains, was cozy. It reminded me of being inside a maid café, which aims to block off reality and create an alternative world.[6] But what sets Garçon apart from maid cafés and typical bars is the masculine presentation of employees like Ikki, a visual reminder of their *dansō* practices and the larger female-to-male cross-dressing culture they represent. Ikki, a dashing, willowy twenty-seven-year-old who sported short dyed-blond hair, described himself as *chūsei*, a term meaning "middle sex/gender" and referring to someone who is nonbinary or locates themselves in between genders.

Garçon's main attraction, Ikki told me, was the *kakkōii* (cool/good-looking) *dansō* staff. Glancing at him and his colleagues, who were similarly attired in white dress shirts, black vests, and black pants, I could see what he meant. Hiyori, a handsome twenty-five-year-old employee with tinted hair styled in the latest "mushroom" or bowl cut, resembled an idol from a K-pop (Korean popular music) boy band. I quickly discovered that this resemblance was no coincidence, as Hiyori was a huge fan of boy bands TVXQ and SHINee. Hiyori used *ore*, the strongly masculine first-person pronoun for men, while simultaneously gesturing toward a nonbinary subjectivity using *chūsei* or *musei*, the latter term meaning "no sex/gender" and indexing someone who is asexual or agender. Like Ikki and Hiyori, the majority of Garçon employees located themselves along a continuum of genders and sexualities.

Doubling as Garçon's manager, Ikki was instrumental to the establishment's day-to-day operations, including training new employees and communicating with the owner, Yuka, a cis woman in her early forties. Although Garçon was among the first *dansō* café-and-bars to open and popularize female-to-male cross-dressing in Akihabara, its proliferation of *dansō* seemed almost incidental. Unlike Miho and Hayashi, who claimed to promote *josō/otoko no ko* out of personal interest, Yuka neither practiced *dansō* nor attended to customers as service staff. From all appearances, she regarded Garçon simply as a business.

Despite designating themselves as "café-and-bars," Garçon and Paradise are more like bars than cafés. At both establishments, customers of all genders alternated among eating, smoking, drinking alcohol, playing games, watching anime, bantering with employees and other patrons, and observing all these activities unfold before them.[7] Although offered, food and drinks weren't the main reason for their patronage—which is perhaps understandable given that food and drink prices at both establishments were at least three times those of typical bars or gastropubs in Tokyo. More than one regular customer explained to me that it made economic sense for them to grab a quick meal elsewhere before arriving at the café-and-bar to drink. Rather, conversation, or what my interlocutors called *seken hanashi*, everyday discourses about society and the world, was the prime service employees provided. In time, I would come to know that the majority of customers—60 percent or more—at Paradise were cis men. The reverse was true at Garçon, where 60 percent or more of customers were cis women. Whereas around one in ten customers came to Paradise in *josō*, I was initially disappointed to learn that few customers (around one in twenty) turned up at Garçon in *dansō*. Garçon encouraged interest in *dansō*, and I had assumed that more customers would practice *dansō* themselves. But this was not the case. Most customers at both establishments were bisexual, pansexual, or heterosexual with a minority identifying as transgender or nonbinary.

This book takes us inside the worlds of these *dansō* and *josō/otoko no ko* establishments, two separate kinds of businesses where employees dress as a different gender, which sprang up in Akihabara beginning in the mid-2000s. Their rise was not random; since the 2000s, Akihabara has become synonymous with the culture of otaku, or fans of anime, manga, and games.[8] Many regulars of Garçon and Paradise also considered themselves otaku. That these establishments are located within sites of popular culture consumption like Akihabara instead of Shinjuku Ni-chōme, Tokyo's gay and lesbian neighborhood, is noteworthy, I argue, for initiating new markets for emergent categories of expression and subjectivity to thrive.[9]

Drawing on extensive ethnographic research of Garçon and Paradise, I chronicle the genders that emerged alongside popular culture—including *josō*, *dansō*, and *otoko no ko*—as well as the everyday life experiences of individuals who operated, worked at, and patronized these establishments. Such emergent genders, I contend, find new ways of flourishing in periods of both economic growth and stagnation, launching new markets for self-fashioning and social interactions. This has implications for both queer theory and transgender studies, particularly an assumed white, northern, anglophone trans studies that has overlooked or barely begun to "engage non-Western forms of gendering."[10] My focus on Tokyo decenters the works of scholars who have emphasized the significance of capitalism for trans studies and queer theory and vice versa, complicating current understandings of these trans capitalist and queer capitalist relationships. I posit that looking at gender innovations transnationally offers different answers to the question of how trans and gender nonconforming individuals survive and flourish in a capitalist context.[11]

*Emergent Genders* shows how my interlocutors at Garçon and Paradise contradictorily threaten the hegemonic and all-encompassing discourses of capitalism and embrace the normalizing influence of work, (self-)commodification, and consumer pleasures that risk them being folded into neoliberal regimes.[12] Discourses of "capitalist hegemony" represent the "virtually unquestioned dominance of capitalism," (4), which J. K. Gibson-Graham criticizes in favor of anticapitalist or noncapitalist politics.[13] However, my interlocutors—many of whom locate themselves as trans, nonbinary, or otherwise—resist such representations of capitalism through defying existing categories and innovating diverse genders while simultaneously contingent on these representations for their vernacular innovations.[14] For the editors of *Transgender Marxism*, the relationship between gender and capitalism is one of "mutual dependence."[15] As they put it, "Rather than merely destructive, capitalism is simultaneously productive of affects, attachments, fierce passions, commitments, and hatred."[16] This gives us hope that in precarious Japan, the flourishing of emergent genders in commercial settings may lead to capitalist renewal, giving birth to new forms of capitalism within a perpetual state of crisis.

## Emergent Genders and the Material

Though *josō* and *dansō* emerged in the twenty-first century, gender and sexual variance aren't new to Japan.[17] Indeed, as I detail in chapter 1, warriors and royal family members occasionally engaged in *josō* and *dansō* practices as far back as the late first and third centuries, respectively.[18] In medieval Japan, *josō* and *dansō* as ritual included acolytes in monasteries and women in white tunics performing "male dancing" in the Kyoto court.[19] *Josō* and *dansō* practices have also gained visibility through the professional performances of the *onnagata* (female roles; performers who play women in Kabuki, traditional Japanese theater using an all-male cast) and *otokoyaku* (male roles; performers who play men in the all-women theater group Takarazuka Revue).[20] Today individuals like Ikki, Hiyori, Miho, and Hayashi have innovated based on these older forms to create modern forms of *josō* and *dansō* to express who they are and what they do in the process of becoming.

In this book I coin the term *emergent genders* to point to the ways older forms are fractured, contested, or recuperated but at the same time invigorated, (re)imagined, and embodied by individuals as new gender practices, categories, and ways of being in their everyday lives. The emergent, as Raymond Williams expounds, is not "merely novel," referring to how "new meanings and values, new practices, new relationships and kinds of relationships are continually being created" vis-à-vis existing categories.[21] I follow Teresa de Lauretis in thinking of gender as continuously socially constructed and potentially deconstructed by representations, practices, and theories but always located in and produced through people's material lives and social relations.[22] I use *genders* to accommodate a plurality of genders, building on Michael Peletz's notion of "gender pluralism," which he uses in the early modern Southeast Asian context.[23] In employing *emergent genders* to describe my interlocutors' inventiveness, I demonstrate how their ambiguous, unstable, and incomplete embodiments cannot be disentangled from Tokyo's recessionary contexts.

Emergent genders at spaces like Garçon and Paradise must be understood, I argue, in terms of Japan's long economic recession throughout the 1990s and 2000s—known as the Lost Decade and Lost Twenty Years—after the nation's rapid postwar economic growth and the subsequent bursting of the bubble in the late 1980s.[24] During this time, Japanese people increasingly faced social inequality, employment irregularities, and precarious living conditions. Their situation was due to the gradual collapse of Japan Inc., a socioeconomic order in which job security and productivity were intertwined with stable living conditions at home, thereby prioritizing social collectivism over individual independence.[25] With the breakdown of Japan Inc., the heteronormative family unit—one in which Japan's social, political, and economic institutions were believed to be entrenched—was increasingly dismissed as a viable basis of productivity.

I contend that categories like *josō*, *dansō*, and *otoko no ko* flourished within alternative spaces of work and consumption in recessionary Tokyo because of—not in spite of—the material conditions brought about by economic stagnation. My interlocutors—the owners, employees, and customers of Paradise and Garçon—were able to innovate and negotiate nonnormative forms of sociality and personhood because when normative ways of being have become impossible, other, nonnormative ways of being, such as diverse gender expressions, can emerge as new possibilities. Renewal thus arises through these new modes of living and survival, or living otherwise.

*Emergent Genders* traces the *josō* and *dansō* practices of trans and nonbinary employees like Ikki and Hiyori, the consumption practices of the mostly cis bisexual or heterosexual customers, and the differing investments of owners like Miho, Yuka, and Hayashi. Their narratives illustrate the complex connections among capital, embodiment, popular culture, and gender and sexual subjectivities. In late-capitalist Tokyo, businesses such as Garçon and Paradise and the commercial culture surrounding them both enable new practices, attachments, and modes of sociality and expression to flourish and potentially fold them into the market. While such gender innovations may threaten the "continuity of capitalism," the potential also exists for them to be turned into a "material force" that generates new forms of capitalism.[26] It is this uneven suturing of emergent genders and the material that interests me most.

The material, according to Petrus Liu, has an "unhappy marriage" with queer theory—one he seeks to "rehabilitate."[27] He characterizes the material as "how a subject comes into existence by virtue of its constitutive outside— what cannot be known or named in advance, what necessarily escapes categories of identity politics."[28] Indeed, many of the *josō* and *dansō* individuals I met at Garçon and Paradise didn't align with LGBT (*eru jī bī tī*; lesbian, gay, bisexual, transgender), neither the label, nor its activism, nor the public and scholarly discourses, including in the Japanese context.[29] They didn't find their own experiences reflected there. As I show in chapters 1 and 4, my interlocutors often defied existing gender and sexuality categories altogether, choosing instead to enact new affects, categories, and socialities at *dansō* and *josō/otoko no ko* establishments. Their refusal to adopt extant categories and their insistence on gender and sexual fluidity is one way of destabilizing Japanese society and its notions of productivity structured by heteronormative family and marriage, as I discuss in chapter 2.

How might we begin the work of tracing and retheorizing ways of being and becoming that do not fit neatly into existing categories? Through a tracing of categories like *josō*, *dansō*, and *otoko no ko* that arose within an economically stagnant late-capitalist Tokyo, I argue that rethinking the relationship between emergent genders and the material enables us to challenge identitarian models of gender and sexuality and theoretical frameworks incubated in a predominantly white, anglophone US academic context.[30] Although trans, queer, feminist, and Marxist scholars have underscored the necessity of bringing queer theory and transgender studies to bear on Marxist politics' and vice versa, many remain loath to engage in queer-materialist or trans-materialist critiques—something I take up in the following pages.[31] As Liu posits, this particular impasse is rooted in US-centric identitarian modes of analyzing gender and sexuality.[32] If we were to move away from this to think with theories and experiences from other cultures and languages, we may just find new spaces for queer- and trans-materialist approaches to gender crossing, gender nonconformity, and emerging categories, all of which this book is concerned with.

Articulating a relationship between emergent genders and the material in what might be considered unlikely sites, *dansō* and *josō/otoko no ko* café-and-bars in Tokyo, I find evidence in these establishments, and the practices of *josō* and *dansō* individuals who inhabit them, of the ways genders are innovated alongside popular culture in material worlds. The development of such worlds hinges on gender experimentation with dress, fashion, and other material objects, but this experimentation has material costs. For my interlocutors, the ability to practice *josō* and *dansō* depends on their economic means. Just as corporations have co-opted and exploited certain gender-variant and sexually variant bodies by incorporating them into neoliberal regimes of markets, rights, and recognition, there are costs involved in frequenting businesses like Garçon and Paradise that turn *josō* and *dansō* individuals into profit.[33]

I contend that markets are an important force for the emergence and embodiment of gender categories in Japan. Intervening in the anticapitalist ethos of US-centric queer theory and trans studies, I argue that engaging in materialist approaches to trans and queer issues and adopting trans and queer perspectives toward the material can allow us to see other possibilities for understanding and articulating genders and sexualities.[34] Rather than seeing capitalism simply as a threat, I maintain it is precisely the commodification of *josō*, *dansō*, and *otoko no ko* that has encouraged attachments to them. With a focus on these attachments, *Emergent Genders* follows an empirically grounded materialist feminist approach to draw on ethnographic data, illustrating how my interlocutors—particularly the trans and nonbinary employees whose stories I tell in chapter 4—reinvent themselves.[35] Importantly, to lean on Nat Raha, who asserts trans labor is necessary for sustaining trans lives, *josō* and *dansō* employees can build a world for people like them to survive.[36] As I delineate in chapter 5, with *josō* and *dansō* becoming increasingly commercialized, consumed, and taken up by young amateurs—what I call "contemporary *josō* and *dansō* cultures"—and expanding beyond Akihabara, beauty and fashion turn into tools of survival for trans, queer, and nonbinary individuals.

I think of sites like Paradise and Garçon as "both in and out" and "simultaneously capitalist and noncapitalist"—what Anna Tsing has called *pericapitalist*.[37] This sense of in-betweenness allows us to see past the dichotomy of noncapitalist and capitalist and imagine what it might mean for them to work together. What happens when we venture outside the confines of capitalist logic and seek "multiple ways forward—not just one?"[38] Pericapitalist economic forms enable us to decenter hegemonic and monolithic notions of capitalism in our lives that, as Gibson-Graham describes, present capitalism as singular and homogeneous.[39] Economic diversity, however, allows us to make sense of value, labor, and the marketplace in new ways, edging us toward renewal. Understanding how innovations like *josō*, *dansō*, and *otoko no ko* operate affectively for those who use and feel attached to them makes it possible for us to rethink existing categories and redraw boundaries of gender and sexuality.[40]

## Mapping Queer- and Trans-Materialist Approaches

A vast scholarship rooted within US-centered politics of identity has long examined the intersections between queer theory and Marxism, even when such connections aren't made explicit.[41] Two queer-materialist approaches in this scholarship bear discussion in the Japanese context.[42] First, scholars have shown how LGBTQ (lesbian, gay, bisexual, transgender, queer/questioning) people are situated within economic structures of Western late capitalism.[43] Many gay and lesbian individuals, particularly white upper-middle-class cis gay men in the United States, are increasingly targeted as affluent consumers—creating what some scholars have called the *pink economy, pink capitalism,* or *rainbow capitalism*.[44] Lisa Duggan has criticized this trend as a "new neoliberal sexual politics" or homonormativity.[45]

As I delineate in chapter 1, in Japan the rise of modern capitalism during the postwar period was accompanied by a pre-Stonewall-era flourishing of gay bars and lesbian spaces.[46] But it is only more recently that this has been hailed as an "LGBT market" (*eru jī bī tī ichiba*). During this "LGBT boom," the acronym LGBT became widespread in public discourses, major newspapers, and television programs to discuss gender and sexual minorities (*seitekishōsūsha*).[47] We can see, for instance, the explosion of pride parades and other LGBT events, the introduction of same-sex partnership certificates, and the passing and revision of bills and policies that prohibit LGBT discrimination across the country.[48] After a 2015 survey conducted by global advertising company Dentsū estimated the value of LGBT people's consumption to be JPY 5.94 trillion (USD 54 billion), corporations similarly jumped on the LGBT bandwagon.[49] In the run-up to the 2020 Tokyo Olympics, for instance, there was an upsurge in interest in and consciousness about LGBT issues across mainstream media, corporations, and state-led initiatives.[50]

Despite this, gender and sexual minorities in Japan have regarded the LGBT boom with equal optimism and suspicion. Their everyday lives have not necessarily improved, and as I found among my interlocutors, some feel disinclined to identify as LGBT, even though the media's popularization of LGBT could potentially foster greater public awareness.[51] Their reluctance perhaps stems in part from the way the marketization of LGBT has contradictorily erased and sensationalized gender and sexual minorities. This new interest in LGBT issues has also elicited the occasional conservative backlash.[52] One infamous example is Liberal Democratic Party (LDP) lawmaker Sugita Mio's repudiation of investing taxpayers' money into policies supporting LGBT people, calling the latter "not productive" (*seisansei ga nai*) for not bearing children.[53] This angered gender and sexual minorities and incited many people to rally against Sugita in front of the LDP headquarters; others took to social media to assert that they, too, contribute to the Japanese economy.[54] However, this controversy raises important questions about what productivity means under neoliberal capitalism. Why have questions of productivity surfaced now, as LGBT discourse gains prominence in the Japanese public imagination? Important to my own study are questions about the appeal of *dansō* and *josō/otoko no ko* establishments within this larger framework. What does their existence reveal about shifts in attitudes toward gender and sexuality as well as socioeconomic conditions in Tokyo?

These questions relate to the second queer-materialist approach, in which scholars like John D'Emilio demonstrated how the emergence of nonnormative sexual identities aligned closely with the development of US capitalism at the turn of the twentieth century, when men and women left the heterosexual family-based economy for waged labor in urban areas.[55] More recently, Christopher Chitty intervenes in the unilinear temporality of a Western history of sexuality theorized by Michel Foucault and compels us to rethink this history, contending that sexual relations between men in proto-capitalist economies in seventeenth- and eighteenth-century Europe came about due to capital accumulation and are thus "world-systemic phenomena."[56] Although focused on European homoerotic cultures, Chitty's arguments are useful in the Japanese context because they establish a much longer connection between capitalism and same-gender relations. Also valuable is the work of transnational queer and sexuality studies scholars who have sought to analyze the asymmetrical ways capital produces sexual subjectivities in specific historical, cultural, and geographic contexts.[57] These scholars observe how global discourses of queers' contradictory relationship with the economy operate differently from those in the US context and demand a more complex materialist understanding of this relationship, pointing to the need to look beyond white gay male desires and their modern sexual identities in the purportedly totalizing force of US capitalism.[58]

*Emergent Genders* offers ways to rethink existing queer-materialist approaches by tracing categories that emerged in recessionary Tokyo and the labor of individuals who embrace these categories. Although there has been abundant scholarship on gender and sexual minorities in Japan in the past three decades, this scholarship has rarely considered their economic lives and work experiences. Though there have been some recent studies, primarily in the Japanese language, that pay attention to gender and sexual minorities' class and labor issues via the LGBT market, they are largely quantitative surveys of workplace experiences.[59] As I detail in chapter 2, these studies demonstrate how, despite their waning as a model of productivity, heteronormative family and marriage still persist as a commonsense ideal and continue to structure the workplace.[60] Some of these studies have called for the private sector and the Japanese government to prevent and prohibit employment discrimination against LGBT individuals.[61] Nevertheless, despite these calls and a growing public discourse, perceptions of productivity remain the same. As LDP lawmaker Sugita's criticism of gender and sexual minorities reveals, to be productive necessitates bearing children to ensure the reproduction of the capitalist labor force. My book challenges the idea that gender and sexual minorities either threaten or reinforce existing structures of productivity modeled on heteronormative family and marriage and argues, instead, that the notion of productivity needs to be reconfigured.

*Toward a Transnational Trans-Political Economy Studies*

Dan Irving, Vek Lewis, and numerous other scholars have begun highlighting the importance of political economy approaches for trans studies through trans-political economy (TPE) studies, a subfield of trans studies that stresses the contradictory connections between capitalism and trans oppression and examines trans individuals' experiences of poverty, job discrimination, and access to welfare and other social services.[62] They have shown how, in establishing "proper trans social subjects," trans activists, scholars, and individuals inevitably contribute to their naturalization as legitimate citizens and productive bodies within exploitative labor relations.[63] Notably, trans people continue to be treated as resources for current regimes of capitalist accumulation, contingent on the production, consumption, circulation, and extraction of "trans."[64]

Within a specifically Asian context, fewer works have mapped the explicit connections between trans issues and the economy, although some scholars, such as Peter Jackson and Ara Wilson, engage in what might be considered TPE studies.[65] Jackson contends that capitalism has played a larger role in generating modern Asian trans and queer cultures and identities than scholars previously imagined.[66] "The market has provided a space for the modern Filipino *bakla*, Thai *kathoey*, Indonesian *waria*, and other transgender identities beyond the West to form around the commodification of modern norms of feminine beauty," instead of being rooted in either local premodern genders and sexualities or US-centric queer cultures.[67] While I agree with Jackson and find his arguments insightful, I also follow Wilson in challenging the reductive logic of transnational capitalism by thinking of plural *markets* instead of a singular market.[68]

*Emergent Genders* contributes to transnational TPE research by investigating trans and nonbinary lives and bodies in recessionary Tokyo. I take a critical approach to capitalism's often homogeneous discourse and representation, following Gibson-Graham, who criticizes this "capitalocentrism" and calls for us to think instead of economies as multiple and heterogeneous.[69] Building on this, I explore how emergent genders might differently shape and be shaped by diverse economies through tracing some of these emerging categories, including *josō, dansō, onabe, new half* (*nyūhāfu*; mixed gender), and *x-gender* (*ekkusu jendā*; neither male nor female, or both).[70] Central to this are the looks, bodies, and practices of employees at *dansō* and *josō/otoko no ko* establishments and the ways they not only become monetized but also open up not-yet-imagined ways of being that surpass how we think about gender, economy, and heteronormative productivity.

Here I lean on scholars who have studied themed establishments in Japan like maid cafés, cat cafés, and host clubs and have called for us to understand productivity differently.[71] These scholars have noted, for example, that otaku who frequent maid cafés and regulars of cat cafés have been characterized as deliberately unproductive, whereas hosts at host clubs similarly struggle to define their masculine subjectivity according to Japan Inc.[72] The *dansō* and *josō/otoko no ko* employees and customers I look at either refuse to be productive or have a complicated relationship with productivity, but something important they do share is the search for ways to survive. Of course, patrons and workers at host clubs and cat and maid cafés are also trying to survive in a cis-heteronormative society, but following TPE scholars, the stakes are much higher for the more marginalized *josō* and *dansō* individuals, especially those who are trans and nonbinary. Although by their very existence such *josō* and *dansō* individuals unsettle compulsory heteronormativity, their survival necessitates and drives the formation of new categories and capitalist renewal in which they can flourish without being labeled nonproductive. Many of the stories I tell in this book are about trans and queer survival, ranging from their gender innovations (chapters 1 and 3) and alternative forms of belonging (chapter 2) to labor as a source of pleasure (chapter 4) and commodified looks and styles (chapter 5).

### Affect and Precarity in Neoliberal Times

I arrived in Tokyo intending to study how the prolonged recession and neoliberal restructuring have impacted the day-to-day existence and employment prospects of individuals who visit or work at *josō* and *dansō* establishments. After the Lost Twenty Years and in the wake of neoliberalism, noticeable social, cultural, and economic shifts can still be glimpsed within people's daily lives, well into the twenty-first century. Under neoliberal ideologies in developed parts of East Asia, changes in labor markets and subsequent declines in government support and social spending meant citizens had to assume the responsibility of ensuring job security, notably through constant self-development.[73] For instance, under neoliberal restructuring, workers in Japan were rendered "free" to succeed or fail and to sell their labor to whomever they chose and, as a result, were frequently uninspired by their work and exploited for their cheap labor.[74] This may be a far cry from the lifetime employment system—guaranteed employment for a minority of "salaryman" (sararīman), or male white-collar office workers during their working life—but flexible work has long been women's experience of work.[75] As Anne Allison illustrates in *Precarious Japan*, many in Japan experience multiple and overlapping precarities, not only in work but also within their everyday lives and relationships with other people.

This was true for the majority of my interlocutors, many of whom, whether employees or customers, held irregular, part-time, and temporary jobs. Yet, when I asked if they felt uneasy (*fuan*) about the recession or worried about the future due to diminishing employment prospects, they often focused on the present and the positive aspects of their jobs. I wondered if my interlocutors, like many patrons and workers at host clubs and cat and maid cafés, normalized precarity.[76] Perhaps they regarded flexible work in terms of individual freedom and an independent lifestyle, deriving these neoliberal ideals from the structural reform (*kōzō kaikaku*) policy introduced in 2002 to tackle the economic slowdown. This policy proposed new measures to accommodate diverse working styles, such as flexible employment independent of age or gender, the ability to switch jobs more easily, and increased opportunities for professional training.[77]

Over the months, however, I came to understand that my interlocutors' optimism was built not on ideals of flexibility but rather on their personal attachments to *josō* and *dansō* and to one another. Instead of understanding their contingent labor and living conditions solely as precarious—from a singular hegemonic capitalist perspective—we might instead imagine, from pericapitalist perspectives, that they attained compensation in different (not necessarily monetary) forms.[78] Among trans and nonbinary employees like Ikki and Hiyori, most saw their care work as more than just an underpaid job, as labor that enabled them to live otherwise through their *josō* and *dansō* practices—something I take up in chapter 4.

The operation of affect, emotion, and intimacy within advanced economies is complex, but leaning on Eva Illouz and Viviana Zelizer, I think of emotion, intimacy, and economy as shaping and being shaped by one another, entangled in ways that structure our everyday lives.[79] For Lauren Berlant, the emotion-economy relationship is complicated by how people's ordinary lives are affectively impacted by capitalism.[80] Through this lens we might begin to see why some customers cultivate intimate bonds with employees and fellow patrons at Garçon and Paradise as a means of surviving life in the outside world. *Dansō* and *josō/otoko no ko* establishments in Tokyo are interesting case studies because they manifest both pericapitalist possibilities and inextricable connections between emotion, economy, and the emergence and circulation of genders.

It bears asking, then, why emergent genders have come out of neoliberal and recessionary Tokyo. Is there something special about the Japanese economy that allows them to materialize? Are there instances when they might be inhibited? Economists and political scientists have written about the Japanese economy as distinct from the Anglo-American model in terms of its Asian developmentalist state model of capitalism, cultural and institutional differences, and companyism—an agreement predicated on labor-management compromise and job security, namely, lifetime employment.[81] Based on these studies, it would appear that the Japanese economy functions to sustain heteronormative family and marriage—something I discuss in chapter 2—instead of encouraging the emergence of diverse genders.

Yet, with a dwindling number of lifetime employees and a rise in flexible workers, such shifts in employment, masculinity, and social class may spur on alternative ways of living, being, and coupling. For example, as I discuss with regard to the documentary film *Shinjuku Boys* (Kim Longinotto and Jano Williams, 1995) in chapter 2, young cis women who gained employment through the flexible workforce in the 1990s were apparently free to patronize *onabe* clubs—establishments staffed by *onabe*, masculine-presenting employees who were assigned female at birth—and date the employees there instead of conforming to social expectations to marry (heterosexually) and start a family.[82] Although *onabe* clubs are located in Shinjuku and distinct from the contemporary *dansō* café-and-bars I explore in Akihabara, there are notable overlaps between these two kinds of establishments, such as categorial innovation and the ensuing booms and boom-based economies. It is this productive tension between emergent genders and the material that this book seeks to illuminate.

## Booms in Japan

Japan has been called a "boom-based society" for its series of intellectual booms, which come in rapid succession and "artificially creat[e] a new difference" each time.[83] In mainstream media, booms are seen as contingent on the mass commodification of difference. While not unique to gender and sexuality, the idea of booms is useful for thinking through the connections between categorial innovation and Japanese media and popular culture.[84] In chapter 1, I trace the historical trajectory of queer and trans booms in Japan, but one example is a pre-Stonewall gay boom during the late 1950s and 1960s, when young Japanese men frequented taverns and coffee shops to seek (sexual) companions, leading to heightened magazine coverage on the *gay boy* (*gei bōi*)—a category of effeminate gay male entertainers—and a subsequent gay boy boom.[85] This succession of one boom after another is characteristic of boom-based cultures.

Much has been written about the relationship between booms and subcultures in Japan and elsewhere, and these scholars have drawn on Dick Hebdige, who argues that while youth subcultures in postwar Britain are subversive and resist hegemonic norms through style, they eventually become commodified, repackaged, and resold to mainstream consumers.[86] For instance, in the 2000s the otaku or manga/anime subculture became "normalized and nationalized in Japan" as a boom.[87] Since the postwar period, Akihabara, where the *dansō* and *josō/otoko no ko* café-and-bars I study are located, has been a hub for the mass consumption of household electric appliances and personal electronic goods like computers and game consoles. However, it was only in the 2000s that Akihabara turned into a site for popular media and culture. These otaku and Akihabara booms are tied to "Cool Japan," the state promotion of the nation as a "cultural superpower" as well as a marketing strategy by content industries through the global spread of popular cultural elements, such as anime, music, and fashion.[88] Cool Japan aligns with Joseph Nye's notion of "soft power," a nation's influence over other countries through its culture, policies, and political ideals instead of force.[89] The circulation of anime products, for example, is aimed at "inspiring desires in global consumers for something Japanese."[90]

Churning out profit through mainstreaming is a vital aspect of booms in Japan. In economic terms, the word *boom* means a high-growth period, such as a rise in business sales and economic output for the nation and its gross domestic product (GDP). The 2010s LGBT boom I described earlier indexes not only the state, media, and corporations visibly taking up LGBT but also the profit gains, consumption, and expanding markets related to this uptake. Such recurring booms appear responsible for encouraging increased consumer spending, rather than enacting any kind of longer-lasting social change, despite the promise of heralding change. Given all of this, the LGBT boom might not be considered entirely novel; perhaps it merely rebranded old ideas as new.[91] This raises the question of whether there is anything inherently innovative about the gender categories I trace in this book. Could they instead simply be explained as recurrent fads, situated in the logics of boom-based economies?

To answer this question, it may help to consider the 2000s otaku and Akihabara booms but this time from consumers' perspectives. Otaku include women, but the majority are men who are "engaged in intimate interactions and relations with manga/anime characters."[92] Although booms shape fans' consumption of anime, manga, and game characters, fans, too, animate the orbit of boom-based cultures.[93] As Mark McLelland points out, consumers play an important role in how they use, access, (re)interpret, and (re) distribute such cultural content—outcomes that may be unintended by the government and content industries.[94] *Josō* and *dansō* individuals' creative consumption—what I call contemporary *josō* and *dansō* cultures and delineate in chapter 3—within the fertile environment of Akihabara demonstrates a different kind of innovation. These individuals' gender-crossing practices trouble Cool Japan's masculinist production and proliferation by male elites and academics for predominantly male otaku, which, as Laura Miller argues, operate to sustain "structures of gender stratification" in Japanese society.[95] They also turn Akihabara into an unexpected site for emergent genders.

For example, extending from their consumption of two-dimensional *otoko no ko* characters in anime, manga, and games, customers and employees alike affectively regard real-life *otoko no ko*. Capitalizing on these desires, the owners of Paradise encouraged customers' increased consumption of and employees' promotion of themselves as *josōko* and *otoko no ko*.[96] The owners' embrace of *otoko no ko* in the real world generated much backlash among otaku who only acknowledge two-dimensional *otoko no ko* existing within game and manga worlds—something I detail in chapters 1 and 3— but despite this, Paradise's employees and customers would go on to shape the game, manga, and internet culture that has informed their practices and consumption. We might think of these productive flows among *josō*, *otoko no ko*, dimensions, and establishments as multidirectional instead of unidirectional.

Far from merely subsuming subcultures under capitalism, as some scholars have contended, booms are a result of continuous coproduction and co-consumption of media, cultures, and communities. They tap into consumers for their contribution while also depending on entrepreneurs like Paradise's and Garçon's owners to initiate the next new thing. The differing investments of owners, employees, and customers all point toward a world where the material unevenly sutures with emergent genders. I find evidence of this in contemporary *josō* and *dansō* cultures at their height in the late 2000s (first wave) and later, when they became more mainstream in the 2010s (second wave). As I limn in chapters 3 and 5, these two waves show how *dansō* and *josō/otoko no ko* establishments are pericapitalist: they are simultaneously sites of resistance and sites of monetized consumption.

## The Politics of Naming Genders

In this book, while I employ certain categories to discuss gender-variant and sexually variant individuals, what they mean and who gets to use them are highly contested, even among those who adopt these terms to describe themselves. Because categories of gender and sexuality are socially constructed and embedded in history and politics, they are never neutral, and our existing vocabulary can fail to accurately express people's diverse genders and sexualities.[97] For *Emergent Genders*, this is compounded by the issue of translating Japanese terms and categories into English for the purposes of publishing in English. For instance, while *toransujendā* (a transliteration of *transgender*) appears to derive solely from, and signals meanings familiar in, the US context, it is located specifically in the Japanese context. Because of this, it is vital I lay out my use of *queer*, its transliteration (*kuia*), LGBT, *trans*, *transgender*, *toransujendā*, and locally specific terms to index emergent genders, including *josō*, *dansō*, and *x-gender*. I pay attention to how these categories may (dis)empower individuals in specific contexts while also being mindful of how they are used within North American queer and trans studies. Throughout my work, I follow the terms and categories my interlocutors used to describe themselves.

### Queer/Kuia

Following Eve Kosofsky Sedgwick, who emphasizes the messiness and social construction of gender and sexuality, I use *queer* as an analytical tool rather than an identity or umbrella term.[98] *Kuia* (a transliteration of *queer*) first came to Japan in the mid-1990s during the "*kuia* movement." Since then, *kuia* has been used primarily among literary and academic circles, not so much in Japanese people's everyday lives.[99] This stresses the importance of bringing theoretical frameworks primarily rooted in US discourse and scholarship published in English into conversation with locally specific terms and their sociocultural context. The gap between academics and gender and sexual minorities can be seen in their (non)employment of LGBT today. During the LGBT boom, academics, activists, corporations, and conservative critics alike increasingly used *LGBT* to advance their respective agendas. Among gender and sexual minorities, however, there has been a refusal to adopt the label, as a form of resistance to the co-optation of gender and sexual diversity.[100]

## Transgender/*Toransujendā*

Gender and sexuality minorities' relationship to *trans* and *transgender* is difficult to articulate and complicated by the aforementioned issues that plague *queer* and *LGBT* as well as intracommunity divisions. The latter was noted by trans activist Mitsuhashi Junko, who, in an interview with gay activist Fushimi Noriaki, remarked on the more vulnerable position of trans people as compared to privileged gay men.[101] *Toransujendā* emerged around the same time as *kuia* and Japan's legalization of sex/gender reassignment surgery (SGRS) in 1996.[102] Following Susan Stryker's broad definition of *transgender* as "people who move away from the gender they were assigned at birth, people who cross over (*trans-*) the boundaries constructed by their culture to define and contain that gender," I note that individuals' moving away and crossing over need not align with the male/female binary.[103] They may identify as nonbinary gender, for example, as in the case of *x-gender*. Likewise, not all nonbinary individuals may identify as trans; they may refuse the categories of cis and binary transgender (i.e., trans man or trans woman) or identify as gender nonconforming.

In Japan as elsewhere, legal and medical discourses of trans people often prescribe gender binarism, resulting in individuals having "mismatched corporeality" and desiring to "fix" their bodies.[104] For example, *seidōitsuseishōgai*, the Japanese translation of *gender identity disorder* (GID), entered common parlance after the Act on Special Cases in Handling Gender Status for Persons with Gender Identity Disorder (*Seidōitsuseishōgai-sha no seibetsu no toriatsukai no tokurei ni kansuru hōritsu*; GID Act for short) was implemented in 2003. The GID Act allowed individuals medically diagnosed with *seidōitsuseishōgai* to legally change their gender in the family registry after fulfilling many criteria.[105] Unfortunately, this medicalized discourse has led to the pathologization of trans people.[106]

## X-Gender

At its inception in the late 1990s, *x-gender* was a reaction to the pathologizing discourses of GID and SGRS—a history I expand on in chapter 1.[107] *X-gender* refers to a gender that is "neither male nor female, or, depending on the definition, both."[108] For instance, individuals would refer to themselves as FTX (female-to-X), MTX (male-to-X), or XTX (in the case of those who do not identify with any gender), following from FTM (female-to-male) and MTF (male-to-female), which are often used by trans people in Japan to describe themselves.[109] *X-gender* seems to resemble *genderqueer*, but based on S. P. F. Dale's historiography of *x-gender*, it may be more accurate to say *x-gender* emerged in Japan around the same time that *genderqueer* did in the United States.[110] None of my interlocutors ever used *genderqueer*, however.

Josō/Dansō

In Japanese the term *josō* (女装) denotes the wearing of women's clothes or adopting a feminine appearance, and *dansō* (男装) indexes a masculine appearance or being adorned in male attire. In this book *josō* and *dansō* refer mainly to male-to-female cross-dressing and female-to-male cross-dressing, respectively, which corresponds with how my interlocutors employed them. Depending on the individual, *josō* and *dansō* might be understood simultaneously as adjectives to describe a person and as labels for their practice, identity, or way of being.[111] Moreover, as I observed with my interlocutors, individuals may disagree about what for them constitutes *josō* and *dansō* and where to draw the lines between *josō* and non-*josō* and between *dansō* and non-*dansō*. In the twenty-first century, *dansō* has also undergone various shifts with individuals being alternately known as *dansō-san* (female-to-male cross-dressing individuals), *dansō joshi* (female-to-male cross-dressing girls), and *ikemen joshi* (handsome girls).[112] Except in cases where I want to bring attention to specific terms my interlocutors used, I use *dansō* throughout to refer to them. Likewise, as my interlocutors used *josōko*, *otoko no ko*, and *josō danshi* (boys) interchangeably, I use *josō* throughout to refer to them.[113]

*Identitarian Discourse and Common Sense–Inflected Morality*

Many studies about the LGBTQ community in Japan have employed human rights and medicalized discourses modeled after scholarship in the United States, emphasizing coming out, queer activism, and LGBTQ social movements as starting points for determining nonnormative identities.[114] Such discourses have significantly impacted demands for legal recognition, social support, and health care access for trans and queer people, but they nevertheless hinge on identitarian notions of gender and sexuality. By focusing exclusively on identitarian categories, we risk losing sight of the individual bodies, practices, and experiences, which may not fit into predetermined categories, particularly in non-anglophone contexts where they do not easily translate.[115]

One example of this untranslatability is *otoko no ko*. Although it refers to male-to-female cross-dressing individuals, it is written with the characters 男の娘 (boy/male daughter) and, when spoken, is a pun for "boy."[116] Such nuances, which showcase the category's creative propensity for ambiguous embodiments, are lost when *otoko no ko* is translated into English. Moreover, starting with one's identity (who one is) instead of one's practices (what one does) may fail to encompass overlaps between gender and sexual variance, which are prevalent in many Asian contexts.[117] For instance, under the sign *dansō*, individuals of all genders and sexualities practice female-to-male cross-dressing. Such diverse individuals as Ikki and Hiyori are bound not by their gender identity or sexual orientation but by their practices of *dansō*.

In Japan genders and sexualities diversified in ways not tied to the liberal politics of inclusion that arose as a reaction to religious moral condemnation. Homosexuality has never been criminalized in Japan nor subject to religious stigmatization, unlike in the United States, where Judeo-Christian beliefs prevail.[118] Japan's two major religions, Shintoism and Buddhism, at best sanction same-gender sexuality and at worst are indifferent to it.[119] This does not mean there is no discrimination against gender and sexual minorities in Japan, only that it is structured by a morality tied neither to legal nor to Judeo-Christian religious discourses. Wim Lunsing contends that common sense (*jōshiki*) as an organizing principle frames how Japanese people perceive constructions of gender and sexuality, including how they are socially expected to behave and judged to fit into these constructions.[120] One example of common sense–inflected morality he discusses is (heterosexual) marriage. Between the 1950s and 1980s, it was considered common sense for people in Japan to be married, and many did; those who did not, such as gay and lesbian people and feminist women, ostensibly operated outside these naturalized ideas.[121] At this time, perspectives on marriage in Japan were similar to those in Britain and the United States.[122] However, that they were not based on Judeo-Christian beliefs means Japan's trans and queer economies function differently. Likewise, our approaches to thinking about emergent genders and the material must be different as well.

To rethink the relationship between emergent genders and the material, we need to first interrogate "*common processes* that affected both Asian and Western sexual cultures."[123] Such an interrogation aligns with scholars who have proposed rethinking "queer Asia" as method or critique as a means of reconfiguring queer and Asian knowledge production.[124] Drawing on Kuan-Hsing Chen's notion of "Asia as method," this reconfiguration aims to recenter frameworks and approaches from within Asia and reassemble Asian societies, subjectivities, and meeting points.[125] This can be done by reconceptualizing "Asia" as nonstatic, displacing queer theory's US-centric biases, and reconstructing queer as key to doing research on Asia.[126]

## Roles and Methods

My positionality as a non-Japanese, non-transgender Asian woman and transnational feminist and queer studies scholar educated in the United States played a major role in my gathering, organizing, interpreting, and reconstructing of the data for *Emergent Genders*. I was always acutely aware of my own submersion in US-centric liberal-pluralist ideology and its identitarian models, suffused as they are within mainstream queer theory, and how this would frame the stories I would tell. My research was primarily ethnographic, consisting of interviews, field notes, participant observation, and close analysis of these field data using interdisciplinary queer and feminist approaches. I join qualitative researchers from anthropology, cultural studies, communication, and gender and sexuality studies in recognizing myself as a "research instrument" with one subjective voice among many.[127]

This book is based on fourteen months of field research in Tokyo. I made three early field visits in 2014 and 2015, each lasting a few weeks. In 2016–17 I carried out long-term fieldwork, living in a city close to Akihabara, my main field site. A few shorter trips scheduled for 2020 were derailed when the coronavirus pandemic struck, bringing on a series of lockdowns and travel restrictions. My data therefore reflect a prepandemic world. I observed the everyday comings and goings at Garçon and Paradise, among the first *dansō* and *josō/ otoko no ko* café-and-bars to open in Akihabara. Because I spent copious amounts of time and money at these two establishments, the relationships I established mirrored those between employees and regular customers, and I found myself relating easily to regulars. At Garçon and Paradise, I always paid my own way, at times buying drinks for employees and occasionally fellow customers in lieu of gifts and money—standard practices in ethnography. I approached employees and fellow patrons directly after forming relationships with them. I conducted semistructured interviews with owners, employees, and a sampling of new, regular, and occasional customers, learning about their perspectives on their *josō* and *dansō* practices, feelings toward gender-crossing culture, and experiences of working at and/or frequenting the café-and-bars.

Initially, as a newcomer to Garçon and Paradise, I was pegged as an outsider. Although my interlocutors knew of my intentions, some remained suspicious I was secretly with an authority that could report them. Although *josō* and *dansō* establishments weren't illegal—something I discuss in chapter 2—I quickly realized anonymity was a serious concern among my interlocutors, most of whom used *adana* (nicknames; pseudonyms). For this reason, Garçon, Paradise, and all names—including *adana*—of interlocutors in this book are pseudonyms, though insiders may be able to guess my field sites.

After several weeks and months frequenting Garçon and Paradise, sometimes multiple times a week and with each visit amounting to two to three hours and setting me back on average JPY 3,000–5,000 (USD 27–45.50), I realized the employees and other patrons had gradually warmed up to me.[128] Friends I brought to the establishments noticed how warmly I was welcomed. I was fast assuming the role of a regular who introduced more customers as a way to help promote these establishments. While all customers were invited to special events like Halloween and Valentine's Day and routine employee birthday celebrations at the café-and-bars, I began to receive invitations to occasional activities hosted outside the establishments, such as Paradise's annual summer barbecue and Garçon's tenth-anniversary party.

In hindsight, I realized a combination of factors may have enabled me to blend into the Garçon and Paradise crowd more easily. Because I visited frequently and because I paid in full for my patronage, my interlocutors approached me more like a regular than a researcher, although they never completely forgot my role as a researcher. Being able to speak Japanese fluently was helpful, as the majority of my interlocutors did not speak a second language. In addition, from my interlocutors' perspective, I did not look unfamiliar—I was sometimes told I didn't feel out of place (*iwakan ga nai*). Perhaps my fair complexion visibly registered as the pale "white" skin tone Japanese people are imagined to have and base their racial identity on, even though they knew I wasn't Japanese.[129] At Garçon, my boyish figure and cropped dyed-brown hair were read as androgynous and visually similar to the employees and customers who practiced *dansō*. This may have encouraged some of my interlocutors to trust me and open up during interviews. Moreover, conversation is the main service of these establishments, which was tremendously helpful for me as I approached them.

However, the same factors that allowed me to be inconspicuous at Garçon made me conspicuous at Paradise. For instance, my short hairstyle, lack of makeup, and casual ensemble of T-shirt and slacks rendered me out of place at Paradise, where the employees and customers who practiced *josō* prided themselves on skillfully applying makeup, wearing their hair long, and modeling the latest fashion. To navigate this minefield, I alternated between my role as a researcher and that of a customer seeking their advice on makeup, hairstyles, and feminine fashion. In the latter, I followed the cue of cis women customers, some of whom were romantically attracted to *josō* individuals, and *josō* patrons who sought companionship and information from like-minded people. My status as an English-speaking foreigner conferred certain privileges and, unexpectedly, facilitated a different role for me in the establishment: an interpreter.[130] I was occasionally roped into attending to non-Japanese tourists who visited Paradise and were unable to speak Japanese. As an unpaid intermediary between employees and foreign customers, I had the opportunity to closely observe these exchanges and bond with employees over the struggles of caring for first-time customers.

To get a broader sense of contemporary *josō* and *dansō* cultures, I also visited other *dansō* and *josō/otoko no ko* establishments and *new half* bars scattered across Ueno, Nakano, Ikebukuro, Akihabara, and the larger Shinjuku area. By my estimate, the number of *dansō* and *josō/otoko no ko* establishments was half or less that of maid or cat cafés.[131] I also attended events organized by or catering to *josō* and *dansō* individuals.[132] Collectively, this hodgepodge of bars, clubs, events, and businesses designated as *josō* and *dansō* make up the *josō* and *dansō* business circles ( *gyōkai*), respectively. The term *gyōkai* is apt for capturing the *josō* and *dansō* commercial scenes and multiple social networks—as opposed to a singular network—of individuals engaged in the ebb and flow of *josō* and *dansō*. While I visited a wide variety of establishments, my deep dive into Garçon and Paradise means my research has a particular focus on young urban individuals interested or engaging in gender crossing and may not be representative of Tokyo's wider *josō* and *dansō* business circles.

## Overview

This book situates emergent genders within Japan's economy as it experiences periods of growth and stagnation. From inside two establishments, Garçon and Paradise, I analyze how the owners, employees, and customers make sense of their work, practices, sociality, and consumption under pericapitalist modes and the roles they play in driving and sustaining categorial innovation. Focusing on what my trans and gender nonconforming interlocutors *do* and how they survive, flourish, and reinvent themselves in spaces that are at once capitalist and noncapitalist, I unsettle North American anglophone queer theory and trans studies.

Chapter 1 begins by examining emergent genders in the historical context of Japan, drawing on the documentary *Shinjuku Boys*. Taking a genealogical approach, I explore how these configurations of gender and sexuality have been foundational to current categories and have also figured complexly within them.[133] Turning to categories like *new half, onabe*, and *x-gender*, I trace the forces behind their emergence during and after the bubble economy. Connecting these categories to my ethnographic data, I show how contemporary categories are complicated by my interlocutors' individualistic practices and understandings. I argue that those pushing for these categorial innovations cannot be neatly contained within identitarian notions of articulating gender and sexuality.

Chapter 2 articulates the relationship between capitalism and the cis-heteronormative home, family, and marriage in the Japanese context and the ways in which Paradise and Garçon as profit-making businesses figure within this relationship. I use a gender lens to explore capitalist development in Japan and the gradual departure from commonsense expectations of marriage and family while also demonstrating how the cis-heteronormative home lingers in the Japanese imaginary. Telling the stories of Paradise's and Garçon's births in Akihabara, I also investigate the café-and-bars' (dis)connections to Japanese sex and night entertainment through what I call *pink economies*, or wider networks of production, consumption, and circulation of goods and services related to how sex, gender, and sexuality have been commodified in both heteronormative and nonnormative sites since the postwar period.[134]

Mapping the rise of *josō, dansō*, and *otoko no ko* since the 2000s, chapter 3 shifts to Akihabara as an important, if unexpected, site for new categories and nonnormative practices to emerge. Although its pink economies are different from those discussed in chapter 2, Akihabara remains a fertile environment for young amateurs' heightened practices, consumption, and commercialization of *josō* and *dansō*—what I call contemporary *josō* and *dansō* cultures. Drawing on conversations with my interlocutors, I posit that their gender innovation was facilitated by Akihabara's pericapitalist material conditions in the mid-2000s through an array of media, services, and establishments by and for *josō* and *dansō* individuals.

Chapter 4 turns to the employees of Garçon and Paradise and the ways their (im)material labor produces and sustains emergent categories of *dansō*, *josō*, and *otoko no ko*. Telling some of their stories, I contend it is not a simple case of labor exploitation, although it is potentially exploitative, with most employees working on a part-time basis; rather, focusing on the experiences of employees who locate themselves variously as trans and nonbinary, I show how, for them, work is more than just work. While Garçon's and Paradise's employees were hired precisely for their capacity to promote *dansō*, *josō*, and *otoko no ko*, they also capitalized on these same categories to strategically position themselves and negotiate their relationships with other people.

Chapter 5 builds on people's consumption at Garçon and Paradise, focusing on style, beauty, and *body work*—the work individuals do on their or other people's bodies.[135] Unlike the first wave of contemporary *josō* and *dansō* cultures, discussed in chapter 3, in the second wave, *josō* and *dansō* practices became more mainstream and embedded in beauty and fashion. How do these embodied modes of consumption offer new ways to think about gender innovation throughout the 2010s? I contend that my interlocutors' co-consumption—the act of consuming together—of fashion, beauty, and popular cultures motivates and sustains the production and circulation of emergent genders and enables the generation of diverse class, sexual, and gender subjectivities under "nonhegemonic formations" of societies and economies.[136]

In the coda, I reiterate the book's central argument that not only are emerging practices, attachments, and modes of sociality and expression potentially enabled by markets, they can also become a material force for generating new forms of capitalism. One of the key takeaways I offer to the reader is the need to reconfigure how we currently understand structures of productivity and to rethink US-centric identitarian models of gender and sexuality, particularly in Asian contexts. I reflect on why emergent genders and living otherwise remain important to think about amid multiple crises around the world stemming from the coronavirus pandemic.[137] These ways of living, dubbed the *new normal*, are characterized by the uncertainty of new rules, mindsets, and behaviors, including movement restrictions and limited or no interactions with other people in everyday life. But what does this mean for the future of my interlocutors and their gender innovation and the survival of *dansō* and *josō/otoko no ko* establishments? Thinking through these questions from the perspectives of gender-variant and sexually variant individuals, I gesture toward new ways of engaging with the material in a (post)pandemic era.

# 1

Categories That Bind

*Gender Innovations and Their*
*Sticky Relations to Capital*

"You think of yourself as a man, don't you?"[1] A young cisgender woman with long, straight black hair poses this question to a masculine-presenting individual named Gaish in a tête-à-tête in a bedroom. "Do you think so? What do you think of yourself as?" repeats the woman, turning to Gaish, who is propped up on the bed where she sits. Gaish has a short curtain hairstyle and wears baggy blue jeans and a loose long-sleeve plaid shirt over a white T-shirt.

"Me (*ore*)? I don't think anything," Gaish replies, looking slightly confused. "I'm just me (*ore wa ore dakara*). I'm not bothered about it," Gaish says coolly and continues, "I don't think I'm a girl (*onna no ko*) and I don't think I'm a boy (*otoko no ko*)."

The woman cracks a joke about how Gaish's personality is so bad Gaish would be better off as a man.

"There are all kinds of *onabe*," Gaish declares, looking at the bed instead of the woman's face. Gaish, who prefers to be thought of as "in-between" (*chūkan-teki*), explains they do not feel like a woman and cannot become "more feminine," nor do they want to undergo hormone replacement therapy to become "a real man."

This bedroom scene between Gaish and their customer raises several questions: Why must Gaish be either a man or a woman and not an in-between? Given Gaish's rejection of both "man" and "woman," why does the category *onabe* remain useful for them, and how does it challenge other gender categories? *Onabe* means "shallow pan" in Japanese and is slang for "nonfemale" individuals or those assigned female at birth who are masculine-presenting and are romantically and sexually attracted to women.[2] This scene is from the award-winning documentary *Shinjuku Boys* (1995), by British filmmakers Kim Longinotto and Jano Williams, which shadows three *onabe*—including Gaish—as they go about their everyday lives and work at an *onabe* bar known as Marilyn (figure 1.1).

Though *Shinjuku Boys* takes place in Kabukichō, an entertainment and red-light district in Tokyo's Shinjuku area catering mainly to straight people, rather than the pop cultural hub Akihabara, where Paradise and Garçon are found, this film is a valuable resource for this book because it is one of the few documentaries on *onabe* and *onabe* bars in Japan, especially in the 1990s. As scholars like Jack Halberstam have long argued, trans masculine individuals have significantly less media representation and are the focus of less academic scholarship than trans feminine individuals.[3] This is no different in Japan, which is reflected in the more extensive research on *josō* individuals, such as Mitsuhashi Junko's *Josō to nihonjin* (Male-to-female cross-dressing and Japanese people), a historical account of *josō* based on her ethnography of working as a *josō* hostess at a bar in Kabukichō in the 1990s. *Shinjuku Boys* has been vital for making visible the experiences and perspectives of *dansō* and trans masculine individuals. Scenes and images from *Shinjuku Boys* pop up in *Emergent Genders* sporadically as a visual and textual reminder of their presence. *Shinjuku Boys* is not unproblematic, however. The film was made by two white British women filmmakers, who heavily dramatized the experiences of *onabe* like Gaish. This raises questions about accuracy and authenticity. However, given the dearth of (ethnographic) research on *onabe*, I find it useful to draw critically on *Shinjuku Boys* as quasi-ethnographic material to build on my own research findings.

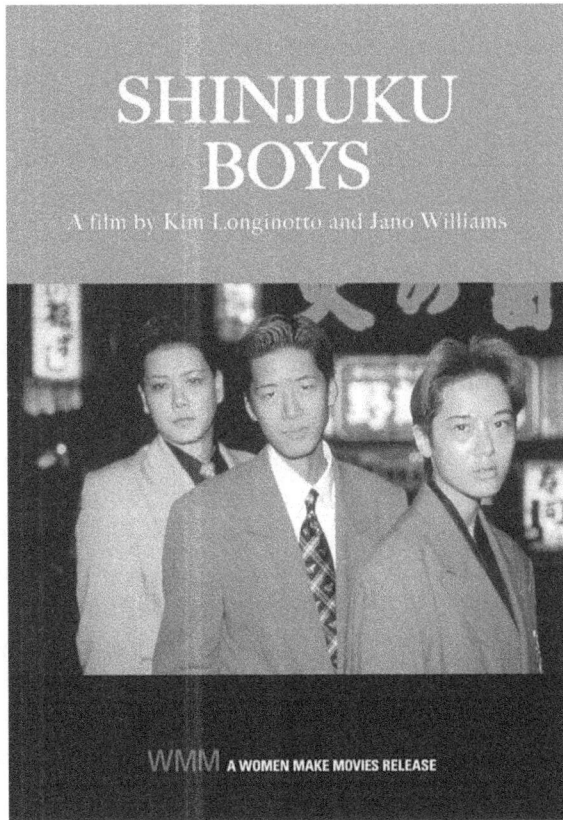

1.1     Kazuki (*left*), Tatsu (*center*), and Gaish (*right*) in the poster for *Shinjuku Boys*, 1995.

Gaish's articulation of who they are can be understood as a form of resistance to the GID (gender identity disorder; *seidōitsuseishōgai*) discourse, a medicalized and rights-based discourse of non-cisgender individuals that was growing in popularity around the time *Shinjuku Boys* was released. Since the GID discourse is predicated on gender normativity, being an in-between disrupts the perceived desire to be a man or a woman. Gaish's frustration also demonstrates the difficulty of articulating their in-betweenness. Although Gaish adopts the strongly masculine first-person pronoun *ore*, they insist on a firmly nonbinary way of being, encapsulated by *onabe*. For Gaish, then, *onabe* appears useful not only as a category to express who they are to other people but also as a form of innovation vis-à-vis existing categories during the 1990s recessionary period, which coincided with the queer (*kuia*) movement. Though they used different language, Gaish's experience reflected those of my interlocutors at Garçon, which raised the question of how *dansō* was located within this longer history. What are the overlaps—if any—between *onabe* and modern-day *dansō*?

In this chapter I investigate the emergence of genders and ways of being in Japan over the decades, including shifting categories, terminologies, and understandings of gender and sexuality. I adopt Michel Foucault's genealogical approach, the process of "excavating the depths" of historical discourses and conditions to show how they produce and continue to shape the present.[4] Instead of recounting a coherent history, I trace the uneven struggles, knowledges, and power relations embedded in the past from which emergent genders developed. Rereading this history from a trans-political economy (TPE) studies perspective, I pay close attention to the material conditions shaping how categories became conflated with and distinguished from one another over the years. Although extensive, this genealogy allows us to see the innovation and evolution of these categories over the arc of time, which my interlocutors worked with and reworked. This informs our understanding of how *josō*, *otoko no ko*, and *dansō* came about in Tokyo in the twenty-first century, demonstrating how emergent genders flourished under capitalism.

Curiously, my interlocutors sometimes hearkened back to this history when speaking about *josō* and *dansō*, as if making such a connection validated their own practices. For instance, as Paradise's owners reminded me, because Judeo-Christian beliefs do not structure Japanese people's *josō* practices, gender crossing is largely disregarded rather than heavily policed. Emerging in twenty-first-century Tokyo, then, is not only my interlocutors' doing and commodification of *josō* and *dansō* but also their embrace of *josō* and *dansō* as a way of being.[5] Instead of being completely disconnected from older Japanese traditions, contemporary *josō* and *dansō* practices are fractured from these earlier forms.

In the rest of the chapter, I first show how in the premodern and prewar era, categories came about mainly through religious rituals and traditions and theatrical performances, then eventually through Western influence, and later, during the postwar period, through the growth of commercial media and public spaces. These categories would set the stage for gender innovations in big cities such as Tokyo and Osaka, and some would eventually evolve into boom cultures from the late twentieth century and well into the twenty-first century. (Readers already familiar with this historical context may wish to skip to the contemporary stories of *josō*, *dansō*, and *otoko no ko* later in this chapter.)

In the 1980s and 1990s—during the bubble economy and after its collapse—categories like *new half, onabe*, and *x-gender* variously proliferated through the mass media and commercial spaces and through individuals' labor in Japanese sex and night entertainment and in their resistance to liberal identity-based categories developed from social movements like GID. I argue that these individuals' material conditions not only enabled them to innovate but also translated into different attachments to multiple desires, bodies, and subjectivities. Drawing on emotional capitalism, I contend that emotion and economy are so deeply intertwined that people's economic lives and practices transform and are transformed by their relationships with one another, thereby shaping the development and circulation of gender categories.[6] What Sara Ahmed calls "stickiness" allows us to rethink how certain gender categories emerge and operate in the present. Stickiness can be seen as an effect of people being bound to the economy, and this stickiness conveys a history and a "transference of affect" to emergent genders.[7] During economic stagnation, individuals may become "stuck," form attachments to certain bodies, or cling to specific desires and subjectivities, which are stickier for some people than others.

The connections between these older categories and present-day categories demonstrate how some individuals at Paradise and Garçon innovated by adopting *otoko no ko* and reimagining *josō* and *dansō* to express themselves. These categories are deeply embedded in popular culture, which I discuss in later chapters to answer the question: Why have *dansō* and *josō/otoko no ko* establishments sprouted in Akihabara? For now, I make the point that similar to *new half, onabe*, and *x-gender*, our understandings of *josō, dansō*, and *otoko no ko* are complicated by the individualistic practices and understandings of the people who inhabit them. Ultimately, I contend that these individuals constantly push at the boundaries of gender and sexuality, challenging how we have come to understand them in the contemporary moment.

## Locating *Josō* and *Dansō* in History

Two of the oldest historical records, *Kojiki* (An account of ancient matters), published in 712, and *Nihon Shoki* (The chronicles of Japan), in 720, make sporadic mention of the *josō* and *dansō* practices of warriors and royal family members.[8] For instance, Yamato Takeru, Prince Ōsu of the Yamato dynasty, active during his father Emperor Keikō's reign, estimated to be between 71 and 130, would infiltrate his enemies' lair as a "*josō* lad" on the day of a banquet.[9] Yamato's apparent attractiveness as a "young maiden" enticed his enemies to let him get close enough to kill them.[10] In medieval Japan, *warawa*, or courtiers who had been taken into service at temples as children, existed as a "third gender" category in between adult men and women.[11] Many *warawa* practiced *josō*—though they avoided this descriptor—by adopting appearances that were indistinguishable from "maidens"; within an all-male community, they behaved and were treated as "women."[12] Both these examples illustrate a close relationship between *josō* and the youthfulness of modern-day gender crossing.

Records mentioning *dansō* practices mostly describe women who wore their hair like men and put on armor to go into battle in a male-dominated world. Examples of such a narrative recorded in *Nihon Shoki* include Empress Jingū during her third-century reign and Tomoe Gozen, a brave and strong woman warrior in the twelfth century who adopted a "male appearance" to fight in a "man's world."[13] Historians have also noted "male dancing" performances in the Kyoto court between the twelfth and fourteenth centuries by women dancers dressed in male costumes.[14] However, since these dancers mainly emulated adolescent boys instead of grown men in ritualized performances, scholars have questioned whether such practices could be considered *dansō*.[15] Though this raises important questions about how *dansō* and *josō* were defined, by whom, and whether their practices were confined to ritual and performance, these examples show that *josō* and *dansō* practices were religiously sanctioned in premodern Japan.

*Josō* and *dansō* practices were also found in the theater. Kabuki theater began in 1603 when Okuni, a shrine maiden at Izumo Grand Shrine, led an all-women cast in a new style of dancing called "Kabuki dance." Until women were prohibited onstage in 1629, Okuni directed her dancers in playing both "male" and "female" roles.[16] Kabuki was subsequently taken up by male adolescents called *wakashu*, many of whom performed in *josō*. Perhaps because *wakashu* also refers to a young male prostitute or younger partner in a male-male relationship, in 1652 *wakashu* were banned onstage for corrupting public morals.[17] Adult men, notably *onnagata*, or male actors who play "female" roles, thus became performers, laying the groundwork for the Kabuki we know today. *Onnagata* continue to be celebrated by both men and women for their "gender crossing skills to entertain," and many are top performers in terms of ranking and salary.[18]

When the ban on women performing onstage was lifted in 1890, women gradually returned to the theater.[19] With traditional Japanese theater such as Kabuki and Noh off-limits to them, these women often performed in

Western-style plays.[20] It was against this backdrop that Kobayashi Ichizō founded the Takarazuka Revue, an all-women theater group, in 1913. Kobayashi did not, however, establish Takarazuka with the aim of supporting women's theater; rather, profit was his main motivation, and he hired young women because they could be paid less. Takarazuka remained an all-women group because the performers and their families objected strongly to the idea of becoming co-ed.[21] Women underwent training to play "male" roles, known as *otokoyaku*, as well as "female" roles.[22] Takarazuka officially debuted onstage in 1914, and its novelty contributed significantly to its eventual popularity.[23]

The theatrical connection is important because during the Meiji era (1868–1912), when Japan began to modernize and adopt Western understandings of civilization, *josō* and *dansō* were briefly banned—for crossing gender boundaries—in all instances except the theater.[24] For example, under the new law, women were not allowed to have short hair, whereas men—as modern national subjects—were called on to cut their hair short and wear Western clothing.[25] Although this prohibition did not last long, the authority's perceptions of *josō* and *dansō* were slow to change, as evidenced by the arrest and prosecution of *josō* and *dansō* individuals in the years following.[26] These laws, and the media coverage of their enforcement, helped to associate *josō* and *dansō* practices with crime and suspicion.

Western influence on *josō* and *dansō* was also apparent in the 1920s during an early sexology boom in Japan. Following World War I, sexual "experts" in Europe developed and perpetuated the field of sexology through discussions of "perverse sexual desires" (*hentai seiyoku*).[27] Spurred by these discussions, Japanese psychiatrists, physicians, and medical researchers began to view homosexual and cross-dressing individuals who possessed "perverse sexual desires" as mentally deranged, publishing widely in various sexological journals and newspapers and magazines intended for readers seeking advice for their "condition."[28] As Mitsuhashi laments, this pathologization of homosexuality and cross-dressing lumped different individuals together and conflated sexual orientation, gender identity, and gender presentation—the effect of which lingers in Japanese society today.[29]

Immediately after World War II, *nanshoku* (male eroticism) culture rapidly revived after being repressed by strict state management of bodies during the fifteen-year war. Originating in the Muromachi period (1392–1568), *nanshoku* refers to "male-male sexual desire," and representations of *nanshoku* in commercial literature and other forms of popular discourse typically portray sexual relations between an adult man and a male adolescent.[30] Besides *nanshoku*, "new kinds of sexual culture" also proliferated during this time of social confusion, and this included a return to "abnormal" and "perverse" (*hentai*) sexualities.[31] For example, as early as 1946, many women and *josō* sex workers could be spotted in Ueno, one of Tokyo's oldest red-light districts.[32] Although *josō* sex work was subsequently shut down, in the early 1950s *josō* sex workers could still be seen in urban areas, such as Tokyo Station, Shimbashi Station, and Shinjuku Station, and always among women sex workers.[33] Also flourishing in the 1950s were "perverse magazines," or commercial magazines that openly discussed "perverse sexual desires" (*hentai seiyoku*), particularly "male and female homosexuality as well as a range of fetishistic behaviors."[34] One perverse magazine, *Fūzoku Kitan* (Mysterious tales about sexual customs), provided a space for *josō* individuals to share their experiences through a regular column, which inspired one of the first clubs for amateur cross-dressers to become established in Shinjuku in the early 1960s.[35]

Postwar perverse publications also occasionally alluded to people's everyday *dansō* practices. An article in the June 1954 issue of *Fūzoku Kitan* titled "*Dansō* Mania" claimed that women developed relationships with other women due to a shortage of eligible men and that one partner would practice *dansō* to "pass" at work.[36] However, the limited interest in *dansō* as compared to *josō* in the perverse press, as elsewhere, means that much less has been written on these practices. We do know that by the late 1950s, the tabloid press started picking up on *dansōsha*—another term for *dansō* individuals—in the entertainment world, individuals who would set a precedent for future female-to-male (FTM) transgender performers in bars and other subcultural spaces.[37]

At the same time, with its popularity continuing to grow, Takarazuka influenced the creation of *dansō* characters in girls' (*shōjo*) manga—one of the first being Princess Sapphire, dressed as a valiant knight in Tezuka Osamu's *Princess Knight* (*Ribon no kishi*) in 1953.[38] Over the years, these androgynous characters morphed into "beautiful boy" characters in the "Boys Love" genre, which explores romantic and sexual relations between men.[39] As I argue in chapter 3, these popular cultural texts would form the basis of alternative worlds in Akihabara.

### Emergence of Genders: New Half and Miss Dandy

In April 1981, Betty, a "gay boy" (*gei bōi*) who worked at the Osaka show pub Betty's Mayonnaise, debuted as a singer with a song titled *New Half* (*Nyūhāfu*). The songwriter, Sōden Keisuke, explained that *new half* refers to a person who is "half man and half woman" (*otoko to onna no hāfu*).[40] The next month, the press described Matsubara Rumiko, a popular *josō* hostess in Ginza who played a small role in the 1981 movie *In the Cellar* (*Kura no naka*), directed by Japanese filmmaker Takabayashi Yoichi, as the "rumored new half."[41] But it wasn't until August 1983 that the women's magazine *Shūkan Josei* (Weekly women) published a section called "This Week's New Half" that the previous term *gay boy* gave way to *new half*.[42] As use of *new half* spread in the media, many bars and clubs eagerly embraced it as a category, leading to a *new half* boom in the midst of the 1980s bubble economy. This accorded some feminine-presenting individuals increased visibility, though often at the price of being rendered spectacles in the public eye.

The *new half* boom followed on the heels of the pre-Stonewall gay boom of the 1950s and 1960s, which triggered the rapid growth of what I call *pink economies*, that is, commodified sex and entertainment industries and gay, lesbian, and gender-variant establishments, such as gay bars, particularly in large cities. Inhabiting these gay bars were *josō* and gay-identified individuals, laying the foundation for contemporary bars and clubs employing *josō* individuals and for the category *new half* to emerge.[43]

However, while the above narrative points to *new half* as an identity marker, it is also considered an occupational category, tied to assumptions about individuals working in Japanese sex and night entertainment—known as *mizu shōbai* (water trade). *New half* individuals often eke out a living as sex workers, hostesses, performers, and entertainers in bars, pubs, and clubs due to employment discrimination and stringent regulations barring them from holding full-time jobs in other sectors.[44] This vicious cycle of discrimination and exploitation has been observed by TPE scholars, where trans women, especially racialized and colonized trans women from the global south, are exploited for their underpaid, irregular, and temporary labor—on which capital accumulation depends—while also being easy targets for criminalization, anti-trans violence, and discrimination in so-called respectable regular and permanent employment with higher wages.[45] As a result, *new half* individuals are frequently stigmatized for their labor and usually not recognized as "proper" trans subjects that can be folded into mainstream Japanese society.[46] This is further complicated by the economic reality that many *new half* individuals who seek hormone therapy and sex/gender reassignment surgery (SGRS) struggle to pay for these medical interventions, again obstructing their recognition as "proper" trans subjects.[47]

What all of this tells us is that although the media's proliferation of *new half* subsequently led to the *new half* boom, boom-based cultures are only one part of the story. We also need to understand how *new half* individuals are situated within the TPE in Japan and how their gender variance has been capitalized on and is thus integral to wealth accumulation.

Following closely on the heels of *new half*, in the mid-1980s and early 1990s, another term entered the Japanese vocabulary and became prominent in the mass media: *Miss Dandy* (*misu dandī*). A transliteration of the English words *miss* and *dandy*, *misu dandī* refers to individuals assigned female at birth who (wish to) live as men and may or may not have undergone SGRS.[48] Unlike *new half*, the category *Miss Dandy* straddled a robust and a stagnating economy, which I find intriguing. Its popularity spanned the height of Japanese economic growth, the bursting of the bubble, and the recessionary era. However, how economic conditions enabled and inhibited *Miss Dandy* is difficult to determine because, aside from sporadic mentions, much less has been written on *Miss Dandy* than on *new half*. In one of the few existing books on *Miss Dandy*, journalist Toyama Hitomi compiled interviews she conducted with masculine-presenting individuals assigned female at birth she called "Miss Dandy."[49] It is important to note that these narratives belong to a diverse group of individuals who either live as men or desire to do so, may or may not be transitioning, and may not necessarily use *Miss Dandy* to describe themselves—Toyama is the one doing the categorization.

One example from Toyama's volume is Mizuno Makiyo's story, which chronicles his life from childhood through adulthood.[50] What I find interesting about this story is the way it traces the different categories Mizuno and the people around him have used over time. For instance, as an adolescent, Mizuno recalled falling in love with an attractive senior in school. This relationship was known as *S* (short for *sister love*), an expression describing two women in an "older sister" and "younger sister" relationship.[51] As he explained, in the 1950s, *rezubian* (lesbian) had not yet become widespread, so *S* was used instead. By the time he opened Kikōshi, a historic *onabe* bar located in Roppongi, in the mid-1970s, *onabe* had already been coined as an occupational category—much like *new half*—to characterize the employees working at bars and clubs like Kikōshi.[52] It is telling that nowhere in Mizuno's story does he refer to himself as *Miss Dandy*, despite the title of Toyama's book. Scholars may have assumed this categorization due to his reference to masculine-presenting employees, the main attraction at various bars in 1960s Tokyo, as "*dansō* beauties" (*dansō no reijin*).[53] Miss Dandies were also typically associated with public characters on television, though the lives of these characters were undoubtedly different from those of individuals like Mizuno, suggesting that *Miss Dandy* was primarily a mainstream media invention to appeal to audiences and catapult a *Miss Dandy* boom.[54]

In her monograph on Takarazuka, Jennifer Robertson associates "Miss Dandies" with Kikōshi (Mizuno's bar) and New Marilyn (the apparent setting of the film *Shinjuku Boys*), the clubs she visited in the late 1980s, and their masculine-presenting hosts, who wore suits and ties and were Takarazuka fans.[55] However, as some scholars have pointed out, these clubs were more accurately *onabe* bars rather than Miss Dandy clubs.[56] While Robertson is not the only one to conflate Miss Dandy with *onabe*—between 1993 and 1996, *Miss Dandy* was used in Japanese mainstream magazines as a moniker for *onabe*—she also collapses the categories of *Miss Dandy* and *otokoyaku* (male roles in Takarazuka) by describing Kikōshi and New Marilyn employees as "basically offstage *otokoyaku* who live their daily lives as men."[57]

The influence of *otokoyaku* on Kikōshi and New Marilyn is clear, but what's less clear is whether the owners were directly inspired by Takarazuka or whether they were inspired by the history of *dansō* bars and just happened to be Takarazuka fans.[58] Regardless, this conflation of categories coupled with the eventual waning of *Miss Dandy* demonstrates the latter's instability. Having developed as a media category that was not embraced by gender-variant individuals themselves, *Miss Dandy* had a short life span, lasting only as long as its boom. Though this particular category was created solely for mass consumption, the rise and fall of *Miss Dandy* follows the Japanese economy, suggesting that categorial innovations are possible during a time of economic flux. *Miss Dandy* leveraged trans difference for profit during a time of economic flux, but it was soon replaced.

### *Onabe* and *X-Gender* during the Recessionary 1990s

Throughout the recessionary 1990s, categories like *onabe* and *x-gender* proliferated in areas already saturated with various commercial establishments. I argue that these categories grew out of particular material conditions and can be distinguished from existing gender categories, practices, and ways of being. The innovation of genders might be regarded as "modern consequences of local market-based processes" where local markets become sites for modern Asian trans and queer cultures and identities to develop that are distinct from so-called precapitalist traditional forms of genders and sexualities.[59] The 1990s brought a prolonged recession in Japan, and labor shifts and neoliberal restructuring turned many young people into *freeters*; part-time, temporary or dispatched workers; or the unemployed looking for work.[60] This was also the time of the queer movement, the legalization of SGRS, the medicalized discourse of GID, and, toward the late 1990s, the popularization of the internet for consumer use. I posit that the recessionary era enabled the innovation of gender categories such as *onabe* and *x-gender*.

Scholars have previously observed the rise of gender and sexuality categories in the queer movement, but they focus mainly on institutionalized and rights-based approaches.[61] For instance, scholars have discussed how activists articulated a *gei* and *rezubian* politics during the 1990s queer movement, which—similar to the spread of *gay* and *lesbian* in late 1960s and 1970s United States—involved gender and sexual minorities (*seitekishōsūsha*) in legal action and the mass media, and increased contemporary and historical scholarship on same-gender desires.[62] Although this seems to suggest the unidirectional influence of US gay liberation on Japan's gay and lesbian activism, queer scholar Katsuhiko Suganuma contends that understanding modern Japanese genders and sexualities requires knowledge of their cross-cultural dimensions.[63]

For example, drawing on the definition of homosexuality from US gay liberation, the Japanese nonprofit organization OCCUR (Organization for Lesbian and Gay Movement) filed and won a discrimination lawsuit against the Tokyo metropolitan government.[64] This led to the first legal definition of male homosexuality specific to the Japanese context. Partly due to increased consciousness of homosexuality in the public imaginary and the embrace of *rezubian* as an identity category during the queer movement, *onabe* became distinct from *rezubian*—a separation between what we now know as *gender identity* and *sexual orientation*. This increased politicization of the queer movement influenced the late 1990s GID discourse and subsequent trans activism, both of which stressed a human rights discourse. Advances in medical technologies also played a large role in changing discourses, coinciding with the advent of SGRS in Japan. This helped to shift the discourse away from the long history of gender-variant people working in Japanese sex and night entertainment—typically as entertainers or sex workers—and toward the pathologizing discourse of GID.[65]

This is not to suggest that these identitarian and institutionalized discourses had no role in the development of gender and sexuality categories, on the contrary, but I also want to consider how capital has shaped these categories in recessionary Japan. While some scholars have noted, in passing, that the 1990s gay boom—characterized by the spread of gay and lesbian media, social spaces, and other enterprises—coincided with the end of high economic growth, few have closely examined this relationship.[66] I give consideration to this relationship, particularly in rethinking the connections between the material and emergent genders and the ways they may offer gender and sexual minorities alternative modes to make sense of their work and consumption at various entertainment establishments using queer- and trans-materialist approaches.

I contend that in responding to the 1990s queer movement and GID discourse, some individuals who resisted liberal politics of inclusion and desired the fluidity and multiplicity of genders and sexualities innovated their own categories. This follows Eve Kosofsky Sedgwick's notion of "queer" where genders and sexualities are plural and can radically transcend existing meanings and categories.[67] For instance, gender and sexual minorities struggled against the gender binary promoted by the medicalized discourse of GID and the clear separation between gender identity and sexual orientation located in the identity-based politics of gay and lesbian activism. This struggle points to the divide between categories that are institutionalized and legitimized by the ability to champion a rights-based discourse, such as GID, and categories that are not, such as *onabe*. Why can some categories be used to advance identity-based politics and not others? What are the politics of adopting certain categories over others as their meanings shift over time? How are these categories and the sites in which they proliferate molded by capital?

To answer some of these questions, I return to *Shinjuku Boys*. Released in 1995, this documentary portrays the lives of three *onabe*, Gaish, Tatsu, and Kazuki, who work at Marilyn. Although *onabe* first emerged in the 1970s and is not new per se, I am interested in how it became a distinct category embraced by certain individuals who engaged in *dansō* in the 1990s, coinciding with the onset of the recession. *Shinjuku Boys* illustrates exactly the window of time in which *onabe* was recognized as a category of its own, after it became separate from *rezubian* and before it became conflated with GID in 1996.[68]

At Marilyn, employees mainly host, serving customers drinks and conversing and singing karaoke with them (figure 1.2). They are also expected to play certain roles. As Kazuki puts it, "Each customer thinks we're her special boyfriend. They're wrong. That's how we do business." Some employees, like Gaish, may also provide sexual services outside the club, which, unlike their formal employment, constitutes paid informal work. Differing understandings of *onabe*, which *Shinjuku Boys* sensitively portrays through the stories of Gaish, Tatsu, and Kazuki, shape their roles as "ideal men" at the club. For instance, in the bedroom scene I began this chapter with, Gaish declares they prefer to be thought of as "in-between," neither a man nor a

1.2     *Onabe* hosts entertaining at New Marilyn. Still from *Shinjuku Boys*, 1995.

woman. In a subsequent scene, Gaish clearly differentiates between lesbian sex and their own sexual relations, proclaiming that unlike "lesbians" (*rezu*), they never take off their clothes or show their body to their sexual partner. Gaish does not want to be seen or touched because they do not have "a man's body," nor will they become "a real man."

Gaish's resistance to many things—the gender binary, GID discourse, lesbian identity, and male and female embodiment—reveals the fluidity of a category like *onabe* as they understand it. This is compounded by there being "all kinds" of *onabe*, as Gaish points out, and diverse understandings of what it means to be an *onabe*. In rejecting the gender binary and arguably the idea of being gendered, Gaish makes us question exactly what these categories of "man" and "woman" are and how limiting they can be. Gaish also distances themselves from *rezubian*, a category indexing a cis-female individual who is sexually and romantically attracted to another female-bodied individual; nor does Gaish think of themselves as playing the man during sex, contrary to the roles of "ideal man" and "special boyfriend" they are expected to enact at Marilyn. Gaish also does not desire to be a "real man" through taking hormones and therefore does not identify with the

GID discourse. That they are not comfortable with another person seeing or touching their body suggests that, for Gaish, sex is a job, transactional, rather than an emotional connection with someone.

Due to its association with bars and clubs, *onabe* is often perceived as an occupational category, which—similar to *new half*—stems from a long history of gender-variant people working in Japanese sex and night entertainment. In the late 1990s, such culturally available narratives of gender-variant individuals abruptly shifted to those of GID. The category GID came out of the queer movement and subsequent lobbying and advocacy by trans rights activists as an identity for trans people in Japan.[69] As early as the 1980s, trans writer and activist Torai Masae began writing in magazines about his experience of taking hormones and subsequently undergoing SGRS in the United States; in 1994 he launched *FTM Nihon*, a "mini communication" meant for GID-identified individuals.[70] Publicly available narratives such as Torai's story informed understandings of GID as being tied to medical interventions and a liberal politics of inclusion. As a category, GID hinges on identitarian models of gender and sexuality.

After the first official SGRS in Japan, performed for a FTM individual in 1998 and a MTF individual in 1999, GID was widely used by mainstream media, due largely to a popular and long-running Tokyo Broadcasting System Television (TBS) drama, *3nen b-gumi Kinpachi-sensei* (Mr. Kinpachi, 3rd year B group; henceforth *Kinpachi-sensei*).[71] In its sixth season (2001–2), *Kinpachi-sensei* portrayed a trans character, Tsurumoto Nao (played by cis actress Ueto Aya), modeled after the life and struggles of Torai, who was consulted for the drama and even met Ueto for her role.[72] Significantly, the season was televised around the time the GID Act was passed. The GID Act allows one to legally change one's gender on the family registry (*koseki*), a right trans activists—including Torai—took years to achieve.[73] As Japanese scholar Yonezawa Izumi notes, *Kinpachi-sensei* shifted perspectives of trans people from "occupational"—as *new half* entertainers and sex workers, for instance—to "a normal person in deep distress."[74] By disassociating trans people from Japanese sex and night entertainment, dramas like *Kinpachi-sensei* helped to raise public awareness of them. But such media also framed the issues in terms of the GID discourse, normalizing this discourse for all gender-variant individuals in Japan. This has apparently translated into people's day-to-day lives, as sociologist Tsuruta Sachie observed during her fieldwork; after learning about GID in the media, an increasing number of individuals sought a GID diagnosis.[75]

The lingering tension in gender-variant individuals' affiliation with both Japanese sex and night entertainment and the GID discourse has impacted how we take up certain categories today. On the one hand, with few employment options available for ambiguously gendered individuals, their affiliation with Japanese sex and night entertainment indexes how they make a living. On the other hand, those who embrace GID are allowed to change their legal gender in the family registry, but those who don't identify as GID or meet the conditions of its medicalized discourse are increasingly left out. It is unsurprising, then, to find individuals like Gaish who hold on to *onabe* to express themselves. Under the gender-normative GID discourse, *onabe* are often stigmatized for their labor within Japanese sex and night entertainment. At the same time, the gender fluidity of *onabe* breaks with commonsense notions of productivity: to be married (heterosexually) and run a household.

The institutionalization of GID accompanied by its spread through mainstream media reflects shifting attitudes toward gender and sexuality during the recessionary 1990s. At a time when young people became increasingly disinclined or unable to marry, trans activists and groups were actively lobbying to bring about legal gender change, eventually succeeding with the 2003 GID Act. It is interesting to observe that trans people who fall outside commonsense constructions of heteronormative marriage and family are fighting to be included on identity documents and the family registry, which includes only Japanese citizens.[76] Indeed, the GID Act currently remains the only legal way for a person to change their gender on the family registry. For this reason, scholar S. P. F. Dale has suggested that *GID* operates as a form of biopower, drawing on Foucault's notion of the power the state has over its population's lives through managing their bodies.[77] In addition to practical considerations such as receiving health care or obtaining full-time employment, the family registry is an important site of contestation for trans people to prove their national belonging and legitimate citizenship.[78] Legally changing trans people's gender therefore symbolizes state recognition, particularly their economic value as "proper" trans subjects. Yet their inclusion in the family registry simultaneously subjects their lives to state scrutiny and surveillance. Instead of questioning Japanese common sense–inflected morality, these trans activists and groups have subscribed to it by pushing for the GID Act, which imposes stringent conditions, such as being over twenty, being unmarried with no children, and having undergone SGRS. Despite these nonideal conditions, Torai and other trans activists pushed for this legislation, believing it was their only opportunity to effect real change.[79]

Since its passing, the GID Act has remained controversial. Some have criticized the GID Act for marginalizing gay and lesbian issues, notably same-gender marriage, whereas others celebrated its implementation as a form of recognition for gender and sexual minorities.[80] Many trans people, too, continue to regard the GID Act as prescriptive in terms of defining a trans person as one who subscribes to the gender binary and desires to undergo SGRS.[81] Within TPE, GID and the discourse surrounding it can be said to benefit only some trans individuals and legitimize them as "proper" trans subjects while leaving out those who do not wish or are unable to conform. In other words, the current recognition of trans people's economic value in Japan is connected not only to citizenship and gender normativity but also to a liberal politics of inclusion embedded in the GID discourse.[82]

X-Gender *and Local Queer Production*

If *onabe* emerged as a fluid category from masculine-presenting employees at clubs like Marilyn in resistance to GID and the gender binary, *x-gender* had its beginnings in local queer production. *X-gender* flourished in the Kansai region toward the end of the 1990s, mainly in resistance to identitarian notions of gender and sexuality but also as a result of people's emotional investments in the media and commercial public spaces for hanging out, such as bars and clubs, and the rise of the internet. Individuals innovated the category *x-gender* (*ekkusu jendā*) to capture those who did not align with extant sex/gender categories; they were "neither sex/gender" (*dochira demo nai seibetsu*) or, depending on the definition, both male and female and hence X.[83] Departing from binary categories of man and woman, *x-gender* individuals countered the GID discourse, which enforced SGRS as a criterion for legal gender change and advocated GID as a liberal identity-based category. In this sense, *x-gender* individuals were less likely to seek out SGRS because they opposed the often gender-normative identitarian models of gender and sexuality GID-identified individuals stood for. *X-gender* individuals' categorial innovation might also be interpreted as a means of engendering new ways of being that differed from existing modes of gender and sexuality. To innovate during the recession means to go against the grain of thinking about economic stagnation, the latter of which is usually accompanied by a lack of growth.

At its birth, *x-gender* developed through independent print and audiovisual media dependent on the emotional investments of queer networks and individuals in Osaka and Kyoto. Examples of such media examined in Dale's historiography of *x-gender* include a 2000 themed issue in *Poco a poco* (Bit by bit), a journal published by LGBT organization G-Front Kansai;

a 1999 documentary titled ♀?♂?♂?, produced by queer activist Tanaka Ray, depicting the stories of three individuals, one of whom identifies as MTFTX; and nonfiction books authored by various writers and scholars, such as Yoshinaga Michiko, Nakamura Mia, and Tsuruta Sachie.[84] As these vernacular media forms circulated, *x-gender* became "sticky." During times of economic stagnation, such "stickiness" may manifest in individuals becoming attached to other bodies, desires, and subjectivities.[85]

Scholars have shown that how emotion operates within advanced economies is complex. Perhaps people's relationship to the economy might be described as what Lauren Berlant calls "cruel optimism," or "when something you desire is actually an obstacle to your flourishing," such as by investing in "bad" objects of desire to attain "the good life" one is attached to.[86] However, countering Polanyian thought of money and markets as fragmenting social life and dismantling human connections, Martijn Konings contends that the economy might instead be perceived as "productive" and "constructive."[87] Following this, emergent genders that develop through social spaces and networks similar to boom cultures are sticky and useful for *x-gender* individuals to express themselves and form attachments with one another. The question then is not only how the recessionary context has enabled or inhibited categories like *x-gender* but, more important, how *x-gender* individuals themselves have adopted, rejected, or responded to these categories under pericapitalist modes.

As more individuals gathered under the sign *x-gender*, they began to share their experiences on blogs, bulletin board services (namely, 2channel), and social networking sites, such as Mixi and Twitter.[88] This coincided with the increased popularity of the internet, which encouraged the spread of *x-gender* as *x-gender* people all over Japan connected and established bonds with one another. Facilitated by local productions, publications, and online social interactions, such sticky synergies about *x-gender* may have been possible precisely because of the material conditions during the recession. By moving away from gender roles and norms tied to notions of productivity in a weakened economy, *x-gender* individuals could begin to consider a life where they weren't gendered. They innovated by finding ways of flourishing that were different from the GID discourse and what it represented.

Although the category of *x-gender* offers hope for opting out of gendered subjectivity, *x-gender* individuals' radical aims of transcending the gender binary have been difficult to sustain, especially in recent years. With GID perpetuated in mainstream media and public discourse as the dominant framework for understanding and talking about trans people, many *x-gender* individuals began using the same language and knowledge to describe and think about themselves to obtain "security in one's identity."[89] By buying into the *x-gender*-as-GID discourse, these individuals gained access to a shared vocabulary for ascertaining who they were, as well as the medical diagnosis and procedures necessary for fulfilling the GID Act, such as obtaining a GID diagnosis of having a "disorder" (*shōgai*; also "disability") and subsequently undergoing SGRS. Hence, *x-gender* individuals who choose to identify as GID aren't freed from trans oppression and discrimination but rather enter into a continued relation of capitalist exploitation.

Despite this trajectory, not all *x-gender* individuals wish to be folded into the GID discourse. For example, many of my interlocutors who were *x-gender* did not (wholly) subscribe to the GID discourse. Saito, an *x-gender* regular customer of Garçon in their late twenties, rejected the gender binary through their gender expression. Looking for unisex clothes that could fit their long limbs and broad shoulders, for example, Saito shopped in both the men's and women's departments. By not distinguishing between men's and women's clothing, Saito can be said to either embrace a mixture of masculine and feminine styles or confine their practices to neither gender. Neither gender was also how Yuta, a nonbinary twenty-eight-year-old employee at Garçon, defined *x-gender*. Yuta described themselves as identifying more strongly with *chūsei* (middle sex/gender) than *x-gender* as they felt more comfortably located in between genders. Scholars have differently translated *chūsei* as "androgynous" and "feeling not quite female/male, but somewhere in-between."[90] Yuta's understanding of *chūsei* likely aligns more with Dale's translation of being "somewhere in-between" as, rather than rejecting women's clothing, they drew on all kinds of styles.[91] Through their nonbinary gender identity and expression, both Yuta and Saito appear to resist the GID discourse, and, to my knowledge, neither wished to transition.

This negotiation with the GID discourse was more complicated in the case of Jiji, a Paradise customer in her thirties who shifted from identifying as MTF to MTX over the months I knew her. Jiji associated her *josō* practices with her desire to become a woman, but although she seemed to be buying into the GID discourse, she claimed she didn't wish to undergo SGRS. Her subsequent identification as MTX further confounds stable understandings of GID, *x-gender*, and *transgender*. Categories are not inherently neutral and are continuously shaped by how individuals use, disavow, or reinvigorate them.[92] Hence, despite the *x-gender*-as-GID discourse's rising popularity in recent years, a number of *x-gender* individuals queer this narrative through their categorial innovations.

## Categorial Innovations in the Present: *Josō*, *Dansō*, and *Otoko no ko*

Miho, one of Paradise's owners, offered the following insight:

> We promoted the expression *otoko no ko* [boy/male daughter]. It's a long story, but in the time after we opened, because we have spread the term widely, individuals became named [*nanoreru*] *otoko no ko*. You may have noticed on Twitter many *otoko no ko* have come out [*detekuru*], right? They all have accounts, I mean. Of course, the phrase *otoko no ko* had already been coined, but our establishment conveyed the sentiment, "It's okay to name yourself *otoko no ko*." A three-dimensional *otoko no ko*—as the term originally refers to the two-dimensional. The thing is, the longer our establishment stays open, the more people know "These kinds of people do exist" or "They're unexpectedly beautiful." Or they might think after watching television, "This establishment exists, and there are people who visit it." At another time, they might also say, "I [*ore*] frequent that establishment" or "Hmm, that looks interesting" or "Oh, I saw this on TV." And someone might acknowledge, "So it is fun." That person goes to that establishment. And that's fine.[93]

From Miho's perspective, Paradise played a significant role in proliferating *otoko no ko* and more broadly *josō*, especially how they were embraced as categories of self-expression. Also, as a cis bisexual *josō* individual in his thirties, Miho has a personal stake in the *josō/otoko no ko* boom. Under pericapitalist modes, emergent genders come about because *otoko no ko* periodically produce and interact with media content to create public awareness of individuals who self-refer as or consume *otoko no ko* at Paradise. As people became more familiar with *otoko no ko*, they began to recognize their visual appearance or claim the label *otoko no ko* for themselves. Here, Miho articulates a different phenomenon of three-dimensional *otoko no ko* (individuals), who out of necessity reinvented themselves as distinct from two-dimensional *otoko no ko* (characters). Transcending the two-dimensional, three-dimensional *otoko no ko* can be described as real-life individuals who practice *josō*, self-refer as *otoko no ko*, and appear on television and at Paradise as well as produce their own content across social media.

The term *otoko no ko* originated during the early 2000s internet boom, when it began to be used and circulated on 2channel, an anonymous internet bulletin board, as a slang to denote two-dimensional *josō* characters.

*Otoko no ko* (男の娘) is a pun and homonym for "boy" (*otoko no ko*; 男の子) as the *ko* (娘) in *otoko no ko* is written with the character for "daughter" (*musume*), which also means "girl."[94] Users discussed *otoko no ko* appearing in games and manga they consumed, such as *Junai Girl* (Platonic love girl), an adult game featuring an adolescent *josō* "heroine" that was released in 2001 by game company RUNE. The company's subsidiary brand, CAGE, would go on to develop ten more adult games all depicting *otoko no ko*, such as *Puru Moenjeru Aidoru Aiko* (Pure *moe* angel idol Aiko, 2007), until RUNE's demise in late 2008.[95] Several manga portraying *josō* protagonists were also published during this time, such as Tsuda Mikiyo's *Princess Princess* (2002–6). First serialized in girls' manga magazine *Wings*, *Princess Princess* chronicles the lives of three first-year protagonists at an all-boys school who are chosen for their good looks and personalities to participate in its "princess" (*hime*) tradition, where they practice *josō* and serve as a school ambassador for a year. In 2006 a sequel manga, PlayStation 2 video game, and anime and drama adaptations of *Princess Princess* were released and reached an international audience.

Although they met with varying success, these media were important for laying the foundation for the *otoko no ko* genre. From the mid-2000s to early 2010s, *otoko no ko* characters appealed to a broader instead of a niche manga readership made up of otaku, or fans of anime, manga, and games.[96] While opening the market to more consumers, these shifts in genre and target audience would become the source of much tension between otaku, who maintained that three-dimensional *otoko no ko* did not exist, and an increasingly visible group of *josō* individuals, some of whom called themselves three-dimensional *otoko no ko*.[97] But why do the dimensions of *otoko no ko* matter in the first place? Part of the reason lies in safeguarding the two-dimensional world, including the *otoko no ko* characters originating from it, as otaku's territory.[98] Despite threatening the two-dimensional world from which *otoko no ko* originated, the mid-2000s emergence of *josō* individuals who began to understand themselves as three-dimensional *otoko no ko* demonstrates their categorial innovations. Within an establishment like Paradise, where cis-heteronormativity and hegemonic femininity and masculinity can be transgressed and individuals can be seen transgressing these norms, emergent genders can come into being. Moreover, that *josō* and *otoko no ko* can be read in diverse ways demonstrates their potential for both unsettling and preserving the gender order in uneven ways.

However, *josō* and *otoko no ko* are complicated by the fact that they may or may not be connected to an individual's gender identity and sexual orientation, and others may read cis straight people's gender crossing practices as reinforcing the gender binary or co-opting trans experiences.[99] For instance, Kaori, a cis heterosexual twenty-year-old employee, initially drew clear lines between his gender expression, gender identity, and sexual orientation, though these distinctions seemed to break down later in our interview. Kaori was slim; had long, straight black hair with bangs; and, like his colleagues, was well versed in makeup. While maintaining he was "a man through and through" (otoko no manma), he told me he did feel "feminine on the inside" (nakami wa onnarashii) while in josō. Working at Paradise enabled Kaori to talk to and be among "fellow women" (onnadōshi), allowing him to take pleasure in establishing emotional contact (fureai) with them. This was the main reason he took the job, despite the low wages, lack of job security, limited employee benefits, and even parental disapproval.

Kaori's experience complicates static and unambiguous ways of interpreting the josō practices of cis straight individuals, who made up half the employees I interviewed at Paradise. The other half located themselves as non-cisgender and nonheterosexual, including transgender, asexual, and bisexual. While Kaori identified as cis and heterosexual, his josō practices simultaneously entailed feeling "like a woman" (onnarashii) and mingling with "fellow women," including himself as one of the "women." His understandings of josō continuously challenge how we make sense of the connections among gender expression, gender identity, and sexual orientation. As a manager of Paradise explained to me, employees' attitudes toward josō may shift over time even if they started out at the café-and-bar thinking otherwise. For example, several ex-employees ended up "graduating" or leaving Paradise to become new half or undergo SGRS.[100] While the time frame of my research makes it difficult to see the evolution of all employees' feelings toward josō, it is clear that individuals' engagement with josō and otoko no ko is a process of continuous reinvention.[101]

*Individualistic Understandings of Dansō*

Although, like onabe, dansō is not a new term per se, what it means to those who practice dansō often differs from individual to individual and is located in a specific time and place. Such an individualistic understanding of dansō is encapsulated by one twenty-seven-year-old employee who had worked at Garçon longer than anyone else, who alternately viewed the practice as being "cool" (kakkōii), "like a mystery" (nazo), and embodying different "dansō ideals." These varied perspectives show how the category is ultimately shaped by those who do dansō. Though we can trace its beginnings to premodern

Japan, *dansō* has become fractured from older forms through continuous innovation by *dansō* individuals. Like *josō* and *otoko no ko*, *dansō* may or may not be tied to an individual's gender identity and sexual orientation.

Garçon's employees were also a diverse group, with the majority describing themselves as nonbinary and gender nonconforming, using the terms *chūsei* (middle sex/gender), *x-gender* (neither male nor female, or both), and *musei* (no sex/gender or "a complete rejection of being gendered"), while the rest said they were questioning or undetermined about who they were.[102] Despite these different subjectivities, they all declared they "ha[d] no preferences" (*kodawari ga nai*) as far as their partners were concerned. Some expressed being attracted to both men and women; a few said they were interested in two-dimensional characters. Although they have gathered under the sign *dansō*, their practices and understandings of *dansō* appear more different than similar, which hints at the category's instability.

Yu, a twenty-one-year-old employee at Garçon, described *dansō* individuals to me as "women [*josei*] who are like men [*dansei*]." By this, he means that *dansō* refers not only to individuals' "appearance" (*mitame*) but also to their "awareness of behaving like men" (*dansei toshite ishiki shiteru*). From Yu's point of view, *dansō* individuals are masculine both on the inside and on the outside. Yet when I asked Yu, who thought of himself as questioning, what *dansō* meant to him, he described himself as "not consciously practicing *dansō*" (*dansō ishiki shiteinai*). On an everyday basis, he enjoyed keeping his hair short and wearing his favorite clothes—usually pants and a shirt. However, Yu never thought of these practices as *dansō* until he started working at a *dansō* café-and-bar and was interpellated by everyone around him—society, his colleagues, and Garçon's customers—as doing *dansō*. This was complicated by Yu's alignment with "questioning," which may well have nothing to do with his nonconscious *dansō* practices. Individuals who are questioning are either ambivalent about their gender identity and/or sexual orientation or "prefer not to label themselves with any particular orientation."[103] Hence, Yu's gender identity and sexual orientation are considered separate from his masculine gender expression.

There seems to be a contradiction between Yu's definition of *dansō* as individuals consciously adopting masculine behavior and appearance and his personal understandings of *dansō* as a nonconscious act. While this raises questions about the differences (if any) between individuals who consciously and nonconsciously practice *dansō* and the ways their *dansō* practices may similarly or differently facilitate their identities, perhaps, in the larger scheme of things, such differences do not matter. Within Garçon, Yu becomes valued by colleagues and customers for doing *dansō*, whether he used the term or not. This labeling is partly due to contemporary *dansō* culture—that is, increased commodification and consumption of *dansō* among younger individuals—but it is also due to the active contribution customers make to contemporary *dansō* culture by eagerly exchanging information about their favorite Garçon employees and *dansō*-related topics, such as idols, fashion trends, and newly opened establishments. These forms of commercial avenues and social networking are as far-reaching as those in contemporary *josō* culture.

The instability of *dansō* may also stem from *dansō* individuals' distance from the queer movement's liberal identity-based categories. Although they appeared accepting of LGBT individuals and located themselves along a continuum of genders and sexualities, most employees at Garçon did not consider themselves LGBT because they felt the label and activism did not speak to their experiences.[104] For instance, Ikki, Garçon's twenty-seven-year-old manager, told me, "I don't consider myself as a part of LGBT. I mean, I know what it is, but I don't think I fit into its categories." Ikki's conscious disavowal of LGBT to describe himself reveals a questioning of constructions like "gay" and "lesbian," much in the same way *x-gender* individuals resisted identitarian notions of gender and sexuality and innovated their own category in the 1990s. Following from feminist notions of the political, we might say that *dansō* individuals have a different kind of politics that is inextricably tied to their everyday practices of *dansō* and involves constantly reinventing themselves to find their place in Japanese society.[105] This sentiment is epitomized by Hiyori, a twenty-five-year-old employee, who said, "I am me" (*ore wa ore*), echoing Gaish in *Shinjuku Boys*, who similarly resisted the idea of being categorized. Gaish and Hiyori are just who they are. *Dansō* individuals' rejection of LGBT is therefore meaningful for challenging existing modes of gender and sexuality and (re)shaping understandings of *dansō*. Their politics are about carving a different path in the world.

### Conclusion: Importance of Categorial Innovations

Charting the genealogy of categories from the premodern era to the contemporary moment allows us to see how emergent genders variously developed through religious rituals and traditions, theatrical performances, and popular culture. Rereading this history from a TPE studies perspective demonstrates how categorial innovations in Japan have shaped the emergence of *josō*, *otoko no ko*, and *dansō* in twenty-first-century Tokyo. The material conditions of the postwar growth of commercial mass media and public spaces were not coincidental to individuals' ability to reinvent themselves.

Individuals adopt *onabe* because the category appears useful for moving beyond extant gender and sexuality categories, including *rezubian* (lesbian) and GID. Like *new half*, *onabe* is considered an occupational category, which means employees' labor in Japanese sex and night entertainment also needs to be scrutinized, as I do later, together with the labor of Garçon and Paradise employees. For now, this chapter has illustrated that these categories became distinguished from other categories—such as *gay boy* and *Miss Dandy*—and proliferated through boom cultures through the labor of *onabe* and *new half* individuals, notably the *new half* boom. Boom-based cultures are only one part of the story, however. Approaching this from TPE studies, we see that *onabe*, *Miss Dandies*, and *new half* individuals occupy different roles—they share different relations to capital.

Similarly, while the GID discourse provided a normalized and institutionalized language and framework for understanding themselves as "proper" trans subjects within a singular hegemonic capitalism, individuals who resisted this discourse, as well as identitarian modes of gender and sexuality, engaged in categorial innovations to express themselves as *x-gender*. In the late 1990s, such categorial innovations were possible only because of shifting gender roles and social expectations linked to commonsense notions of productivity. *X-gender* individuals could begin to regard themselves as X, which simultaneously represents a resistance to the gender binary, institutionalization, rights-based movements, a neat separation between gender identity and sexual orientation, and, perhaps more important, the very idea of categorization itself. This rejection of labeling and being labeled is also something I found with my interlocutors at *dansō* and *josō/otoko no ko* establishments. By expressing their refusal to be categorized, they intervene in categories popularized by mainstream media and market-driven discourses of LGBT.

These new gender categories emerged and operated through individuals' emotional investments in mass media and commercial public spaces—and through their engagement with pink economies. Individuals' emotional and economic investments also play a large role in categorial innovations within contemporary *josō* and *dansō* cultures in the 2000s and 2010s. The mass enterprise and consumption of popular culture present a starting point for emergent genders to develop in alternative worlds where people constantly reinvent themselves and become "stuck" in generative ways.

# 2

## Doing Business in Japan's Pink Economies

*Enacting Home, Family, and Alternative*
*Forms of Belonging*

One evening, I found myself at Paradise for a casino-themed birthday bash for Shigure, an employee in their early thirties originally from Hong Kong. Paradise organized special events like this two to three times a month, to celebrate employees' birthdays and "graduations" and public and commercial holidays like Halloween and New Year's Day.[1] These events ensured a 25 percent increase in the mandatory cover charge, which was usually JPY 1,500 (USD 13.50) per customer and included the first drink. While, on average, regulars would frequent an establishment once or twice a week, spending JPY 5,000–6,000 (USD 45–55) each time, for special events patrons could easily spend in excess of JPY 10,000 (USD 90) in a night.

That night, Paradise was transformed into a casino. Behind the event's concept was the exoticization of Hong Kong as a site for casinos and gambling.

Instead of the usual bar-like setting where customers sat next to each other and faced the standing employees, tables were rearranged so they could be used for playing poker and blackjack. This freed up space on the floor for playing roulette and cee-lo, a dice game. Since such forms of gambling are legally prohibited in Japan, customers played the games using chips named after Shigure, "Shigure dollars" (SD).[2] Employees doubled as dealers and wore colorful cheongsams—traditional Chinese costumes for women—in various designs.[3] Shigure, who wore a two-piece deep purple corset and miniskirt with matching boots and a long wig woven into braids, became the event's centerpiece. Included in the cover charge were one drink and SD 100 to play games or buy food and drinks, but customers could purchase or win more chips. The menu also featured Hong Kong–style food not usually served at Paradise, such as Chinese dumplings (*shumai*) and a small assortment of dim sum, each for SD 125 (about JPY 1,190, or USD 10.90). Customers spent much of the evening drinking, snacking, and gambling. Of all the special events I attended during my fieldwork, none epitomized the establishment's profit making more than this one. Turning Paradise into a casino symbolized the desire for both the owners and customers to win big.

Even when special events were not held, Paradise maintained a business model largely motivated by profit. On weekends, late nights operated differently from evenings at the establishment. Officially, Paradise was open until 11 p.m., but its owners sold the time slots between 11 p.m. and 5 a.m. to certain employees, who would run the place and earn extra income. When I mentioned this to Rin, a regular customer and cisgender woman in her thirties, she pointed out that this was the business model when Paradise first started. Back in the day, the owners rented a space in Akihabara where they worked the bar late at night on weekends. By offering the same opportunities to their employees, the owners secured additional revenue and provided more flexibility in terms of staffing and managing the establishment.

Once, I followed Rin to Paradise after we had dinner together elsewhere and arrived just in time to witness the shift change. The manager closed the cash register, and employees cleared the tables for the next shift, preparing to clock out. A different set of two employees started their shift, helping customers to settle in for the late night. It was assumed that these customers would be staying the night; likely they had missed their last train and couldn't afford to take a taxi home or stay the night at a nearby hotel.[4] For instance, present that night was Noriko, a cis woman in her late twenties and a regular whom Rin had befriended at Paradise. Noriko lived in Yokohama and, after missing her last train, had no choice but to remain at the café-and-bar. Taking a taxi home would easily cost tens of thousands of yen (a few hundred US dollars), which was much more expensive than sticking around the establishment. Customers spent less during late-night sessions and were charged a flat fee for an all-you-can-drink (*nomihōdai*) course: JPY 2,000 (USD 18) for soft drinks and JPY 2,500 (USD 22.50) for alcoholic drinks. Customers could pay an additional JPY 300 (USD 2.70) for an all-you-can-eat (*tabehōdai*) course. Drinking, eating, and chatting continued in these later hours, albeit in muted tones. Some patrons eventually became so drunk or sleepy that they would take a nap until closing time.

This chapter examines Paradise and Garçon as profit-making businesses in relation to capitalism and the cis-heteronormative home and family in Japan. Japanese capitalism has historically been intertwined with gender in various ways, and I begin by tracing its trajectory, particularly how constructions of the nuclear family and home became embedded in Confucian patriarchal ideology during the Meiji period (1868–1912) and were vital for developing the political economy. This historical context is important for understanding how gender roles were shaped by capitalist development in Japan and why they shifted in the 1990s. Through a discussion of what I call *pink economies*, that is, wider networks of production, consumption, and circulation of goods and services related to how sex, gender, and sexuality are commodified in both heteronormative and nonnormative sites in Japan, this chapter illuminates the (dis)connections between Paradise and Garçon and Japanese sex and night entertainment. In doing so, I highlight the ways these establishments are pericapitalist, or "simultaneously capitalist and non-capitalist."[5]

Under pericapitalist modes, the establishments are profit driven and leverage *josō*, *dansō*, and *otoko no ko* as new phenomena, yet the individuals involved make sense of their experiences in ways that aren't always monetary in nature. To demonstrate this, I delineate Paradise's and Garçon's births as among the first *dansō* and *josō/otoko no ko* café-and-bars in Akihabara and the owners' initial struggles with founding the establishments. I explore how customers have enacted alternative forms of belonging or "homes" inside the café-and-bars as a means of living otherwise and what this means for the cis-heteronormative home and family outside. How do some customers negotiate their patronage with their masculinity and familial obligations? I argue that although businesses like Paradise and Garçon may present alternative social formations, they also operate to reinforce the status quo outside.

## Japanese Capitalism and Gender

Capitalist development in Japan has its roots in the Meiji Restoration (1868), a period that saw the formation of a modern nation-state and colonial expansion with the nation's rapid militarization and industrialization.[6] As a late-developing capitalist state, Japan drew on Western models of empire to annex Korea, Taiwan, Manchuria, and parts of China and the Pacific Islands, but it also departed from these models to form an Asian imperialist state.[7] Japan established an "emperor system" built on patriarchy, which promoted the emperor as the nation's father who had full authority over his subjects, while "maintaining an appearance of constitutionalism."[8] The patrilineal household system and family registry were established in 1871, making a man the head of each household.[9] Such Confucian patriarchal ideologies were also employed to justify Japan's military and colonial pursuits and formed the basis for women's subjugation, particularly through their roles as wives and mothers in the family.[10] In this way, Japanese capitalism, much like capitalism everywhere, instrumentalized women's reproductive labor.[11]

During the postwar era, Japan shifted from a militarist state to an industrial state, focusing on export-led manufacturing of steel, electronics, and automobiles.[12] While men contributed their labor to these industries, women were expected to do so at home. This "reproductive bargain" was significant for the Japanese political economy because of a social exchange between a male breadwinner, who was guaranteed certain benefits in his employment, and his financially dependent wife, who was responsible for child-rearing and household management.[13] Japanese companies depended on this gender division of labor because male middle-class white-collar office workers—known as *salarymen*—demonstrated their loyalty to their corporate family by working long hours and, in return, received benefits such as promotions, pay raises, and lifetime employment.[14] Modern Japanese capitalism was achieved on the backs of women's unpaid domestic and care work.

Since the bubble burst in the early 1990s, however, the reproductive bargain no longer seems viable, and the *salaryman* is decreasingly the hegemonic masculine ideal. Despite scholars' valorization and exoticization of Japanese capitalism and Japanese-style management vis-à-vis the Anglo-American model, many cracks that began to appear during the long recessionary period have continued to grow into the present.[15] For instance, since the 1990s and postindustrialization, there has been an increasing number of homeless people on the streets, the majority of whom are male middle-aged and elderly blue-collar and nonregular construction workers who were cast off during the industry's stagnation in Tokyo.[16] Homelessness as a social problem is compounded by precarious employment among men and women in their twenties and thirties; unlike in the postwar period, when companies guaranteed job security for *salarymen*, today few people have permanent long-term employment.[17] In the 1990s sociologist Yamada Masahiro famously coined the term *parasite single* to describe young unmarried people, especially women, who live at home with their parents, depend on them financially, and engage in luxury consumption.[18] Refuting Yamada's claim, economist Genda Yuji argued that due to labor market deregulation, young people have fewer opportunities for stable and regular employment, giving them little choice but to depend on their parents financially; for him, the "emergence of parasite singles among young people is not a cause, but rather a consequence" of these structural changes.[19] Although the label is problematic, as scholars discuss, *parasite single* demonstrates a fundamental shift from thinking about marriage as a given to considering singlehood as a practical option.[20]

Today many precarious young adults are called *freeters* and continue to live with their parents, which keeps them off the streets and conceals the degree of poverty and unemployment in Japan.[21] In particular, women, who form the majority of irregular and temporary workers and would otherwise be homeless, are absorbed into the home and family.[22] The young precariat's plight is exemplified by Amamiya Karin, an advocate for freeters, who goes beyond labor and poverty issues to highlight the disconnection freeters experience with other human beings.[23] As Anne Allison puts it, precarious youths are "bereft of a place that feels homey and secure (*ibasho*)."[24] They lack a felt sense of existence, which hinges on some form of acknowledgment from other people, and when this is not received, they feel displaced. No longer the ideal site for economic production nor even a place of belonging, the Japanese home and family now operate to sweep such social and gender inequalities—contradictions inherent in capitalism—under the rug.

### *Shinjuku Boys*: Understanding Marriage in a Stagnating Economy

In one scene in the film *Shinjuku Boys*, Gaish casually chats with a customer, at one point broaching the topic of marriage.[25] They are not at Marilyn, Gaish's workplace, a bar staffed by *onabe* employees, but are at what looks like a hotel restaurant the morning after. The customer, an attractive cis woman who has long, straight hair with bangs and looks to be in her twenties, de-

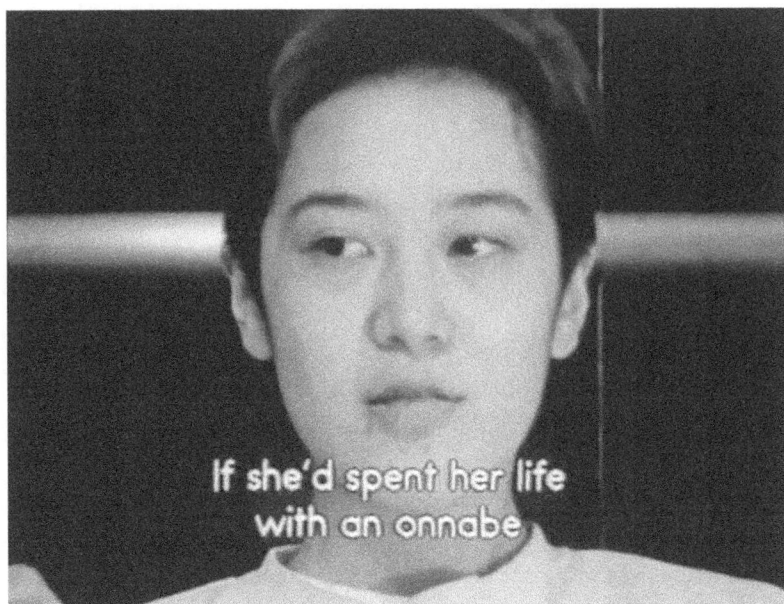

**2.1** Gaish discussing their first relationship, which was with a high school teacher. Still from *Shinjuku Boys*, 1995.

clares she has no intention of getting married. "Besides," she jokes playfully, "I can't marry you." An amused Gaish agrees with her and asks, "Why don't you want to get married?" She replies that she just does not.

The camera cuts to an interview with Gaish, who sits on a bed in casual clothing, as they discuss their first relationship, which was with their homeroom teacher in high school (figure 2.1). After three years together, Gaish and their teacher broke up so the latter could go through with an arranged marriage. Despite looking heartbroken while telling this story, Gaish reasons, "If she'd spent her life with an *onabe*, she would have been an outcast. It was better for her to marry and lead a normal life rather than be with me."

These two scenes show changing attitudes toward cis-heteronormative marriage and family. The bursting of the bubble and ensuing recession in the 1990s shaped people's commonsense ideas surrounding heterosexual marriage and other (nonheterosexual) alternative social formations not defined under the rubric of marriage. When Gaish was still in high school, more young women were predisposed to getting married, as was the case for their homeroom teacher. However, since the 1990s, a growing number of young women have become disinclined to marry, exemplified by Gaish's customer. From an economic standpoint, we might contend that with more young women gaining financial independence through the flexible work-force, they have less incentive to marry.[26] Young women like Gaish's customer hold some form of employment, enjoy their own time, and spend part of their income on leisure, such as at establishments like Marilyn. They no longer have to depend on the men they marry for their livelihood—the main role, in economic terms, of marriage.[27]

Despite rising numbers of men and women not getting married, however, Yoko Tokuhiro contends that Japan remains a "society where marriage is the norm" (*kaikon shakai*).[28] In her ethnography of marriage based on interviews with mainly elite college-educated unmarried Japanese women in their thirties, Tokuhiro observes they have internalized social expectations of marriage as an ultimate goal.[29] It is unsurprising to find them holding on to such ideals. Even before cracks started to appear in Japanese capitalism, the reproductive bargain was primarily open to and embraced by middle- and upper-class individuals like Tokuhiro's interlocutors. Such commonsense ideas of marriage persist in Japanese society, as seen in Gaish's decision to leave their homeroom teacher so she could marry a man and "lead a normal life." From Gaish's perspective, being in a relationship with an *onabe* remains heavily stigmatized in comparison to heterosexual marriage—the bastion of normality.

Perhaps instead of simply indicating that the institution of marriage is either weakened by existing economic conditions or reinforced by social norms and cultural traditions, this demonstrates a widening gap between people's (often unrealistic) expectations of marriage and the reality that marriage is becoming increasingly unaffordable and hence unattainable for many individuals. This can be seen in the case of Gaish's customer, who seeks other ways of fulfilling her sexual and emotional desires, such as establishing a casual relationship with Gaish—one they both know will not end in marriage. Gaish's customer's lament that she cannot marry an *onabe*, although said in jest, reveals a lingering contradiction between the breakdown of marriage as an institution and the way it is safeguarded as a heterosexual privilege.

That said, the destabilization of marriage coupled with shifting gender roles and social expectations shaped by a weakened economy opens up the possibility of alternative social formations. If it was previously unthinkable to date or form a lifelong attachment with an *onabe*, such evolving conditions have gradually enabled these possibilities for Gaish and their customer. That this occurred in the 1990s, concurring with the onset of the recession and with *onabe* becoming a category of its own, is no coincidence. On the one hand, stagnation has encouraged the rethinking of relations outside the heteronormative marriage and family and indeed the reproductive bargain.[30] Being single is not merely an economic choice; it's also a personal choice and a form of resistance against commonsense expectations of marriage in Japanese society. On the other hand, this shift has also allowed for new understandings of social formations that sites like Marilyn engender. They are vital spaces for *onabe* and *onabe*-loving individuals to interact and remain emotionally invested. The club depends on customers' regular patronage and, perhaps more important, their—often sexual and romantic—attachments to specific employees. Ultimately, this hinges on patrons' willingness to spend a sizable amount of time and money at Marilyn.

Although Marilyn is not the same as Garçon and Paradise, we might consider these establishments in similar ways. With shifts in attitudes toward marriage, gender roles, and capitalist productivity, *dansō* and *josō/otoko no ko* café-and-bars become sites where, as we shall see, regulars spend copious amounts of time and money to enact alternative homes and forms of belonging. Deviating from a sociality tied to the home, school, or workplace, they generate alternative social formations that are nonnormative and potentially destabilize such notions of productivity. At the same time, some customers negotiate their *josō* practices within their obligations to the cis-heteronormative home and family and, in so doing, reinforce the status quo.

## Pink Economies in Japan

What I call *pink economies* are closely related to the *pink yen*, which, like the *pink dollar* and *pink pound*, is used to measure the spending power of gay and lesbian people. As scholars have eloquently argued, while the pink dollar or pound conjures the image of gay identity adhering to money, this relationship is in itself unstable.[31] Instead of *pink yen*, I use *pink economies* to index broad networks of production, consumption, and circulation of goods and services related to the commercialization of sex, gender, and sexuality in the media and Japanese sex and night entertainment. Since the postwar period, which coincided with the beginning of rapid economic growth, goods, services, and money have flowed across cis-heteronormative and nonnormative commercial media and sex-related and entertainment sites, including gay, lesbian, and gender-variant establishments.

Neither *pink yen* nor *pink economies* is commonly used in Japan. However, since the 1960s *pinku* (pink)—both the word and the color—has been used in multiple terms to indicate "erotic nuances or connotations."[32]

Examples include pink salons or cabarets, establishments offering various sexual services except for penetrative sex (e.g., fellatio), and *pink mood*, from *Pink Mood Show* (*Pinku mūdo shō*), a late-night program broadcast by Fuji Television in the 1960s portraying strip dancers' erotic performances at the Nichigeki Theater.[33] Due in part to heightened public discourses on sex surrounding the Prostitution Prevention Law—a law abolishing the prostitution of women—and the demise of the Japanese film studio system owing to dwindling audiences, Japanese cinema began to increasingly represent sexual issues. This led to the early 1960s rise of the pink film (*pinku eiga*), a genre of "soft-core, independent cinema of Japan," or sexploitation films produced on a shoestring budget.[34] The experience of "seeing" pink films involved offscreen sexual encounters among spectators at pink theaters, linking them to pink salons and pink cabarets.[35]

In using *pink economies*, my aim is twofold. First, I wish to underscore the productive connections between cis-heteronormative and nonnormative commercial media and sex-related and entertainment sites in Japan. Despite the abundant scholarship on these sites, most scholars research the cis-heteronormative sites separately from the nonnormative ones.[36] Two exceptions include Mark McLelland and Mitsuhashi Junko, whose works trace the historical intersections between the sex trade and same-gender and gender-variant spaces of consumption in the 1950s and 1960s.[37] They demonstrate how during the postwar period, these sites were initially fluid and overlapping and developed with the growing economy. This backdrop helps us understand how genders sometimes emerge from the intersection between nonnormative spaces of consumption and sites of cis-heteronormative sex-related and nighttime entertainment.

Second, I wish to locate Japanese pink economies within transnational economies of sex, gender, and sexuality. Here I am not advocating a kind of "global queering," or the globalizing spread of gay identity-based politics modeled after the United States.[38] Instead, I wish to show how pink economies inform and are informed by the contradictions of queer globalizations, the plural and multidirectional global processes of turning nonnormative genders and sexualities into commodities while also empowering these individuals in creative ways.[39] These contradictions align with those of neoliberal capitalism, which enables "new modes of inclusion and exclusion" by making some queer and trans consumers visible in the marketplace while rendering others invisible.[40]

Pink economies in Japan are fundamentally shaped by two laws enacted during the postwar period: the Businesses Affecting Public Morals Regulation Law (*Fūzoku eigyō torishimari hō*, often abbreviated to *Fūeihō*) in 1948 and the Prostitution Prevention Law (*Baishun bōshi hō*) in 1956. The Businesses Affecting Public Morals Regulation Law regulates businesses providing food, alcohol, and entertainment.[41] Prominent examples of such establishments include hostess and host clubs, which became popularized during the expansion of consumer-oriented postindustrial capitalism and neoliberal reforms in 1970s Japan. Hostess clubs are establishments where cis women or feminine-presenting employees provide conversation for mostly male customers, typically *salarymen*; host clubs are the male parallel. Although these establishments offer different services, they are all required to register with the municipal public safety commission to operate. Other than policing these businesses, the law also normalizes the commercialization of sex and other kinds of services.[42] Previous scholarship has firmly situated hostess clubs outside Japan's sex industry, arguing that they provide corporate entertainment, a form of entertainment aimed at bolstering masculine bonds within or between companies.[43] However, other scholars have argued that the lines between sex work and companionship aren't always clearly drawn.[44] Regardless, both kinds of labor—hostessing and sex work—contribute to larger economies of pink. And as some scholars have shown in less elite Filipina hostess bars in Japan, pink economies are complicated not only by issues of gender and sexuality but also by class, race, and ethnicity.[45]

The Prostitution Prevention Law, which women's groups succeeded in getting the Japanese government to pass, cast prostitution as a "social evil" to maintain so-called public morals instead of directly penalizing sex workers or their customers.[46] This can be seen from the law's narrow definition of prostitution as a woman having vaginal intercourse with an "unspecified person"—that is, a male nonacquaintance—in exchange for payment.[47] Despite the law's implementation and the crackdown on red-light districts in 1958, commercial sex did not completely disappear; instead, it diversified to offer various nonpenetrative sexual services, manifesting as pink salons, pink cabarets, and "soaplands."[48] Soaplands charged clients an entrance fee for the public bathhouse, but once inside, clients negotiated with women employees for massage and sexual services and paid them directly.[49] This shifts the responsibility to sex workers and skirts the rule banning sex between nonacquaintances on the grounds that clients and employees become acquainted during the massage. These sites were all distinct in their own ways, but they had in common the avoidance of penile-vaginal intercourse. More important, because the definition of prostitution as coitus was interpreted as not applying to sexual relations among gay men, lesbian women, and non-cis individuals, establishments providing such services were not considered illegal and indirectly benefited from the abolition of cis-heteronormative prostitution.

For example, the mass closure of brothels in the larger Shinjuku area made way for the pre-Stonewall gay boom in the 1950s and 1960s, during which *josō* and gay-identified individuals occupied the same commercial spaces, as did *dansō* individuals and women-loving women. This enabled a shared culture of consumption and the forging of new relationships. During this time, many bars staffed by *gay boys* or employees who were beautiful gay-identified adolescents and *josōsha* (male-to-female cross-dressing individuals) sprouted up all over Tokyo, including in Ueno, Ginza, Shinjuku, and Shimbashi.[50] Though these two worlds split in the 1960s, this reflected a dynamic period of experimentation for individuals who blurred the distinctions between gay and *josō*. In Shinjuku Ni-chōme, originally a heterosexual red-light district, *homo bars*—short for homosexual-style gay bars—staffed by non-*josō* gay-identified adolescents began to appear.[51] *Josō*-style gay bars staffed by *josō* individuals also opened in Kabukichō, catering to a wider clientele than the niche group of homo bar patrons, who were mostly gay-identified men who knew one another. This split between homo bars and *josō*-style gay bars would not only create ontological distinctions between the categories gay and *josō* but also shape Ni-chōme as the gay neighborhood it is today and the larger Shinjuku area as a site for sex-related and nighttime entertainment, including *josō* bars and clubs.

Equally popular were lesbian spaces, such as bars, circles, study groups, "mini communications," and social interactions on the internet.[52] These spaces informed one another and were not only platforms for socializing but also—in the case of bars—economic institutions where individuals were employed. For example, emerging in the mid-1960s were *dansō* establishments (*dansō no mise*)—retrospectively called *les (rezu) bars*, *onabe bars*, or *boyish (bōisshu) establishments*—which were spaces where cis women customers could mingle with *onabe* bartenders and one another.[53] Located variously in Roppongi, Asakusa, Ueno, and other areas in Tokyo, these establishments encouraged the patronage of customers in *dansō*. For instance, the famous *onabe* bar Kikōshi welcomed many *dansō* lesbian women after opening its doors in 1973. Although there was no eventful split between *onabe*, *dansō* individuals, and lesbian women, as for *josō* and gay individuals, operating within these spaces were various divides such as male/female, active/passive, and butch/femme, which, while not complicating the gender binary and heteronormative gender roles, may blur these tidy boundaries.[54]

However, much less is known about the *dansō* establishments that preceded the women-only lesbian bars in 1980s Ni-chōme.[55]

Arguably, these *dansō* and lesbian establishments and homo and *josō*-style gay bars where like-minded individuals interacted eventually shaped the 1970s women's liberation movement and lesbian feminism and contributed to the 1990s queer movement and subsequent trans activism, on which much has been written.[56] This historical context in which postwar gay, lesbian, and gender-variant spaces of consumption developed from certain legal, cultural, and economic shifts allows us to understand how cis-heteronormative and nonnormative commercial media and sex-related and entertainment sites were at one time fluid and overlapping. My concept of pink economies is thus useful for indexing such transformations, connecting them to twenty-first-century *josō* and *dansō* sites of consumption. Furthermore, pink economies situate Garçon and Paradise within works on homo, queer, and trans economies to rethink the relationship between emergent genders and the material.[57]

## The Births of Garçon and Paradise

### Garçon's Beginnings

In a short video produced by Yuka, Garçon's owner, she ambles along the dimly lit streets of Akihabara in the evening as she speaks about her experience of running the café-and-bar. A cis woman in her early forties with glasses, a surgical mask, little to no makeup, and her long dyed-brown hair tied into a ponytail, Yuka looks nondescript in a dark down jacket. Turning a corner, she stops in front of a construction site, a multistory building that had been torn down earlier that year. Pointing to the projected plan of the new building, Yuka announces that Garçon was born on the fourth floor of the previous building. She recalls how the ground floor used to be a ramen restaurant and that above Garçon was a cosplay goods shop.[58]

Yuka then walks to a nearby building, where Garçon is housed, bumping into a few regulars on their way out. As nondiegetic music starts to play, the camera cuts to a montage of videos and images taken at Garçon over the previous ten years. The camera then cuts to a slide show displaying the photographs and names of all the employees—about forty or so—who had worked at the establishment. On the last slide were the words "Thank you for ten years."

This video was presented by Yuka at Garçon's tenth-anniversary party, which I attended in December 2016. Held in a rented ballroom, the party was an annual celebration for employees and customers, who dressed to the nines. That evening, the employees were decked out in sharp suits and ties, and customers wore a colorful array of suits, blazers, and evening gowns. Yuka herself wore a traditional cream kimono with dark gray contrasts and pastel green flower prints—a significant change from her nondescript appearance in the video.

After the video ended, Yuka gave a short speech reminiscing about how far they have come since opening in 2006. Garçon had a rocky start, and in the early days, few people knew of its existence. When the café-and-bar was still housed at its old location—the first building Yuka approached in the video—they had as few as three customers a day. A few years later, just as Yuka thought business was finally taking off, she heard about the closure of several *dansō* establishments in Ikebukuro, including one called B:Lily-rose, and once again felt uncertain about Garçon's future. In an effort to keep the business alive, Yuka decided to persuade a few anime- and game-related companies to collaborate with Garçon to do tie-up events, resulting in a 2009 themed event based on the anime series *Neon Genesis Evangelion* (Anno Hideaki, 1995–96).[59] The success of these tie-ups paved the way for later collaborations and helped Garçon overcome the crisis and acquire many loyal customers. Since then, Yuka has envisioned Garçon as one of the top establishments within *dansō* business circles.

As one of the oldest *dansō* café-and-bars in Akihabara in the mid-2000s, Garçon's birth was timely for heralding the first wave of contemporary *dansō* culture—and it capitalized on *dansō* as a new phenomenon. But Garçon's future was threatened when, in the late 2000s, maid cafés and other themed establishments declined in popularity.[60] The anime tie-up events enabled it to turn the tide. One longtime customer, a cis heterosexual woman in her twenties, told me her first encounter with Garçon was through one of these events, a themed event based on Kawamori Shōji's mecha anime franchise *Macross*. Because she enjoyed the experience so much, she decided to return for a second visit. Despite this, I argue that these tie-ups alone do not account for Garçon's survival, especially in the 2010s during the second wave of contemporary *dansō* culture when such events became less common—the last *Macross*-themed event was held in early 2011. As one employee told me, they have become far too busy attending to customers to orchestrate tie-ups. I posit that Garçon's enduring success stems more from the everyday construction of alternative worlds where diverse genders and nonnormative social formations could be enacted. Because of its place as a hub of anime, manga, and game culture, Akihabara is an ideal site for such alternative worlds.

Toward the end of Garçon's tenth-anniversary party, I asked Ken, a long-time cis-male customer in his forties, to introduce me to Yuka. Over the months I conducted fieldwork, I had only gotten a glimpse of Yuka once or twice when she quickly dropped by the establishment, but I never had the opportunity to speak with her. Yuka regularly traveled for work and was so busy it was even hard for her own employees to meet her in person. For matters pertaining to running the café-and-bar, Ikki, Garçon's twenty-seven-year-old manager, usually communicated with Yuka over the phone. This meant that most of the time Yuka left the day-to-day operations to Ikki. But I wanted to understand why someone who didn't practice *dansō* would start the first *dansō* establishment.

When I approached Yuka with Ken, she was reserved and politely refused my request for an interview, citing her busy schedule. Undeterred, I asked her there and then why she thought of opening a *dansō* café-and-bar back in 2006 when Akihabara was still saturated with maid cafés. At my question, she shrugged noncommittally: "It's Akihabara after all and the first *dansō* establishment at that." She stopped short of explaining herself and quickly excused herself from the conversation. It seems that other than intuiting that a *dansō* café-and-bar might be popular with individuals frequenting Akihabara, Yuka didn't have a strong reason for running Garçon. Besides, according to Ikki, Garçon was only one of many projects Yuka oversaw. Yuka ran a parent company based in Akihabara that offered a variety of services, including consulting, product planning, events planning, costume design, restaurant management, application and home-page design, fan club operations and management, and sales and production of promotional goods. I initially imagined her to be managing a chain of *dansō*-themed establishments, but this wasn't the case—something corroborated by Ikki.

Regardless of Yuka's intentions, her ability to turn Garçon into a viable enterprise where many others have failed was a feat. Her prediction that Akihabara and not elsewhere would be a generative environment for a *dansō* café-and-bar reveals great foresight and a knowledge of what was happening in the neighborhood at the time. Yuka's decision, I contend, was also strategic in two ways. First, by the 2000s Akihabara had the infrastructure from recent redevelopment efforts to support a relatively large and lucrative anime, manga, and game fan base. The otaku boom brought about more positive public impressions and media representations of these anime, manga, and game fans, who now made up an attractive consumer market. In a past interview with a Japanese scholar, Yuka declared that fundamental to Garçon as a business was its specialization in *moe*, a term typically expressing male otaku's "affective response" to cute girl characters.[61] *Moe* can also characterize women fans' emotional attachments to *dansō* and beautiful boy characters, which manifests in Garçon when women patrons find like-minded individuals who possess a similar level of interest in *dansō* as themselves.[62] From Yuka's perspective, it was Garçon's promotion of *moe* that enabled Garçon to prevail as a *dansō* café-and-bar and inspire other *dansō* services and establishments.

Second, beyond the popular culture connection, locating the café-and-bar in Akihabara and not, for example, in Shinjuku enabled Yuka to disassociate Garçon from *onabe* clubs, lesbian bars, and *dansō* host clubs—a new kind of establishment staffed by *dansō* hosts.[63] Marta Fanasca's ethnography of *dansō* escort services, which are also located in Akihabara and provide one-on-one romantic and allegedly nonsexual dates with escorts who are in *dansō*, similarly found that managers seek to "tone down [*dansō*'s] queer potential."[64] It should be noted that *dansō* escorts are distinct in various ways from the *dansō* employees I encountered at Garçon, which I discuss later. Garçon's physical location in Akihabara allowed it to be read more in terms of a popular cultural space directed at anime, manga, and game fans than as a haven for LGBT people and the commercialization of sexual services. This apparent distance from the sex and nighttime entertainment industries distinguished not only Garçon's clientele but also the services its employees provided. In addition, the laws governing the business are different from those for host and hostess clubs. For instance, although the Businesses Affecting Public Morals Regulation Law regulates businesses providing food, alcohol, and entertainment, including the sex industry, *dansō* (and *josō*) establishments tend to fall into a gray area. Garçon appears to have escaped this regulation mainly because it was perceived as targeting otaku—something Yuka reinforces with her allusion to *moe*.

### Founding Paradise

Unlike Yuka, the owners of Paradise were personally motivated to found Paradise by their everyday *josō* practices. Hayashi and Miho first became acquainted through *josō* business circles. Similar to Garçon, the early days of Paradise were a struggle, in part because contemporary *josō* culture had only begun to make waves. Just a year before Paradise opened, in August 2007, a monthly event called "*Josō New Half* Propaganda" was initiated in Kabukichō. This event consisted of a variety of activities, such as live music shows, talks by invited speakers, and dancing to professional disc jockey remixes. On its website (figure 2.2), Propaganda, which operated the

2.2    Screenshot of Propaganda's home page featuring its last president, Satsuki, taken on April 1, 2019. propaganda-party.com (no longer available).

last Saturday of every month, was described as "Japan's largest *josō* event" and a "free space" where people could wear whatever they want without being restrained by their gender.[65] At first, only a handful of individuals within *josō* business circles, like Miho and Hayashi, knew of Propaganda through word of mouth and social networking. However, its attendees, who were said to be "all men," quickly grew from one hundred to over four hundred.[66] Differentiating themselves from the Shinjuku-based Propaganda, Miho and Hayashi decided to set up their business in Akihabara, merging perhaps for the first time the otaku world and *josō* business circles. They could therefore capitalize not only on the growing interest in *josō* galvanized by Propaganda but also on otaku's consumption of anime, manga, and games featuring *otoko no ko* characters.

In 2008, when Hayashi was still an employee at Hibari-tei, the first *otoko no ko* pop-up maid café to open in Akihabara, they tried to persuade its owner to turn the irregular business—operating once a month—into a regular one.[67] When this failed, an ambitious Hayashi decided to take matters into their own hands and started a one-person *josō/otoko no ko* bar. But this was not easy. Hayashi held a full-time job as a model and could only run the bar one weekend night per week, which meant that, like Hibari-tei, Hayashi's *josō/ otoko no ko* bar had undetermined opening hours. One night, when Miho was at the bar as a customer and business was brisk, Hayashi asked Miho to help, improvising as they went along. Finding the collaborative experience fun, Hayashi raised the idea of managing the bar together, and Miho agreed.

In subsequent months, Hayashi and Miho continued their daytime jobs—Miho was then a web director—and after a full day of work, they would serve customers at the bar. As Miho explained to me, they were unsure if the new business would succeed and needed the steady flow of income just in case. A few months later, in mid-2009, Miho and Hayashi changed the bar's name to Paradise, officially establishing the company that would manage the first *josō/otoko no ko* café-and-bar in Akihabara.[68] Over the years, as business picked up, Miho and Hayashi relocated Paradise to a bigger commercial space and hired a cook, bartender, and *josō* employees to serve customers alongside them.

Hayashi's initial struggle to become independent might be read alongside the waning of maid cafés in the late 2000s. The reluctance of Hibari-tei's owner to expand might be interpreted as caution at a time when customers' enthusiasm for maid cafés was rapidly cooling. But Hayashi's decision to forge ahead was based less on profit than their dedication to promoting *josō/otoko no ko*—surely their daytime job would offer them a better salary than selling a few drinks at a one-person bar. However, this does not mean Miho and Hayashi weren't concerned about making a profit. Indeed, their initial plan to hold on to their full-time jobs suggests just the opposite. Because they wanted to turn Paradise into a profitable enterprise, they waited until they were confident the business and *josō/otoko no ko* culture would take off in Akihabara. Their motivation to innovate complemented their business model. Employees and customers alike have relayed to me some of these "origin stories" of how Miho and Hayashi singlehandedly created and nurtured a space like Paradise. These legendary narratives are encouraging to young *josōko/otoko no ko* who aspire to become successful like Miho and Hayashi in terms of both their career and their contribution to *josō* business circles.

Locating Paradise within Akihabara was crucial for two reasons. First, Miho's and Hayashi's identification as otaku meant they could tap into an existing consumer base they were already a part of. Their goal of establishing Paradise as the place to find "Japan's cutest *otoko no ko*" was enticing to consumers already interested in anime, manga, and games featuring *josō* characters.[69] Miho described Paradise to me as a part of the "*moe* industry" (*moesangyō*)—a term coined by Japanese economist Morinaga Takurō to refer to the marketing of *moe* as a product to consumers through goods and services related to anime characters, such as games, figures, and themed establishments.[70] Using Morinaga's term, Miho illustrated his awareness of a lucrative otaku market that has existed since the mid-2000s. Aside from cute cis girl characters, otaku were also attracted to cute *josō* characters. Leveraging such feelings and the burgeoning enthusiasm in *josō* Propaganda generated, Miho and Hayashi set up their business in Akihabara. Bringing the otaku and *josō* worlds together expanded Paradise's customer base, though the emergence of three-dimensional *josōko/otoko no ko* has not been well received by some otaku.

Second, this strategy enabled Miho and Hayashi to differentiate themselves from the Shinjuku-based Propaganda and to skirt the Businesses Affecting Public Morals Regulation Law, which typically governs much within *josō* business circles. Like Garçon, Paradise fell into a gray area. For example, more than one employee told me that because they did not sit next to customers to attend to them in the way hostesses do—they remained standing at all times, like maids at maid cafés—they were not flouting the law. The law appears to be interpreted literally as governing establishments where employees provide designated customers with food, alcohol, and conversation of a sexual nature in a venue smaller than five square meters (fifty-four square feet) with dim lighting below ten lux.[71] At Paradise, as for other establishments, this was easily resolved by having brighter lights, not having customers designate a host or hostess (known as *shimei*), and having employees circulate through the space, which was much bigger than five square meters, engaging in small talk with multiple customers instead of only one or two.[72]

Enforcing physical distance between customers and employees was also important for discouraging romantic and sexual relationships between them, which both establishments forbade. Miho had previously dismissed employees for dating customers and had banned said customers from Paradise. As I understand it, the reason for this prohibition is not that it conflicts with morality—neither legal, Judeo-Christian, nor the Japanese common sense–inflected morality—but that putting sex and love on the table is bad for business. While "no-touch" flirting and romantic gestures between employees and customers were allowed—even encouraged—at Paradise, as one interlocutor put it, who would want to patronize the establishment anymore if they could date or casually meet employees for sex outside? The monetization of love and sex here appears calculated to promote customers' return visits. In this way, we can see the ways in which markets and the Businesses Affecting Public Morals Regulation Law complexly shaped how Paradise was run and what services were and were not offered. Conversation was purportedly the main service employees provided, and their exchanges with customers were everyday discourses about society and the world (*seken banashi*), which are not regulated by the law. Yet, by nurturing employee-customer sociality, these seemingly mundane conversations beckoned patrons to come back for more.

Despite the disassociation the owners of Paradise and Garçon tried to enact between their establishments and Japanese sex and night entertainment, they remained connected in several ways. Understanding Garçon and Paradise in terms of pink economies locates them within a much longer history of cis-heteronormative and nonnormative commercial media and sex-related and entertainment sites. From this perspective, Garçon and Paradise were not entirely new, though they were sites of experimentation to generate booms and categories in the twenty-first century. Yet Garçon and Paradise were simultaneously disconnected from a time of rapid economic growth, emerging instead from prolonged stagnation. In precarious times, *josō* and *dansō* individuals have become empowered to express themselves through consumption. Such contradictions inherent in Japanese capitalism would mean of course that not every *josō* or *dansō* individual has the means to do so, but those who do would pave the way for transformation.

### Home and Belonging Otherwise

Many regulars told me they considered Garçon their home, using various terms that mean "home," such as *ie*, *uchi*, and *hōmu*. For instance, Saito, an *x-gender* regular, described the café-and-bar as "like another home" using the Japanese phrase *igokochi ga ii*, which indexes feeling comfortable in a particular space. A temporary employee (*haken shain*) working in an office, the twenty-nine-year-old had an androgynous appearance, much like some of the employees at Garçon. Saito felt Garçon was "totally different" because of its "atmosphere" (*fun'iki*) as compared to 80 + 1, a popular *dansō* establishment in Ikebukuro that closed its doors in 2015, and ordinary coffee joints like Starbucks and Excelsior. Saito enjoyed conversing with fellow customers—a dynamic not always present in establishments like 80 + 1, which actively forbade conversations among customers unless they were friends outside the establishment.[73] Saito found this rule awkward, leaving patrons to silently sip their drink while waiting for their turn to chat with employees. Another regular, a thirty-one-year-old cis woman, supported Saito's claim, saying she found the "atmosphere" (*fun'iki*) at other *dansō* establishments like 80 + 1 "strained" (*gisu gisu*), whereas at Garçon she experienced a "feeling of being at home."

One special event I attended that enacted this familial environment was the Garçon Family event, so called because it took place during the first week of May, when Mother's Day and Children's Day are celebrated in Japan. During this event, employees wore plain clothes instead of their usual uniforms and greeted customers with *okaeri* (welcome home) instead of *irrashaimase* (welcome). Garçon also sold a plate of two rice balls with Japanese pickled vegetables and fried chicken morsels priced at JPY 1,000 (USD 9). Although this cost is twice that at gastropubs, regulars knew it was special because employees took turns personally preparing the pickled vegetables before coming to work and would make the rice balls by hand before their very eyes.[74] Molding the rice into shape becomes a performance to feast on, and the finished product takes on deeper meanings about being cared for as though by a family member. In the Japanese home, rice balls are typically handmade by mothers for their children. Therefore, behind the event's concept is the idea that customers and employees are part of a big family at Garçon.

The Garçon Family event was also informed by the knowledge that, barring special occasions, the establishment did not usually serve food. When Garçon first opened, Ikki told me, employees served simple food—side dishes or finger food that could be prepared easily or beforehand—but eventually the establishment became too busy to manage the preparation of food, and they started focusing on drinks. Aside from not having enough hands on deck to attend to customers, Garçon had neither a chef nor a full kitchen, leaving food preparation (if any) entirely to employees.

As at Paradise, Garçon's special events, held at least once a month, attracted a larger crowd and required customers to spend more than they usually would. On average, regulars frequented Garçon two or more nights a week and spent JPY 2,000–4,000 (USD 18–36) per night. During special events, regulars could easily spend twice or more this amount, depending on how long they stayed. Although Garçon did not have a cover charge, customers were required to order one drink—either alcoholic or nonalcoholic—for every hour they remained at the café-and-bar. This could add up, considering a nonalcoholic drink like soda or iced tea was upward of JPY 500 (USD 4.50) and alcoholic drinks such as *chūhai* (short for "shōchū highball," a fruit-flavored cocktail made up of soda and shōchū) cost JPY 1,000 (USD 9) on average, three or more times the cost at gastropubs. Besides, special events typically revolved around employees' birthdays and various public and commercial holidays, such as New Year's Day, when employees would shed their uniforms and dress up for the occasion. Devout followers of specific employees would certainly be present at their birthday events from opening to closing, but even regulars would feel obliged to show up and partake in the celebrations.

Regulars' characterization of Garçon as homely and homelike demonstrates how mingling with other people enables them to experience a sense of belonging. This *ibasho*, or "homey and secure" place, is something precarious youths in twenty-first-century Japan sorely lack and need.[75] The meaningful conversations regulars engender and participate in constitute Garçon's *fun'iki*, a term that means "atmosphere" but more accurately denotes individuals' mood or feeling within a specific setting in everyday life.[76] This can be seen from their description of Garçon as eliciting good feelings of ease, comfort, and pleasure. For regulars, the *fun'iki* of a place is vital. *Gisu gisu*, on the other hand, is a Japanese onomatopoeia used to convey an unsociable environment as well as relationships among people who don't get along well. The articulation of 80 + 1 as *gisu gisu* indicates an unpleasant *fun'iki* and implies that people within the space were either distant from or in conflict with one another.

Other terms regulars used to describe *fun'iki* are equally affective, notably *igokochi ga ii*, a phrase often used to express one's sense of comfort with a place—including one's home, school, and workplace as well as parks, shops, streets, and restaurants—or even a person.[77] For Saito, this located Garçon as an alternative home where they could drop by at any time to relax and chat with whomever they wished and then leave. However, this turn away from a sociality tied to the home, school, or workplace also represents a critique of the cis-heteronormative world outside Garçon. The postwar Japanese familial model of sociality and capitalism remains based on the patrilineal household system and state ideology and is tied to "my-homeism," where one's sense of belonging is centered in the home and workplace, which supports the nuclear family, corporate capitalism, and the gender division of labor.[78] At Garçon, however, a different kind of relationship to home existed when regulars like Saito found their place in the establishment. This alternative form of sociality has the potential to destabilize hegemonic and monolithic notions of capitalism, leading to possible renewal.

One episode that comes to my mind is when Ken, an otaku and a cis heterosexual regular in his forties, related to us his experience of attending a *dansō*-performing "strip show" of *King of Prism* (Hishida Masakazu, 2016) in Shinjuku. *King of Prism* is an anime film spinoff of *Pretty Rhythm*, which is a multimedia franchise produced by Syn Sophia and Takara Tomy first launched as an arcade game in 2010 that loosely follows the stories of young women who aspire to become idols. In the strip show Ken attended, the characters were young men (instead of women) played by *dansō* performers. A big fan of *King of Prism*, Ken told an enraptured audience at Garçon he felt overwhelmed by the live performance, which was more artistic than lewd and mostly attended by women, presumably *fujoshi* (BL women fans). In an interview afterward, Ken told me Garçon was his "second home" because there he could speak freely about his passion for *King of Prism*—something he does not share with those outside the café-and-bar. As otaku like Ken continue to be regarded as social rejects for their "inappropriate consumption," Garçon provided him with a safe space to share interests the outside world may frown on.[79]

Although Ken was invested in his "inappropriate consumption," he was also building a home away from home. We might ask why the image of home persists even in reference to Garçon. After all, the idea of a second home alludes inevitably to a first home, modeled on my-homeism and the patrilineal household system. As the breadwinner for a family of three, Ken may appear irresponsible for spending so much time and money at Garçon, but according to him, his wife supported his patronage as a means to destress after work. Besides, he reasoned, it was better than going to a hostess club or some other place he couldn't afford on his modest salary. One might argue that a bit of deviation goes a long way in maintaining the status quo. Ken's narrative certainly fits into the productive logic of the "healing" (*iyashi*) boom, where visiting Garçon restores him to work the next day.[80] Put differently, Ken's second home sustained his first home. It would appear that even in deterritorialized forms of sociality and pericapitalist relations of production, the home lingers.

At the same time, challenging this productive logic is Saito's idea of home. Instead of sustaining the cis-heteronormative home and family, home and sociality for Saito appear synonymous with feelings of ease and comfort tied to nonproductivity and unburdened companionship. This may make sense if we follow queer diaspora and migration scholars in envisioning home not as a static site of territorialized sociality and capitalist productivity but in terms of multiple kinds and (re)interpretations of homes.[81] For queer migrants, for instance, home can be thought of as a "destination rather than an origin" and reimagined for women as a site for queer diasporic female subjectivity.[82] In doing so, queer migrant and diasporic subjects rupture hegemonic representations of home and capitalist social formations, motivating a reimagination and reinvention of these forms of belonging—that of belonging otherwise.

Although most Garçon customers weren't queer migrant and diasporic subjects, the idea of home could be similarly reconfigured for those like

Saito. For instance, even though Garçon provided Saito with important networks of support, they were not obliged to fulfill familial responsibilities or maintain the connections they made inside the café-and-bar, which is characteristic perhaps of capitalist social formations. Although Saito could sustain these bonds if they wished, they were also free to suspend them once they stepped outside the establishment. This freedom enabled Saito to remake home as a site for nurturing alternative forms of sociality. As for many young people in Tokyo who live alone, Garçon represented somewhere for Saito to arrive at and belong to through their patronage. Here they could live and belong otherwise. Garçon as a home therefore remained a safe space for such explorations and not-yet-here ways of being and living.

### Negotiating Masculinity in Pericapitalist Realms

I first met Yokohama, a cis heterosexual *josō* customer in his twenties, just before the Japanese New Year, the most important national holiday. Paradise was packed. Most customers had time off from work and dropped in at the café-and-bar before and after *bōnenkai*, drinking parties meant for forgetting all the year's hardships. Amid the hustle and bustle, Yokohama was seated next to me, and we ended up chatting. Outside Paradise, the newly married Yokohama conformed to the social expectations of being a man in Japan, married to a woman, and providing for the family as a *salaryman*. Decked in a frilly dress, knee-high socks, long light brown hair, and full makeup, Yokohama explained how dressing as a woman made him "feel at ease" (*raku ni naru*). I was surprised to learn he had secretly borrowed the dress from his wife, never mind that he was thin enough to fit into it. It was only at Paradise that he seemed free to explore his desire to practice *josō*—something his wife had no clue about.

Yokohama's experience is not singular; several middle-class cis male customers confided in me how they felt a sense of "ease" (*raku*) and "freedom" (*jiyū*) when they visited Paradise. But what exactly did they feel free or at ease from? It appears that Paradise facilitated their (temporary) deviation from hegemonic masculinity, the dominant model of masculinity epitomized by the *salaryman*.[83] The *salaryman* has long been idealized as a form of masculine success, productivity, and national identity.[84] Despite major labor shifts since the 1990s and many men's inability to obtain full-time employment, *salaryman* ideologies continue to haunt the Japanese sociocultural imaginary in the twenty-first century.[85] Granted, this means Yokohama is privileged by *salaryman* masculinity. But perhaps precisely because of such hegemonic expectations, he was unable to openly engage in *josō* or speak to other people about these interests except at Paradise.

One way of interpreting the café-and-bar space from his perspective may be through what Mikhail Bakhtin calls the "carnivalesque," or a "marketplace style of expression," where individuals participating in this space experience the "suspension of all hierarchical rank, privileges, norms, and prohibitions," allowing them to communicate openly with one another during this time.[86] We might say that Paradise was a carnivalesque space where Yokohama freely indulged in his self-transformation, and when he left, he was expected to revert to the roles that allowed him to maintain a cis-heteronormative home and family. Yet, writing about unruly women, Natalie Zemon Davis posits that even outside carnival time, people simultaneously reinscribe and transgress the established order because their engagement is not only a temporary form of liberation but also "part of the conflict over efforts to change the basic distribution of power within society."[87] Instead of simply reading Yokohama's *josō* practices and interactions with other people at Paradise as carnivalesque, we might regard them as a renegotiation and reconfiguration of these hegemonic masculine ideals and ideologies.

Masako, a fifty-two-year-old longtime customer of Paradise who had long been involved in *josō* business circles—mostly in a non-cross-dressing capacity—stands out in my mind as emblematic of such a renegotiation. When Masako decided to take the plunge to begin practicing *josō* three years previously, it upset the entire family, especially their wife.[88] Masako was married with children and grandchildren, was romantically attracted to women, and self-identified as LGBT with the understanding that the category *josō* counted under LGBT. Although Masako's family objected to and were ashamed of their gender crossing, Masako forged ahead. They have not looked back since, reasoning that since they had done their duty to provide for the family for twenty years, now was finally the time to start living for themselves. Unlike Yokohama, Masako was not a *salaryman* but had worked in various jobs and was now a health care administrator. With the children all grown up and financially independent, Masako could now practice *josō*—something they couldn't do while carrying out family commitments. Masako's *josō* practices therefore illustrate not a temporary suspension of masculine productivity but a departure from the status quo after many years of abiding by it.

Masako, who was around five feet, three inches tall, went to great lengths to become what they imagined to be a "beautiful" woman. One of the oldest and most stylish *josō* customers, they would arrive at Paradise with carefully applied makeup in soft, muted colors to highlight their small face—a

Japanese beauty ideal. Like other *josō* customers I was acquainted with, Masako spent a substantial sum on new clothes, makeup, shoes, and accessories. They also had an eye for detail and meticulously planned their outfits in advance, drawing ideas from the women's fashion magazines they regularly consumed. Masako shared with me how they considered various factors like the season, weather, and matching certain colors and materials. For instance, their spring fashion outfit consisted of mustard and baby blue tones, including a mint green floral print skirt, khaki ankle boots, and a navy trench coat to keep the rain off. During Paradise's Halloween event, they came dressed as a witch, wearing dark eyeliner and lipstick, a black organza dress, and a matching conical hat with wide brim.

Unlike Yokohama's more exploratory practices, I see the much older Masako's *josō* practices as located within self-fulfillment and a desire to lead an autonomous life, short of getting a divorce. Masako's rationale that they deserve "me time" after two decades of familial obligations suggests a sense of dissatisfaction with the cis-heteronormative home and family where one puts family above oneself. For many years, Masako played the stereotypical breadwinning role expected within Japanese postwar society's gender division of labor. In this older model of sociality and capitalist productivity, one could trace their lineage to stem-families and their homes and, for a man, identify as a male employee in a company and as a father and husband in a nuclear family. Now, however, Masako appeared unwilling to continue taking on these roles. What Paradise seemed to offer Masako was a site to cultivate the individual self—away from such social expectations—through experimenting with a different gender presentation. As compared to Yokohama, who borrowed his wife's dress and snuck off to Tokyo to practice *josō*, Masako invested time and money in their outfits, which they methodically planned and put together. Yokohama struck me as new to the scene; most *josō* customers I met during my fieldwork were like Masako, purchasing their own clothing and adornments. Their body work—the work one does on one's body—involved a concerted effort to fit their own style and figure.[89]

Masako and Yokohama remained privileged by their perceived cis straight middle-class male position as compared to *josō* individuals who were working-class freeters and located themselves as trans and gender nonconforming. As Masako and Yokohama fulfilled their obligations of maintaining cis-heteronormative homes and families as full-time employees, their *josō* practices potentially queered or ruptured such modes of masculine productivity. Their practices transgressed hegemonic masculinity—an issue scholars have long discussed in terms of a "masculinity crisis" shaped by the 1970s feminist movements and continuing into the 1990s economic recession, often manifesting in young men's inability or disinclination to pursue the *salaryman* ideal.[90] However, instead of masculinity in crisis, we might think about the entire gender order as being in crisis, which changes how we regard masculinity.[91]

In the context of contemporary *josō* culture, anxieties over gender crossing, loss of male privilege, and gay and transgender identification have led to extensive mainstream media coverage of *josō* individuals proclaiming in no uncertain terms that they are cis heterosexual men. While this proclamation seems to bring the threat *josō* poses under control and restores dominant masculinity, the continued popularity of contemporary *josō* culture provides Masako and Yokohama with a commercial space to differently construct alternative models of masculinity and negotiate the boundaries between femininity and masculinity. Here I align with scholars who contend that hosts and maid café regulars have similarly defied masculinist productivity.[92] Whereas maid café regulars refuse to be productive, hosts redefine their masculinity by playing the role of a "commodified yet entrepreneurial" seducer to their cis women clients.[93] Although different from hosts and maid café regulars, Masako and Yokohama, through their *josō* practices, likewise reconfigured productivity in pericapitalist realms by destabilizing cis-heteronormativity as a model of masculine success.

In an interview with Yokohama nearly two years later, I learned he had stopped practicing *josō* altogether because his wife threatened divorce. Having discovered the knee-high socks Yokohama wore when we first met, his wife demanded an explanation. As Yokohama recounted to me, half laughing, he had to confess either to practicing *josō* or having an affair. Apparently, his wife was more horrified that he had spent the night dressed as a woman than she would have been if he had spent it with another woman. Despite the notion that some of my interlocutors—especially the cis straight men—have that practicing *josō* makes them more attractive to women, this wasn't the case for Yokohama. Unfortunately for him, his wife found *josō* more unthinkable than adultery.[94] She was, perhaps, horrified by the presumed loss of masculinity.

This was how, by the end of my fieldwork, Yokohama became a non-*josō* customer who vicariously consumed through others' *josō* practices. Although Yokohama was still interested in *josō*, he also wanted to stay married to the woman he loved. He insisted this was a small price to pay and reasoned that being among and watching *josōko* and *otoko no ko* at Paradise remained "enjoyable" (*tanoshii*). As Yokohama's and Masako's stories suggest, *josō* can safeguard the heteronormative home and family for a privileged group. Yet, as Yokohama's case also makes clear, customers don't have to practice *josō* themselves to contribute to *josō* business circles.

## Conclusion

As the backbone of capitalist productivity since the Meiji period, the patrilineal household and nuclear family were vital to Japanese military and colonial expansion and subsequent rapid industrialization and economic growth. However, with the bursting of the bubble and the resulting stagnating economy throughout the 1990s, such ideals and ideologies, including *salaryman* masculinity and the institution of marriage, stopped being viable. This created space for alternative social formations, such as between *onabe* and *onabe*-loving individuals, as captured in *Shinjuku Boys*.

In twenty-first-century Tokyo, alternative forms of belonging have emerged from people's patronage at Paradise and Garçon. Instead of reinforcing hegemonic capitalist social formations, Garçon regular Saito reconfigured home as a site for consumption and categorial innovation, enabling them to live and belong otherwise. For another Garçon regular, Ken, however, his second home was a means of compartmentalizing his life by separating his otaku interests from his cis-heteronormative home and family. Similarly, Yokohama and Masako differently negotiated their *josō* practices at Paradise with their masculinity and familial obligations. Ultimately, although Paradise and Garçon may have encouraged alternative social formations to develop, their manifestation also functioned to maintain the cis-heteronormative home and family as the status quo.

Paradise and Garçon must be understood in terms of pink economies situated within both nonnormative and cis-heteronormative commercial media and sex-related and entertainment sites in Japan, which have historically overlapped in productive ways, particularly in the 1950s and 1960s. Both establishments were deliberately set up in Akihabara and not in the Shinjuku area to distance Paradise and Garçon from establishments there, including gay bars, *josō* and *new half* clubs and events, *onabe* clubs, lesbian bars, and *dansō* host clubs. Rather than being connected to these bars and clubs, the owners of Paradise and Garçon maintained they were in the business of selling *moe*, a term describing people's emotional attachments to anime, manga, and game characters, making Akihabara an ideal site for their businesses and allowing them to capitalize on the otaku boom—as we see in the next chapter. Despite the owners' attempts at disassociation, however, I have argued that the café-and-bars remain connected to Japanese sex and night entertainment, being shaped by laws and markets.

# 3

## Alternative Worlds in Akihabara

*The Rise of Contemporary* Josō
*and* Dansō *Cultures*

Mako, a cisgender woman in her thirties, cheerfully recounted to me her first visit to Paradise in 2011. She was supposed to visit a maid café but had gotten off on the wrong floor. She laughed, her big eyes sparkling, as if this was a funny old story she had told many times. Maid cafés are establishments where costumed cis women attend to predominantly male customers, though Mako also frequented them. With her bubbly personality, I could picture her chattering happily with maids. Once inside Paradise, she immediately knew something was different because, although the employees looked like women, many had deep voices. Since she was already there, however, she thought she might sit inside for an hour before venturing upstairs. That evening, Mako chatted with Miho, the charming co-owner of Paradise

**3.1** Akihabara at night. Courtesy of Xavier Portela, xavierportela.com.

and a *josōko* (male-to-female cross-dressing individual). She found Miho so captivating and their conversation so interesting she never made it to the maid café. She stayed until Paradise closed for the night.

Mako's story reveals an alternative world in nighttime Akihabara (figure 3.1), where interactions with individuals practicing *josō* (and *dansō*) are not only possible but also affective and stimulating. After this first visit, Mako told me, she was hooked, describing herself as "Miho-*oshi*," someone who was a fan of Miho. The word *oshi* (pushing for somebody or something) derives from Japanese idol culture but is also used by fans of anime, manga, and games to express their enthusiasm for certain artistes and characters. Mako returned continually to interact with Miho. Two years later, after Miho stepped back from serving to manage Paradise full-time, Mako became a *hako-oshi*, a fan of the place. In idol and otaku culture, *hako-oshi* is a slang word for supporting the entire idol group instead of a certain member, which Mako used to reference her devotion to Paradise. Over the course of my research, she continued to frequent the establishment as a regular customer not so much to see any specific employee but to chat with other regulars. If someone was a regular, chances were she would know the name they went by. She was well connected, and her outgoing personality meant she was well liked by employees and other customers and was able to embed herself in any conversation. Mako was the epitome of a *hako-oshi*—which encourages different forms of sociality among customers.

Alternative worlds at Akihabara are often created by themed establishments like Paradise and Garçon, which are also known as *concept cafés*, or eating and drinking places driven by a particular concept.[1] Frequently, they are embedded in anime, manga, and game culture by having employees wear costumes while they serve customers. Arguably the first concept cafés were maid cafés; the "first permanent maid cafe" set up shop in 2001.[2] Between 2005 and 2007, numerous maid cafés began sprouting up all over Akihabara; they became so popular customers had to wait to get inside, creating a maid boom.[3] Some maid cafés branched out to become a chain store or diversified thematically, such as the high school girl cafés I noticed near Garçon.[4] Concept cafés aren't staffed only by women or even humans, although women do perform most of the labor; butler cafés, for example, which first opened in Tokyo in 2006, are staffed by cis men who take on the role of butlers.[5] At butler cafés, employees attend to the needs of primarily young cis women, some of whom are *fujoshi*, or women fans of Boys Love (BL) media, a narrative genre featuring male homoerotic relations.[6] There are also cat cafés, which opened around the same time in Tokyo, where cats perform healing (*iyashi*) labor for their human customers.[7] In essence, the services such establishments offer aren't too different from one another, but they differ in terms of themes, clientele, and the ways customers respond to them.

Just as these customers at concept cafés find the employees appealing, Mako found herself attracted to *josō* employees like Miho. Akihabara is an important site for alternative worlds where individuals like Miho can move beyond the boundaries of how we currently define and understand genders and sexualities. The development of emergent genders in Akihabara should perhaps not come as a surprise. Beginning in the mid-2000s, *josō* and *dansō* have become increasingly commercialized, consumed, and taken up by young amateurs—what I call "contemporary *josō* and *dansō* cultures" to demarcate the fracturing of early capitalist forms of *josō* and *dansō*, such as the 1960s *josō*-style gay bars and *dansō* establishments discussed earlier. *Josō* and *dansō* café-and-bars also distinguish themselves from these other establishments by location; Paradise and Garcon are in Akihabara rather than in Shinjuku's gay and lesbian neighborhood or its sex and night entertainment district.

In this chapter I explore why *dansō* and *josō/otoko no ko* establishments have sprouted in Akihabara and in particular what material conditions enabled contemporary *josō* and *dansō* cultures to emerge at this time and why. I also address what the rise of *josō/otoko no ko* and *dansō* might mean for anime, manga, game, and BL fans like otaku and *fujoshi* as well as trans and gender nonconforming people who seem removed from this setting. Although this chapter is set in Akihabara, where Paradise and Garçon are located, the stories I tell reveal a different dimension of Akihabara that most scholars have not written about.[8] Indeed, I argue that Akihabara was ideal for gender innovation. Its relatively recent shift to become a popular culture market encouraged many individuals to publicly embrace gender crossing and set up *josō* and *dansō* establishments in the mid-2000s.

Earlier, I contended that Paradise's and Garçon's owners were able to create whole new markets for consumption and gender innovation where individuals could openly practice and consume *josō* and *dansō* within a highly visible and commercialized context. Such businesses were entrepreneurial in nature and run by enterprising individuals like Miho who capitalized on *josō* and *dansō* as new phenomena. To sustain these markets, the owners inevitably exploited their employees' labor by transforming them into commodities for customers to consume; however, at the same time, they opened up more jobs to *josō* and *dansō* individuals. In this way, I argue, *josō* and *dansō* individuals are simultaneously subject to intense commodification and empowered by the incongruities of neoliberal capitalism.

Although distinct from sex and entertainment and gay, lesbian, and gender-variant businesses in the larger Shinjuku area, Akihabara was and continues to be connected to pink economies because it was a market for mass consumption in Tokyo from the postwar period into the 2000s. Akihabara was a rich site for nonnormative media and practices to emerge in the twenty-first century, offering pericapitalist material conditions in the mid-2000s—a period I call the first wave of contemporary *josō* and *dansō* cultures—through an array of services and establishments by and for *josō* and *dansō* individuals, as well as media depicting *josō* and *dansō* protagonists, notably anime, manga, games, popular music, and television programs. This was apparent at Garçon and Paradise, where individuals innovated categories like *josō*, *dansō*, and *otoko no ko* not only to offer alternative worlds and different ways of expressing oneself but also to proliferate and sustain these categories through consumption. Through chronicling the stories of regulars' fandom, attachments, and alternative forms of sociality at the café-and-bars, I illustrate how they must be read alongside anime, manga, and game fandom as well as queer interpretations of popular culture.

## Akihabara, Mass Consumption, and Pink Economies

To extend my earlier discussion of pink economies as the larger Shinjuku area's commercialization of sex, gender, and sexuality, Akihabara's pink economies are encapsulated by *moe*, or fans' euphoric feelings or affective response to cute characters. Although scholars have examined Akihabara and Shinjuku separately, which are distinct in terms of their location, clientele, business regulations, and goods and services, I am interested to see where they might overlap.[9] One example within Akihabara's pink economies is the cute erotic (*kawaii ero*) aesthetic in anime and manga first created by manga artist Azuma Hideo in the 1970s, which sexualizes beautiful girls (*bishōjo*) for its predominantly male consumers.[10] But Akihabara's pink economies aren't limited to male otaku's consumption of cute girl fictional characters— they also extend to women's consumption of beautiful boy (*bishōnen*) characters.[11] Girls' (*shōjo*) manga were originally drawn for women consumers and have since evolved to include BL narratives featuring homoerotic relations between male characters; women also consume cute commodities like Hello Kitty and, during the mid-2000s, *dansō* individuals.[12] However, there is more to Akihabara's history as a productive and profitable site for nonnormative media and practices in the twenty-first century.

Akihabara's reputation today as a world imagined by otaku and a hub for anime, manga, and games is preceded by its place as a market for the everyday consumption of goods and services. As the economy was starting to pick up after World War II and the mid-1950s US occupation of Japan, Akihabara appealed to everyday consumers with its low-priced household electric appliances. Dubbed "three sacred treasures," the refrigerator, washing machine, and black-and-white television became highly desired commodities in every Japanese home.[13] Many advertisements for Sanyo and Matsushita home electric appliances promoted the "American way of life" by depicting housewives as both consumers and "agents" in charge of their homes.[14] While associating technology with domesticity might have been new, locating women's subject position in the home is a familiar discourse. During World War II, the Japanese ideology of "good wife, wise mother" was promoted to dictate women's social roles of child-rearing and home and family management to boost national policies and the economy.[15] Although this ideology waned during the postwar period, it continued to shape Japanese femininity in society and state policies, notably in the areas of sexuality and reproduction.[16]

In 1956 Akihabara accounted for 20 percent of the country's home appliance sales, linking women's gendered self-making through consumption to a neighborhood known for having the best prices for home goods.[17] "Akihabara is cheap," many a customer would remark at the time, and masses flocked from all over Japan to purchase home appliances, with tens of stores specializing in home electronics opening to meet the rising demand.[18] By the end of the 1960s, Akihabara was saturated with hundreds of such shops, many of which were housed in the new Akihabara Radio Kaikan, an impressive eight-story building, ushering in the end of Japan's economic recovery. From a materialist feminist perspective, Japanese housewives' agency and gender roles during the postwar period cannot be regarded as separate from their unpaid labor in the home and middle-class consumption of home appliances in Akihabara.

As the Japanese economy soared and standards of living continued to rise in the 1970s, more—especially young—individuals became interested in leisurely consumption, adopting more divergent attitudes toward life.[19] Riding this wave of consumption, Akihabara shifted its focus from household electric appliances to other digital products, such as personal computers (PCs), video game consoles, and videocassette recorders. In 1976 PC manufacturer Nippon Electric Company (NEC) introduced TK-80, the first computer kit model in Japan, and set up a service center on the seventh floor of Radio Kaikan. This attracted numerous hobbyists and computer specialists—mainly young men—to Akihabara.[20] These young men did not venture into girls' manga or their cute girl characters, nor were they called *otaku* yet; this label came into use only in 1983 when columnist Nakamori Akio applied it in a derogatory manner to "manga maniacs"—crazy fans of fictional characters—in his magazine column "'Otaku' Research" ("'Otaku' no kenkyū").[21] Throughout the 1970s and 1980s, animators who had watched anime as children began creating anime aimed at teenagers and adults, likely with the aim of growing capacity for more diversified markets after toy sales from anime tie-ups declined—but also as the result of increasingly seeking to shape production.[22] As Patrick Galbraith observes, "market strategies provided materials that made possible myriad forms of otaku activity, some of which would later engender serious social anxiety."[23] At the height of the economy, otaku sexuality—male otaku's desire for cute girl characters—developed, in part due to market logic, encouraging us to think about the relationship between the material and emergent genders in new ways.

Also originating in the early 1970s were BL narratives. Women artists began creating girls' manga and developed a new subgenre to negotiate the subject of sexuality—taboo in Japanese society at the time.[24] As manga critic and gender theorist Yukari Fujimoto argues, BL enabled young women readers to "escape from the social realities of gender suppression and the avoidance of sex(uality)."[25] Against gender norms and negative perspectives on women's sexuality in Japanese society, such manga offered them imaginary spaces to "play with sex(uality) (*sei o asobu*)" or actively engage with their sexuality.[26] For instance, *dansō* and beautiful boy characters appearing in girls' manga were said to resemble *otokoyaku* (male roles) in Takarazuka, which would in turn inspire the production and consumption of numerous media and theatrical stagings.[27] Following the publication of Ikeda Riyoko's *The Rose of Versailles* (*Berusaiyu no bara*) in 1972, *dansō* protagonists were portrayed in many girls' manga, anime, and *otome* games, a dating-simulation game genre targeted at women.[28] The first girls' manga depicting *josō* protagonists—a new category called *josō manga*—were also published in the 1970s.[29] Over the years, modern BL narratives have become increasingly experimental, not only inventing new genres and categories of male-male romance but also mixing and transgressing genders.[30]

Although much scholarship has explored cis straight Japanese women's consumption and production of BL media, some scholars have also argued for these texts' queer potential, particularly for nonheterosexual readers.[31] These scholars have pointed out how characters' ambiguous presentation of gender and sexuality in BL narratives leaves them open to interpretation, depending on who consumes them.[32] This is consistent with scholars who have long argued for the queer and nonnormative potential of popular culture, in which consumers' reimagining and reinterpretation of popular culture potentially innovates genders and sexualities.[33] The uptake of *josō* and *dansō* practices in the 2000s can thus be seen as partly drawing inspiration from BL media and girls' manga representations more generally. However, I argue that BL narratives and girls' manga aren't the only factors influencing the emergence of contemporary *josō* and *dansō* cultures. These cultures are also embedded within Akihabara's economic and sociocultural context. Emergent genders in Akihabara represent a shift in terms of not only physical location but also, and perhaps more significantly, people's imaginaries during the 1990s recessionary period.

"Do 'otaku' love like normal people?" Nakamori poses provocatively in his July 1983 *Manga Burikko* column, interpreting otaku's attraction to cute girl characters instead of "real" women as meaning that they lack "masculine ability" (*danseiteki nōryoku*).[34] Because they were perceived to cross male/female and real/fictional lines, otaku became feminized in Nakamori's account;

he even called them *okama*, a derogatory term for effeminate gay men that often conflates gender and sexuality.[35] As manga and anime featuring cute girl characters are typically meant for young women, men who indulge in such media are often feminized for their "unnatural" and "inappropriate consumption."[36] Moreover, otaku, who appear to be unproductive and "weird" "failed men," are considered the opposite of *salarymen*—typically cis heterosexual men who epitomize hegemonic masculinity and embody class, national, and gender ideologies.[37] The otaku is an interesting figure who disturbs not only heterosexuality and gender roles, especially those of cis straight Japanese men, but also relationships with "real" humans and divisions between gender and sexuality.[38]

The otaku figure contributes much to my argument that alternative worlds embedded in anime, manga, and game culture encourage gender innovation. Indeed, otaku sexuality, which is often regarded as "abnormal" for "consuming across gender/genre boundaries," can be thought of as one kind of innovation.[39] In 1989 the mass media depicted otaku as social rejects after Miyazaki Tsutomu, a twenty-six-year-old man, was arrested for kidnapping and murdering four little girls. Key to this moral panic was the association between the pedophilic, socially withdrawn, and "psychologically disturbed" Miyazaki and his consumption of cute girl characters and pornographic anime.[40] Although Nakamori's criticisms and Miyazaki's crimes are distinct issues, both were incorporated into pathologizing discourses about otaku sexuality.[41]

My aim in reprising these two examples is not to agree or disagree with how scholars have construed them but to think about how markets played a role in proliferating otaku sexuality through anime and manga consumption while simultaneously casting it in terms of social deviance and sexual violence. The 1980s market success of anime and manga appears to depend on such tensions of otaku sexuality, notably engaging in nonreproductive and nonconforming practices (otaku's attraction to cute girl characters) and transgressing hegemonic norms (otaku's perversions turned into sexual crimes). After the bubble burst, the 1990s saw the rise of an otaku subculture in Akihabara. This coincided with the internet boom, productive discussions among otaku around definitions of *otaku* and otaku identity, and the self-building of Japanese youth through increased hobby consumption, such as anime character figurines.[42] Previous attacks on otaku and the moral panic over Miyazaki's crimes did not completely fade but came to be read differently during the recession, when the consuming otaku was seen as contributing to the economy. This is similar to the 1990s gay boom and spread of gender categories discussed earlier, in which the economic downturn coincided with the flourishing of gay and lesbian media, social spaces, and other enterprises and the emergence of *onabe* and *x-gender* as persistently fluid categories and gender-variant ways of being.[43] Like otaku, the stigma attached to nonnormative cultures and people didn't disappear overnight but became channeled into markets, where the commodification and consumption of queer practices and individuals bolstered a stagnating economy.

In August 1998 a pop-up café where costumed cis women served customers—not yet called a *maid café*—opened at an anime and game character event to promote the dating-simulation game *Pia kyarotto e yōkoso!! (Welcome to Pia Carrot!!,* 1996).[44] Due to popular demand, the first brick-and-mortar maid café opened in 2001, ushering in a maid boom and an era of change in Akihabara. Under the Cool Japan policy in the 2000s, Akihabara started to undergo massive redevelopment as a part of city officials' plans to advance Japan's digital and creative content industry and boost tourism.[45] In 2005 Daibiru, a high-rise building housing a hub of electronic stores, convention hall, and office spaces for information technology companies, opened in front of the Akihabara Japan Railway station. This was followed by the launch of Tsukuba Express, a newly inaugurated train route and station and, next to it, electronics giant Yodobashi Camera's largest branch.[46] These major structural changes cemented Akihabara's status as a "symbolic site of Cool Japan."[47]

Akihabara began to be represented in mainstream media as the site of a positive otaku boom and Akihabara boom, in which both otaku and their town became perceived as "cool."[48] This changing public discourse on otaku followed on the heels of two major research reports released in 2005 by Nomura Research Institute and Yokohama Bank Research Institute, which investigated the worth of an otaku consumer market.[49] The shift to a more positive otaku image was due not only to the popularity of maid cafés, the emergence of a new consumer market, and the redevelopment of Akihabara as a part of Cool Japan but also the transnational spread of otaku alongside anime. For instance, when anime fans in the United States called themselves *otaku*, they reinterpreted the term's derogatory nuances to locate their identification within anime fan culture.[50] Important to note here is the role fans—both domestic and international—play in consuming and (re)interpreting cultural content in ways that may be unintended by the state and/or content industries.[51]

Originating as a market for postwar mass consumption, Akihabara became a fertile environment where otaku's nonnormative practices and consumption could thrive. Understanding this history is necessary for tracing the emergence of categories like *josō*, *dansō*, and *otoko no ko* to a different genealogy, that of popular media and culture situated in Akihabara, as well as to the material conditions that made gender innovation possible in the 2000s and 2010s. At the same time, *moe*-inflected pink economies were not only unevenly spread across Akihabara but also linked to Shinjuku's commercialization of sex, gender, and sexuality. Although scholars have focused predominantly on male otaku and their attraction to cute girl characters, women otaku and *fujoshi* also contribute to Akihabara's pink economies through their consumption and production of *dansō* and beautiful boy characters. Individuals who innovated *dansō* in the 2000s were not outside of these economies any more than those who innovated *josō* and *otoko no ko*. That these categories emerged and proliferated in Akihabara around the same time is therefore not a coincidence. As a historically rich site for mass and popular cultural consumption, Akihabara encourages the creation of alternative worlds where individuals feel free to reinvent themselves and push at the boundaries of gender and sexuality.

### Contemporary *Josō* and *Dansō* Cultures: The First Wave in the Mid-2000s

A popular story my interlocutors told me was that *josō* and *dansō* came out of the mid-2000s maid boom. One regular related to me the excitement of spotting an occasional *josō* employee donning a maid costume and serving customers alongside cis women employees even before the first *josō* establishment had set up shop in the neighborhood. Another lamented the saturation of maid cafés—the abundance of maid cafés encouraged regular customers like him to look for entertainment elsewhere, which was how he ended up at a newly opened *dansō* café-and-bar. Perhaps this high demand for maid cafés incited proprietors to offer something different from their competitors, such as introducing a *josō* employee in a maid café. Other proprietors diversified their businesses to sustain consumers' shifting interests, and at the height of the maid boom, maid cafés paved the way for other themed establishments to emerge. In the mid-2000s, a broad network of themed establishments, including butler cafés and *josō* and *dansō* café-and-bars, began taking form across Akihabara, Nakano, and Ikebukuro.[52]

It is hard to tell of course if consumer demand preceded novel forms of entertainment or if new kinds of businesses spurred consumers to demand different services and products. From the perspectives of some customers I spoke to, they were trendsetters for discovering *josō* and *dansō* before their spread in Akihabara, but Garçon's and Paradise's owners claimed they were the ones who laid the groundwork for contemporary *josō* and *dansō* cultures. Perhaps it is more accurate to say both owners and consumers contributed to the rise of *josō* and *dansō* in different ways. Underlying this origin story of *josō* and *dansō* as deriving from the maid boom are changing labor and economic conditions that shaped these new businesses and intensified gender-crossing media, practices, and consumption. Within a recessionary context, material conditions molded the imaginaries of consumption and neoliberal ideologies surrounding labor, generating new themes, like having butler characters attend to customers, as well as important sites for *josō* and *dansō* employees to interact with their patrons.

The first wave in the mid-2000s saw the first *dansō* and *josō/otoko no ko* concept cafés, café-and-bars, and enterprises open their doors in Tokyo. In April 2006 a *dansō* café known as 80 + 1 set up shop along Otome Road, a famous street in Ikebukuro sometimes dubbed "women's Akihabara" for its concentration of anime and manga merchandise. In a *Tokyo Shimbun* article, 80 + 1 staff were described as "idols" (*aidoru*) who had burst out of the manga *The Rose of Versailles* to serve mainly women, who made up 90 percent of their customers.[53] Opening in quick succession after 80 + 1 were Garçon and B:Lily-rose, a BL *dansō* café in Ikebukuro resembling an *otome* game, as well as non-*dansō* concept cafés, such as Swallowtail, the first butler café to open in Japan.[54] A year later, in 2007, Garçon to issho, a *dansō* escort service in Akihabara now rebranded as W's Collection, started offering predominantly cis women customers walking dates for a fee.[55]

In January 2008 Hibari-tei, the first *otoko no ko* pop-up maid café, opened as an irregular business on certain weekends at rented locations all over Akihabara. Although, as one of my interlocutors observed, the occasional *josō* employee had been working at regular maid cafés since the early 2000s, Hibari-tei was the first to be fully staffed by *josō* employees. Hibari-tei was thought to create a virtual experience for customers, 60 percent of whom were men.[56] Hibari-tei's owner first conceived the idea of including *josō* employees in August 2007 while managing a regular maid café and facing a shortage of cis women employees.[57] This prompted the owner to employ a *josō* employee called Hibari, after whom the new café was named. In late 2008 one of Hibari-tei's then employees, Hayashi, ventured out and started a *josō/otoko no ko* bar by renting a venue at the multistory building Dear Stage in Akihabara.[58] Like Hibari-tei, Hayashi's bar initially had undetermined opening hours, but as the business expanded in 2009, it was renamed Paradise and became the first *josō/otoko no ko* café-and-bar in Akihabara.

Besides café-and-bars, the first wave of contemporary *josō* and *dansō* cultures was characterized by the rise of popular music groups and numerous anime, manga, games, and light novels depicting *josō* and *dansō* characters. By the 2000s Akihabara had the infrastructure from recent redevelopment efforts to support a relatively large and lucrative anime, manga, and game fan base. The otaku boom brought about more positive public impressions and media representations of otaku, who now comprised an attractive consumer market. During this time, anime and manga featuring *dansō* protagonists were typically set in high schools, such as Hatori Bisco's *Ouran High School Host Club* (*Ōran kōkō hosuto kurabu*, 2002–10), or in an alternate historical period, reflecting premodern Japanese narratives of *dansō* warriors. The settings of these anime and manga also materialized at *dansō* café-and-bars as school-themed events where employees wore schoolboy uniforms, and subsequently at Edo-style themed *dansō* café-and-bars in the second wave of contemporary *dansō* culture. The schoolboy trope was also adopted in the 2008 debut of Fudanjuku, a *dansō* unit under Teichiku Records, similar to a boy band, whose members resembled adolescent characters in girls' manga. Originally formed from members of the Nakano Fujo Sisters, a girl group made up of *fujoshi*, Fudanjuku became a permanent ensemble after garnering favorable responses from their fans, 70 percent of whom were middle and high school girls.[59]

Prominent examples of *josō* games, manga, and anime released in the 2000s include *Maidens Are Falling for Me* (*Otome wa boku ni koishiteru*, 2005) and Miyano Tomochika's *Fingertip Milk Tea* (*Yubisaki miruku tī*, 2003–10), which Sharon Kinsella has examined.[60] These works typically featured high school boys in *josō*, which became a familiar motif for representations of *josō* individuals doing teenage girl activities on variety television in the late 2000s, such as visiting Shibuya and eating crepes.[61] The schoolgirl trope also manifested at *josō/otoko no ko* café-and-bars, such as in school-themed events where employees donned sailor-style uniforms typically worn by middle and high school girls.

All these examples illustrate the myriad flows among establishments like Garçon and Paradise and media and popular culture within the first wave of contemporary *josō* and *dansō* cultures. Although located in similar spaces during the 2000s, *josō* and *dansō* media, events, and businesses structured by Akihabara's pink economies developed separately from each other. I take these differences as productive not so much to compare contemporary *josō* culture with contemporary *dansō* culture, although inevitably comparisons will be made, but to think about them together as differently embedded within the relationship between the material and emergent genders. In the late 2000s, although business picked up for establishments like Garçon and Paradise, things began to slow down for others. For example, the popularity of maid and cat cafés in Akihabara and other parts of Tokyo declined during this time.[62] In Ikebukuro several *dansō* cafés closed their doors, including B:Lily-rose in 2009. This heralded the second wave of contemporary *josō* and *dansō* cultures, which, as I chart in chapter 5, can be characterized as an expansion of businesses beyond Akihabara to mainstream media and popular culture, especially in fashion and in idol music and fandom, where *josō* and *dansō* flourished.

## The Alternative Worlds of Garçon and Paradise

One of the first things customers saw when they walked through Garçon's front door was a modestly sized flat-panel television silently playing anime or old black-and-white movies on repeat. The café-and-bar area was long and narrow, covering only about 15 square meters (161 square feet). At the back was a small bar with five stools and a floor-to-ceiling glass display of bottles of spirits, liqueurs, wines, beers, and nonalcoholic mixers. Adjacent to the bar and hidden from view by a long black curtain hanging from the ceiling was a small efficiency kitchen with a microwave oven. In front of the bar, a long black sofa lined one of the walls, accompanied by black coffee tables and swivel armchairs facing the sofa. Garçon's layout facilitated the consumption of alcohol, media and popular culture, and other people, particularly *dansō* employees. Its lack of windows and bright lights created a cozy atmosphere for a slew of activities amid the hustle and bustle of Akihabara.[63] Customers were able to unwind with a drink and a smoke, play games on their smartphones or portable gaming devices (sometimes with other people), watch anime or old movies on the screen, converse with others about their favorite anime, gaze at and speak to *dansō* individuals, and engage in everyday conversation about society and the world.[64]

Considering Garçon's location in Akihabara, I had expected anime, manga, and games to appeal to all patrons. After all, one employee described *dansō* café-and-bars to me as establishments staffed by "2.5-dimensional *dansō* individuals." His understanding of *2.5-dimensional* stems from "2.5-dimensional space" (*nitengojigen kūkan*), a space in between the two-dimensional, such as the world of anime, manga, and games, and the three-dimensional, the real world.[65] This follows from discourses of otaku, who consider maid cafés to be between two worlds, and their maids to be 2.5-dimensional, that is, in between human and character.[66] Within the 2.5-dimensional world of *dansō* café-and-bars, then, employees appear as if they have stepped straight out of a manga. They also embody the reimagination of space as the in-between, not only between two- and three-dimensional and between human and character but also between femininity and masculinity. In-between spaces, Jack Halberstam posits, allow us to "explore alternatives and to look for a way out of the usual traps and impasses of binary formulations."[67] In what he calls "low theory," in-between spaces are inhabited by unintended paths, unanticipated turns, and spontaneous departures that, while not refuting the binary, do not reinforce its formulation.[68] As the in-between, *dansō* individuals are persistently ambiguous, and their bodies can inhabit multiple genders and dimensions.

Despite this characterization of Garçon and its employees as 2.5-dimensional, some customers were less invested in anime, manga, and games than they were in *dansō* culture. However, such differences did not appear to divide customers, who seemed eager to learn from one another about their diverse interests. Aside from socializing, Garçon's open-concept layout was also ideal for customers to observe other people. Looking and being looked at were common in an establishment where most customers knew one another, if not the names they went by. Unlike in maid cafés, employees actively encouraged interactions among customers in a bid perhaps to outsource their labor of keeping everyone entertained when the café-and-bar was crowded.

On average, regulars frequented Garçon two or three times a week, typically in the late afternoon or in the evening after work. A few regulars told me they sometimes visited the establishment every night. This could be expensive, with drinks at Garçon costing at least three times more than at regular bars and gastropubs in Tokyo. Despite this, many regulars weren't deterred and spent an average of JPY 2,000–4,000 (USD 18–36) per night. The normalization of Japanese drinking culture, especially in corporate settings, is well documented as a means to overcome social hierarchy and promote "human relations" (*ningen kankei*) among individuals who drink together.[69] Although not colleagues, regulars at Garçon (and Paradise) cultivated bonds with each other through shared consumption of alcohol, which was for many an important part of their experience. Customers sometimes paid an additional JPY 500 (USD 4.50) for a bar seat, which allowed them to interact more intensely with employees. The bar was the heart of the action at Garçon as customers and employees centered on the discussions taking place there, rendering these seats a coveted spot for many regulars.

Similar to at Garçon, Paradise's windows were tinted and covered with dark drapes. This prevented passersby from seeing into Paradise and made it difficult to tell what kind of establishment it was. Only a standing neon signboard on the first floor, which featured co-owner Hayashi in a checkered dress with "Paradise *Otoko no ko* Cafe and Bar" in Japanese, indicated its existence. Perhaps because of this, those not in the know tended to overlook the establishment. Once, as I lingered downstairs, I overheard a young cis white man conclude, on inspecting the signboard, that Paradise was just another maid café and persuaded his friend to go elsewhere. In contrast, regulars related to the signboard differently. On one occasion, a regular I was visiting Paradise with noticed the signboard's absence and promptly dragged it outside and plugged it into a power outlet so its screen came alive with colors. As we rode the elevator upstairs, I remembered being impressed with the regular's thoughtfulness to help out employees who must have forgotten to display the signboard.

Most customers arrived at Paradise either immediately after work or later in the evening after eating a quick dinner elsewhere, staying until the establishment closed. On Fridays and Saturdays, opening hours were extended to 5 a.m. Regulars frequented Paradise once or twice a week, sometimes on consecutive nights. As at Garçon, food and drinks at Paradise cost two to three times more than at a gastropub. As such, some regulars advised me it would make more (economical) sense to eat before arriving at the café-and-bar to drink. On average, customers would spend JPY 5,000–6,000 (USD 45–55) each time, which included the cover charge, some drinks, and sometimes nibbles. Every now and then, regulars would invite employees to partake in drinks or food, bringing the total cost up. It was accepted and even common at Paradise for patrons to purchase drinks and food for (their favorite) employees. While this was nowhere on Paradise's menu or website, it was a tacit agreement familiar to and practiced by regulars, a practice I learned about from watching how regulars interacted with the employees they were fond of. On other occasions, employees would ask customers for a drink or two, for which they would receive a small commission (10 percent). Such a system encouraged employees to persuade customers to spend more while they were at the establishment.

Paradise was twice the size of Garçon—approximately 30 square meters (323 square feet)—and was wide, spacious, and dimly lit with orange lights, giving it a warm ambience. The space accommodated a full kitchen and a small bar top filled with spirits, liqueurs, beers on tap, and nonalcoholic mixers. Unlike Garçon, Paradise employed a full-time chef who prepared the food, including an appetizer given to all customers. With a full kitchen, Paradise offered a wide assortment of food, ranging from finger food, such as potato fries and fried chicken (JPY 600–850, or USD 5.50–7.50), to entire meals, such as Japanese-style spaghetti, omelet rice, and grilled mackerel with rice (JPY 1,000–1,500, or USD 9–13.50). The bar was only large enough for the part-time bartender to stand and prepare the drinks. Most of the space was taken up by many small tables lined up side by side so customers could sit next to each other and face the employees, who remained standing in front of them, as if on display. This setting facilitated exchanges between patrons and employees as well as strangers—fellow customers sitting beside them. However, if customers arriving with friends preferred to sit in groups, they could occupy the regular tables behind the bar-like setting. Amid the chattering, strains of music—often from an anime soundtrack—could be heard in the background. Other than participating in conversation, customers could also watch anime and YouTube videos, which played on two large flat-panel television screens hung on the wall behind the standing employees. Sometimes, if a customer wanted to play video games with an employee or customer, one of the screens would be utilized for this purpose. Below the screens were a cash register and open shelves cluttered with CDs, DVDs, books, magazines, playing cards, board games, and console games. At the establishment's far end was an enclosed corner where employees could do their makeup and change their clothes.

Occasionally, sometimes at the behest of a favorite employee, a regular would splurge, spending tens of thousands of yen (a few hundred dollars) in a single night on multiple drinks and food items. These regulars were humorously known among employees and customers as *heavy users*, a term used in common parlance to describe those who spend a lot of time on games, online media, and other consumer technologies. An example of a heavy user is Toyotaro, a regular in his late twenties who fell in love with Eriko, a stunning twenty-eight-year-old *toransujendā* (transgender) employee. Eriko was shapely and light-skinned and wore a fashionable bob hairstyle. Toyotaro, a soft-spoken bespectacled cis heterosexual man, although introverted, was articulate and knowledgeable when engaged in conversation on topics that interested him, such as *josō*. A *salaryman* who lived and worked outside of Tokyo, Toyotaro commuted for three hours or more every weekend just to see Eriko. Having previously dated only cis women, his strong feelings for her surprised even him—he would wake up each morning and think, "I want to see Eriko" (*Eriko ni aitai*). Before meeting her, he told me, he would behave like an ordinary customer, who might go to the establishment without any specific aim. Since getting to know Eriko, however, he had quickly become a regular with his frequent weekend visits and high expenditure. Despite the exorbitant prices, Toyotaro didn't appear to think twice about indulging in food and drinks. Most regulars purchased a few drinks and limited their food intake to what they were willing to pay, but not him. Once, another regular showed me Toyotaro's bill, and we gawked at how many zeros were in it.

The reference to *heavy user* indexes some of my interlocutors' description of Paradise and Garçon as a 2.5-dimensional space. Thinking about Paradise's dimensions is complicated because the mid-2000s emergence of *josō* individuals who began to understand themselves more as three-dimensional *otoko no ko* has threatened the two-dimensional world from which the category *otoko no ko* originated. Part of the reason lies in conservative male otaku safeguarding the two-dimensional world by maintaining that its *otoko no ko* characters exist only within manga.[70] These male otaku did not welcome the three-dimensional *otoko no ko* that establishments like Paradise housed and promoted. Such sentiments reflected deep-seated concerns about male otaku's own "failed" masculinity as well as their "abnormal" sexual desires for fictional characters, resulting in feelings of transphobia and homophobia toward *otoko no ko* in the real world.[71] Although less has been written on this, I also observed how three-dimensional *dansō* individuals did not seem fazed by *fujoshi* in the way that male otaku were affronted by three-dimensional *otoko no ko*. On the contrary, their immense popularity among these women fans suggests three-dimensional *dansō* individuals were well received; however, more work needs to be done on this.

The rise of *josō* and *dansō* in Akihabara through popular culture has various implications for trans and gender nonconforming individuals. Aside from more job opportunities outside of Shinjuku opening up to them, increased awareness of contemporary *josō* and *dansō* cultures from intense media coverage would mean the commodification of trans and gender nonconforming people's embodied practices and desires at commercial sites such as *dansō* and *josō/otoko no ko* establishments. Unsurprisingly, the turning of *josō* and *dansō* people into commodities has not agreed with many LGBT groups and activists due to the potential threat this poses to their advocacy. At the same time, locating trans and gender nonconforming individuals' experiences in popular culture enables new possibilities through the innovation of gender categories, particularly in Akihabara, as they traverse gender and real/fictional boundaries in their practices and consumption. For *josō* and *dansō* individuals who identify as trans and gender nonconforming, these connections to anime, manga, and game fandom transform how they think about themselves through the popular cultural texts they consume instead of through LGBT activism and discourses in Japan. As I discussed earlier, some of my non-cisgender and nonheterosexual interlocutors have openly rejected any kind of association with LGBT, including the label *LGBT*. This demonstrates the importance of highlighting how Akihabara's *moe*-inflected pink economies have shaped their subjectivities and imaginaries differently from Shinjuku's pink economies.

### *Adana* (Nicknames) and Naming in Alternative Worlds

The practice of self-naming, Alisa explained to me, is important because individuals are free to choose their own names. The tall, cis heterosexual thirty-two-year-old employee at Paradise wore light makeup and his long, straight black hair down. Alisa reasoned that because parents picked their names at birth, children usually had no say in the matter. It was therefore imperative that people like him express themselves by giving themselves whatever names they desired and wearing whatever clothes they liked. Since Alisa did not practice *josō* on an everyday basis, he deliberately chose a "girl-like" (*onna no koppoi*) name to distinguish it from his real name, using the latter when not in *josō*. While working at Paradise and as a lead vocalist for his visual *kei* (style) band, he used Alisa instead.[72]

Alisa's perspective on names and naming reflects that of customers and employees at Garçon and Paradise, who only ever used *adana*, the nicknames or pseudonyms they chose for themselves or for other people, never their real names. This is unlike other settings, where people are usually known by their given names. My interlocutors assured me real names were rarely applied, even if known or accidentally let slip. At the café-and-bars, naming oneself represented who one was and was synonymous with choosing the clothes one liked to wear. For *josō* individuals, asserting a nickname or *josō* name—akin to a femme name—aligned with their practices of embracing a different gender from the one they were assigned at birth. Although this was different for Alisa, who was cis and heterosexual, his trans and gender nonconforming colleagues could articulate who they were through their *josō* name. Similarly, at Garçon, all of the employees told me they chose their *adana* carefully to express their everyday *dansō* practices, different personalities, and styles of wearing men's or androgynous fashion, such as harem pants and oversized shirts.

Other than offering the potential to transcend gender boundaries, names and naming practices at Garçon and Paradise functioned as a kind of equalizer and were another way to manifest alternative forms of sociality. To build on my earlier discussion of home, family, and belonging, alternative socialities are nonnormative in enabling individuals to construct a way of being and sense of belonging that neither is centered on the home, school, and workplace nor adheres to the productive logic governing how they develop their subjectivity and social networks. This shift from "territorialized" to "deterritorialized" forms of sociality means attachment is no longer rooted in one's status in society, such as which company one works in, which schools one graduated from, or what reputation one's family name holds, but develops as a result of not knowing any of these things.[73] Unlike real names, *adana* aren't connected to one's family, background, or social status but index a completely different set of characteristics, like one's *josō* and *dansō* practices or, in the case of otaku and cosplayers, their fandom and consumption of popular culture.[74] The absence of real names and identifying information accommodates the different ways people can belong, be that through anime fandom, interest in contemporary *josō* and *dansō* cultures, or something else altogether.

At the café-and-bars, *adana* operate much like given names, sounding more informal and friendlier than the more common use of family names in polite Japanese society. When used in Japanese society, given names are typically exchanged only among family, partners, and close friends, not so much with strangers. By overturning these naming conventions, Garçon and Paradise engendered feelings of proximity among customers and employees. Through the casual use of nicknames, customers had a more or less equal status at Garçon and Paradise regardless of the positions they held in Japanese society. When customers visited Garçon and Paradise, employees were less concerned about who they were outside the establishments than who they were inside, which their nicknames played a role in enabling.

The *adana* convention is not unique to Garçon and Paradise but derives from existing practices of taking up aliases within the *josō* and *dansō* business circles, stage names in entertainment (including idol and cosplay culture), and handles in the digital world, such as in social media and game culture. Scholars have discussed how self-chosen nicknames and nicknames bestowed within a certain group or community potentially allow individuals—including the name givers—to express their social identity and truer notions of the self.[75] In game culture, one study found that players had "strong emotional attachments" to their character names, which function as identity objects and enable them to sustain relationships with other players.[76] Although they aren't birth or legal names, nicknames remain meaningful for individuals and the people around them who adopt them.

Some of the reasons my interlocutors preferred to use nicknames were similar, such as desiring online anonymity, namely, avoiding perceived threats to their real identity, and managing social boundaries among different groups, networks, and environments.[77] For Jiji, a trans-identified Paradise customer in her thirties, her *josō* name allowed her to safely express different genders. Anonymity was important to Jiji because she experienced some form of discrimination both within and outside *josō* business circles—a story I tell in chapter 5. For Ken, a longtime customer at Garçon and cis heterosexual man in his forties, his *adana* allowed him to compartmentalize his relationships, separating his friends, colleagues at work, and family members from those he knew at the café-and-bar. In both these cases, patrons used nicknames to assert their preferred selves and genders within the spaces of Garçon and Paradise.

Some of my interlocutors articulated how they felt about using *adana* in "stickier" terms. In what Sara Ahmed calls "affective economies," "emotions work as a form of capital," and nicknames like Alisa, Jiji, and Ken become sticky signs.[78] Within the affective economies of Garçon and Paradise, affects developed not from inhabiting the bodies of employees and customers but from the circulation of signs and objects of emotion, such as nicknames and *josō* and *dansō* practices, within an organized system. For instance, one employee at Garçon related to me how calling each other by their *adana* helped everyone to "get along well" and "close the distance between people" (*kyori chikaku ni naru*). Using the same turn of phrase, *kyori chikaku ni naru*, Eriko, a Paradise employee I discussed earlier, expressed similar sentiments of becoming closer to other people when using nicknames. In Eriko's words, "it's an outpouring of love/attachments" (*aichaku ga waku*). These two perspectives illustrate how *adana* shorten the distance between addresser and addressee by encouraging deterritorialized forms of sociality.

The use of nicknames appears to be effective for establishing closer bonds among strangers because they are able to engage with one another more candidly, free of the usual familial and institutional obligations that characterize Japanese society. Eriko's use of *aichaku ga waku* depicts the intensity of how love or attachments between people can well up and spring forth, suggesting that *adana* bind a person not only to their own subjectivity but also to the people around them. In hailing or addressing another person using a nickname, we bring them closer to us. Affects travel back and forth among individuals' bodies, nicknames, and *josō* and *dansō* practices, forging a sense of intimacy. Attachments flowing out also suggest that with increased circulation, nicknames accrue affective value. For instance, Jiji's *josō* name provides the means for her to affirm her subjectivity and *josō* practices, and for those at Paradise to relate to her. Over time, the name "Jiji" becomes sticky, and their attachments to her deepen. When names bind us to other people, they are instrumental for sustaining bonds based on the selves crafted within that setting.

Not all individuals at Garçon and Paradise chose their own *adana*. Saito, an *x-gender* twenty-nine-year-old regular, told me how they came to be called Saito. When Saito first visited Garçon six years ago, one of the employees decided to call them Saito after an entertainer because the name they had been given was considered "troublesome" (*mendokusai*). Saito reckoned that because their new nickname rolled off the tongue easily, once they were introduced to other patrons and employees, it stuck. "It wasn't that I liked it necessarily when everybody called me Saito as they pleased [*katteni*], but I don't mind. It makes us feel close [*shitashii*]." When I asked if Saito might have felt uncomfortable at any point, they replied, "Not at all, it feels as if the distance between us has become shortened [*kyori ga chikakunatte yōni*]." Saito gave an example of how they often hung out with fellow customers outside Garçon, having meals and even going on trips across the country, so their legal names would have been exposed at some point. Even so, Saito maintained they continued to address one another by their *adana* because it felt more intimate.

As was true for Eriko, Saito's experience shows how nicknames can engender a sense of proximity between them and other individuals. At Garçon and Paradise, employees sometimes invented new *adana* for others by shortening or making puns out of someone's chosen name. Some customers told me they enjoyed this practice and continued to use these nicknames because it made them feel attached to the employee who named them. Other customers and employees were quick to catch on to these concocted nicknames and readily adopted them to address individuals, as in Saito's case. Precisely due to the continuous and persistent use of names that were either self-fashioned or fashioned by others, customers and employees felt close to one another. Through the circulation of affects among the person who names, the named individual, and the people who use the nickname, bonds develop. *Adana* and the processes of naming are therefore central to customers' subject making and relationships with other people.

## Healing and Finding Alternative Sociality

A self-identified *fujoshi*, Tanaka regularly visited Akihabara to buy manga, after which she would check in at Garçon to "take a breather" (*kyūkei suru*). The shy and soft-spoken cis bisexual woman in her late twenties, who held a full-time job in the food industry and adopted a sophisticated and feminine kind of street style, such as wearing a black leather biker jacket, long skirt in muted tones, and khaki high-top combat boots, had been a customer since Garçon opened in 2006. Like Tanaka, who would take her time to sit, chat, smoke, play games, and drink alcohol at midday, most regulars regarded Garçon as a place for respite, arriving at the café-and-bar after work to unwind.

Tanaka's perspective of Garçon as a place for relaxation alludes to establishments that supported the "healing boom" of the late 1990s, where a wide range of healing (*iyashi*) commodities, including "healing style" (*iyashi-kei*) beings, were marketed to generate "calm for (and in) the consumer."[79] Situated in a longer history of healing booms in modern Japan, the 1990s healing boom occurred in the wake of the 1995 Kobe earthquake and Aum Shinrikyō sarin gas attacks and coincided with the economic recession and restructuring efforts.[80] Some related examples of services and establishments that offer healing include animal cafés, host clubs, sex work, and *dansō* escort services.[81] At animal cafés, for example, customers could escape from the outside world through healing, which "brings together feelings of pleasure and intimacy and a release of tension," derived from interactions with animals.[82] Similarly, when engaging the services of *dansō* escorts, clients gain improved mental well-being through receiving care and "forget[ting] about their obligations and social roles."[83] *Iyashi* can therefore be thought of as contributing to capitalist productivity by recuperating customers' emotional health and helping them to cope with social life so they can go back to work the next day.

However, customers like Tanaka who frequent Garçon not only seek relief from work-related stress or healing for productivity's sake but, more important, come for conversation and socialization with other people. This can be seen in a story Tanaka told me about her experience of visiting Makotozakaya, a *dansō* café-and-bar in the neighborhood where employees donned traditional garments like men's *yukata*. "They were just like hosts," Tanaka complained, referring to employees at host clubs. At this, she frowned at the memory of being "courted like a woman" (*onna kudoku*). She recalled how Makotozakaya's employees tried to "act cool" (*kakkō tsukeru*) and repeatedly heaped praise on her, such as "You are cute [*kawaii*]." This was decidedly different from the more natural (*shizen*) behavior of employees at Garçon and made her uncomfortable. That same evening, she fled from Makotozakaya to Garçon so she "could be healed" (*iyasaseru*).

Tanaka's escape back to Garçon to heal reveals how her experience at Makotozakaya was so stressful and unpleasant that she needed to be restored back to health. Her experience also illustrates the contrast between how customers at Garçon were approached more like friends—which she perceived as natural behavior—and less like potential lovers, which she perceived (correctly) as disingenuous. That Garçon's employees treated customers naturally was corroborated by another cis woman regular who maintained they were unpretentious compared to employees at other *dansō* establishments she visited, including the now-defunct 80 + 1 and B:Lily-rose. Despite being grouped together as a genre of business, *dansō* café-and-bars are in reality diverse spaces that hold different potential for customers, which could explain Tanaka's and this regular's preference for Garçon over others.

From Tanaka's perspective, what she didn't enjoy about her experience at Makotozakaya was the commodification of desire, which was akin to a host club, where masculine-presenting hosts would seduce and romance her for her spending ability. For clients to have a "highly personalized and intimate relationship that can evolve into a romantic commitment" is one main difference highlighted by Marta Fanasca between *dansō* escort services and *dansō* café-and-bars.[84] Since these businesses are diverse in nature, meaning not all *dansō* café-and-bars are the same, and I would venture to say the same for *dansō* escort services, I would caution against such an easy comparison. In Tanaka's case, this might have been true because she was not looking to cultivate a romantic relationship with *dansō* individuals, which resulted in her feeling stressed at Makotozakaya. However, as I discuss later with regard to two cis women regulars, their experiences illuminate more nuanced ways of engaging with *dansō* employees, which is fascinating for thinking about the different contours of alternative socialities they seek.

Tanaka was more interested in interacting with other individuals based on shared interests in games, manga, and *dansō* culture. One example of this at Garçon was her co-consumption—the act of consuming together—of *IDOLiSH7*, a rhythm game and visual novel mobile application developed by Bandai Namco Online. *IDOLiSH7*, which allows players to assume the role of managing an idol group, is popular among regulars. Some employees spent several hours chatting with Tanaka about *IDOLiSH7*, getting to know her, and nurturing bonds with her. At Garçon, Tanaka could be said to have enacted patterns of relatedness with strangers who share similar interests in *IDOLiSH7*.

Like Mako, the Paradise regular I began this chapter with, Tanaka might be described as a *hako-oshi*, or a fan of the place. Unlike regulars who were fans of certain employees, Tanaka frequented Garçon not because she wished to see anyone specifically but because she was invested in the establishment as a site for relaxation and socialization. She had an affective relationship to Garçon that might be characterized in terms of what Kathleen Stewart calls "ordinary affects" or "varied, surging capacities to affect and to be affected that give everyday life the quality of a continual motion of relations, scenes, contingencies, and emergences."[85] Leaning on Stewart, I argue that Garçon could be considered a contact zone or meeting point, where day-to-day flows and encounters among objects, customers, and employees took place.

At the same time, its "atmosphere" (fun'iki) was conducive for healing. As Ben Anderson reminds us, the term atmosphere more accurately means "diffusion within a sphere," where such exchanges are contained but by no means concluded.[86] Perhaps quite aptly then, hako-oshi alludes to a space that not only encases things—where hako means a box or a receptacle that things are put into—but also envelops people. At Garçon, hako-oshi patrons like Tanaka became healed and thrived under different forms of sociality, but filling the same space were also idol-employees who were surrounded by their fan-customers, the stories of which I tell next. Together, they generate an affective atmosphere. Having said that, I want to stress that for many customers like Tanaka, the point of frequenting Garçon is not healing in and of itself. Instead of restoring customers back to work under stagnating economic conditions where normative ways of being have become impossible, healing is significant here because it enables those who frequent these establishments to develop alternative selves and deterritorialized forms of belonging.

### Pushing for Your Idols at Garçon

Hikaru, a twenty-one-year-old cis straight woman, frequented Garçon as often as five days a week after work to chat with twenty-seven-year-old Ikki, her oshi, or someone she was pushing for. A freeter who juggled various part-time jobs, Hikaru regarded Ikki as more like an "idol" (aidoru) than a "person of romantic interest" (ren'ai taishō). Beside her, her best friend, Sakura, who was the same age and a cis bisexual woman, begged to differ. Whenever Sakura was around Yu, a twenty-one-year-old employee who identified as questioning, she said her heart throbbed (tokimeki) and twinged (kyun to suru). Sakura, a final-year student at a university in Tokyo, visited Garçon at least once a week after job information sessions to catch a glimpse of Yu, her favorite employee. Hikaru and Sakura first knew each other outside Garçon because of their mutual love for dansō idols but became much closer friends after they both began visiting the establishment regularly in 2016. Since Hikaru and Sakura appeared to my eyes inseparable, I was surprised to learn they usually visited Garçon separately. Sakura explained that while I had sometimes seen them at Garçon together, their meetings were mostly accidental.

Through their co-consumption of contemporary *dansō* culture, Hikaru and Sakura develop alternative forms of sociality. Unlike how most people are acquainted, Hikaru and Sakura knew each other not from work, school, or friends in their social networks. In fact, removed from the context of *dansō*, Hikaru and Sakura were very different people who did not share similar backgrounds. Sakura was a college student aiming for full-time employment, whereas Hikaru was a freeter and high school dropout. Even on the subject of *dansō*, they were not of the same mind. Hikaru perceives her favorite *dansō* individual as an idol, not someone to actually fall in love with, while Sakura disagrees. For Hikaru, who occasionally practiced *dansō*, frequenting Garçon was not simply a matter of pursuing her *oshi*, the person she was a fan of. If Ikki weren't working that day, Hikaru would spend the time chatting with other employees and fellow customers. But for Sakura, her feelings for Yu were more than those for *aidoru*. The term *aidoru* has specific resonances in the Japanese context; although idol culture coincides with celebrity culture, desire for and consumption of *aidoru* are amplified for fans.[87] Extending beyond *aidoru*, Sakura described her admiration for Yu as *tokimeki*, when one's heart leaps in excitement, and *kyun to suru*, or the temporary tightening of one's chest when experiencing powerful feelings. Although, unlike Hikaru, Sakura would be disappointed if Yu wasn't working on a day she visited Garçon, she would use the time to talk about him instead; after all, she was only able to engage in "discourses of pushing for Yu" (*Yu osu no hanashi*), or fan discourses about Yu, with other employees and customers when her favorite employee was not around. Despite these differences, Hikaru and Sakura characterized themselves as "Ikki-*oshi*" and "Yu-*oshi*" to denote their support for Ikki and Yu, respectively. This shared experience of having someone to support is ultimately what drew these two women to Garçon and what brought them together as best friends.

Building on my earlier discussion of healing (*iyashi*), home, and belonging, I contend that alternative socialities also manifest affectively through idol-fan relations. Hikaru and Sakura's co-consumption facilitates alternative socialities with diverse individuals, enabling emergent genders to flourish within Garçon. The idea that these spaces can help people heal from something suggests that alternative socialities can be recuperative; customers are restored to health and returned to their roles in society, ensuring their contribution to capitalist productivity. But as the narratives of engaging with other employees and customers show, their fandom is less about healing or cultivating a sense of belonging, although this may be part of it. Rather, decreasing dependence on older patrilineal models of capitalist productivity driven by territorialized forms of sociality encourages economic diversification in sites where alternative socialities can be built. As the examples of Hikaru and Sakura illustrate, customers are engaged in a pericapitalist economy, where they "move back and forth between non-capitalist and capitalist forms."[88] On the one hand, Hikaru's and Sakura's idol-fan relations might be understood as a noncapitalistic labor of love to support their respective *oshi*. On the other hand, the large amounts of time and money spent at Garçon demonstrate their capitalist relations. Under pericapitalist dynamics, the co-consumption of fan-customers functions to sustain, if unevenly, alternative socialities.

Once a month, Hikaru participated in live events of *dansō* idol groups like Fudanjuku and THE HOOPERS, who became popular during the second wave of contemporary *dansō* culture. Hikaru also frequented other *dansō* café-and-bars, but because of Ikki, Garçon was her favorite. Her expenses would add up, with each visit to Garçon including the cost of drinks and numerous Polaroid photos, called *cheki*. Each time, Hikaru ordered from five to upward of twenty Polaroids of Ikki or the two of them together. At JPY 500 (USD 4.50) each, twenty Polaroids cost USD 90. Polaroids were desirable for customers because they were one-of-a-kind and allowed them close proximity to and special attention from employees. Although a paid service, the Polaroid is arguably one of the few services that allow employees and customers to materialize a relationship through physical contact, which was otherwise not permitted. In the Polaroids Hikaru showed me, she could be seen hugging, holding hands with, or engaging in extended conversations with Ikki. To nonfans, this may appear an unreasonable amount of money to spend on Polaroids, but to her, it was entirely justifiable. This was where she spent her disposable income.

As an independent young working woman, Hikaru was conscious of spending her disposable income in spaces where she could center her fan identity and derive pleasure. As a freeter with two or more jobs who lived in her parental home and commuted to Tokyo—even one in which she worked mostly late-night shifts, which paid 20 percent more than daytime shifts—Hikaru would not be considered wealthy. In today's socioeconomic environment, Hikaru joins many young people in their twenties who are *kakemochi*, working two or more nonregular jobs because they are not able to find regular employment. Despite this, Hikaru chose to make the most of her interactions with Ikki through the Polaroid pictures. Encased in time, the physical Polaroids and the memories they hold for Hikaru not only give her pleasure but also connect her tangibly to Ikki. If she has to spend her hard-earned money to build intimacy with her idol, that makes perfect sense to her.

Limited by her financial situation as a student receiving parental support, Sakura's experience as a fan-customer differed from that of Hikaru. Beyond the occasional Polaroid photo with Yu, Sakura seldom veered from the mandatory one-drink system. Sakura considered Yu her ideal romantic partner, whom she characterized as "cat type" (*neko-kei*), a person who has cat-like characteristics such as being whimsical and independent.[89] In her study Fanasca discusses *dansō* escorts' designation as different *kei* (types or styles) by themselves and their clients; this culture derives from anime, manga, and games, and the suffix *kei* is defined as "a set of physical and psychological features, behaviors and style in clothes representative of a specific class of individuals."[90] This is useful for explaining Sakura's designation of Yu as *neko-kei*, which stems in part from Akihabara culture. Indeed, it is not unusual for customers like Sakura to assign their favorite *dansō* employees a certain *kei*, which the latter may or may not agree with.

Since Garçon forbade dating between customers and employees, Sakura's case was one of perpetually unfulfilled desire. Every time she visited Garçon, she desired to see and talk to Yu. If he wasn't working that day, she would chat with other employees about him. As Sakura's crush on Yu was an open secret at Garçon, other employees would engage her by recounting funny stories about him or dropping hints on what he might like for his birthday. For example, they might start rather conspiratorially with "Did you know that the other day, Yu did this?" Sakura told me she treasured these stories and appreciated other employees' help with selecting Yu's birthday present. These connections among Sakura, Yu, other employees, and fellow customers in turn shaped her own subjectivity and belonging. Although attached to specific employees, Sakura and Hikaru shared the experience of being a fan-customer and visiting Garçon. Such alternative socialities were significant for enabling their subject formation through the spread of contemporary *dansō* culture.

## Concluding Thoughts: Popular Culture and Gender Innovation

Tracing Akihabara's postwar history of mass consumption, we can see that the neighborhood is not an unexpected site for innovating gender categories. Due in part to its shift to become a haven for popular culture in the 2000s, Akihabara became a rich site for reconfiguring our understandings of genders and sexualities inflected through anime, manga, and games. As Stuart Hall argues, popular culture is "the ground on which the transformations are worked," a shifting domain where power relations and tensions between cultural forms are negotiated.[91] Just as we might consider popular culture productive for generating gender categories and shifts in individuals' subjectivity in Akihabara, we might also think of these same categories as reworking popular culture and its cultural forms. On the one hand, the combination of twenty-first-century state-driven redevelopment efforts and individuals' personal investments in anime, manga, and games has encouraged a (re)turn to *josō* and *dansō*, repackaging gender crossing in new ways and enacting new meanings and relations to other people. On the other hand, the rise of *josō* and *dansō* has not only informed and constituted contemporary *josō* and *dansō* cultures but also changed how popular culture is consumed, circulated, and (re)produced.

The first wave of *josō* and *dansō* illuminates this relationship between popular culture and gender innovation. For example, while the explosion of *josō*- and *dansō*-related media, events, services, and establishments follows similar patterns of commodification as popular culture, it has also transformed how consumers—especially fans like otaku and *fujoshi*—perceive and interpellate gender-crossing individuals and their practices. This echoes what Hall calls the "double-stake" or "double movement," in which popular culture goes back and forth between containment and resistance.[92] This tension between containment and resistance also characterizes the relationship between popular culture and gender innovation, which is neither entirely contained as fixed, traditional forms of culture and gender nor completely resistant to dominant culture and heteronormative gender. *Josō, dansō,* and *otoko no ko* can be said to embody in-between spaces that rearticulate popular culture as inhabiting vacillating forms of the knowable and not-yet-knowable.[93] Establishments like Garçon and Paradise capitalize on these categories to create alternative worlds that both employees and customers sustain through their practices and consumption.

We can see this, for instance, in regulars' affective naming practices and use of *adana* (nicknames) at both establishments, which enabled them to reinvent themselves, express who they were, and materialize alternative forms of sociality and attachments to employees and other customers. We also see it in regulars' perception of Garçon as a place not only for healing and fandom but also for deterritorialized forms of social belonging, expressed through the slang *hako-oshi*, which paints their ardent support for the space. The need for nicknames, healing, and idol-fan relations at the café-and-bars suggests a desire to construct a space away from the suffocating, cis-heteronormative outside world. Although such spaces ensure capitalist productivity through recuperating these individuals, I contend that because my interlocutors' experiences do not always line up with capitalist logics of productivity, they have the potential to disrupt these modes. Indeed, the selves and attachments they develop at Garçon and Paradise appear increasingly more genuine, gratifying, and meaningful than those they develop in the world outside.

Structured by the material conditions of Akihabara's pink economies, *josō*, *dansō*, and *otoko no ko* are marketed to individuals who engender nonnormative forms of sociality and personhood, merging the otaku and *fujoshi* worlds with the *josō* and *dansō* business circles. While the alternative socialities my interlocutors enact gesture toward economic diversification rather than a dependence on older models of capitalist productivity, they are nonetheless enacted within a capitalist system. Contemporary *josō* and *dansō* cultures can never be completely outside of capitalist relations of production and consumption; instead, they are pericapitalist—something I continue to explore in the next chapter in relation to trans and nonbinary employees.

# 4

## More Than Just Work

*Trans and Nonbinary Employees*
*Capitalizing on Their Labor*

What Hiyori loved most about working at Garçon was the "depth of social connectedness [*tsunagari*] with other people." I was therefore surprised to learn the twenty-five-year-old employee was initially resistant to working at a *dansō* café-and-bar. Hiyori, who was *chūsei* (middle sex/gender) or *musei* (no sex/gender) and practiced *dansō* on an everyday basis, regarded *dansō* as "an ordinary thing." When I asked for Hiyori's preferred pronouns, Hiyori told me to go with anything. I uneasily settled for *they/them*, despite Hiyori's use of the masculine first-person pronoun *ore* (I; me), because these gender-neutral pronouns best reflect their nonbinary subjectivity.[1] One of Hiyori's friends had recommended they give the job a try based on their "masculine" (*otokoppoi*) appearance. Hiyori was slender and light-skinned and wore their dyed-brown hair in a fashionable K-pop "mushroom" hairstyle. After looking up *dansō* café-and-bars online, Hiyori decided it might be fun after all and took the plunge.

By the time I interviewed Hiyori, they had been working at Garçon for eighteen months. Before coming to Garçon, they had held various contract and part-time positions in sales, at restaurants, and even at a call center and were therefore not new to service work. What set Garçon apart from these other service roles, however, was how the café-and-bar allowed for more interaction with customers, particularly through informal speech. Hiyori gave the example of how they could establish bonds with customers by using casual speech (*tameguchi*), which was rare in the Japanese service industry, where honorific speech (*keigo*) was usually employed. For this reason, Hiyori declared there were few jobs like being a *dansō* employee.

Hiyori's experience of working at Garçon reveals feelings of pleasure—and at times pride—in a site that can be described as pericapitalist, "simultaneously inside and outside capitalism."[2] Although transactional work is done—Hiyori earns a wage from attending to customers—the value created from providing such services is not about the pay received. In fact, the value of their job seems to have less to do with work than with intimate bonds between employee and customer. This can be seen from their use of *tsunagari*, a term denoting blood ties or close relations between people, to describe the social connectedness they establish with customers who are initially strangers. Such interactions are done by engaging customers in conversation through informal speech, which they appear to enjoy. Under pericapitalist modes, they find meaning in working as a *dansō* employee because it exceeds notions of earning money. For Hiyori, it is more about nurturing connections with other people and enacting a sense of belonging at Garçon.

This does not mean, however, that the job comes without issues of exploitation and inequalities. But it is not a simple case of Garçon and Paradise exploiting employees for their labor, although it is potentially exploitative, as the majority work part-time and earn minimum wage. For this reason, I use the terms *labor* and *work* interchangeably not to conflate them but to signal how my interlocutors complicate clear definitions of *labor* and *work*.[3] Although most employees, like Hiyori, find their work pleasurable in the ways I have described, they also face labor exploitation and the struggle to make ends meet. Profit remains important to Garçon and Paradise, which can be seen from how employees and their *dansō* (Garçon) and *josō* (Paradise) practices are marketed to customers as each establishment's primary form of appeal. Within such a business, one might say that exploitation is almost inevitable because it depends on a match between customers' sustained consumption of *josō* and *dansō* and employees' nonmonetary motivations to continue working.

At the same time, employees like Hiyori have agency in constructing different meanings from their work, particularly in loving what they do. In her ethnography of Filipina hostesses in Tokyo, Rhacel Parreñas argues that although these women are often trafficked and face structural constraints, their agency should not be overlooked.[4] While Filipina hostesses and Garçon and Paradise employees have little in common beyond the shared service work, there is overlap in how employees perceive their own labor. Many *josō* and *dansō* employees regarded themselves as benefiting from their jobs in some—often nonmonetized—ways even as the café-and-bars tapped them to drum up profits. This calls for more complex understandings of *josō* and *dansō* employees beyond an exclusive exploitation framework.

Under pericapitalist economic forms, emergent gender categories can flourish, shaped differently by employees, customers, and establishments. For instance, while *dansō* emerges from the everyday practices of employees like Hiyori, Garçon values and taps into employees' masculine presentation to attract customers, who in turn proliferate contemporary *dansō* culture. Drawing on José Esteban Muñoz's extended understanding of surplus, value might be understood in both monetary and nonmonetary terms.[5] Reading surplus value not merely in terms of profit within capitalism, Muñoz reinterprets surplus as a different kind of excess—one that departs from "conventional forms, [and] conveys other modes of being that do not conform to capitalist maps of the world."[6] To lean on Muñoz, emergent genders can be regarded as a kind of surplus that potentially exceeds capitalist flows and deviates from cis-heteronormative reproduction and forms of belonging.

Connecting to earlier chapters on categorial innovations and pink economies, this chapter focuses on the work experiences of Garçon and Paradise employees who locate themselves variously as trans and nonbinary and the ways they develop emergent genders through their labor. Using their workplace as a site for reinventing themselves, employees push at the boundaries of gender and sexuality. I contend that work in these pericapitalist worlds becomes productive for trans and nonbinary employees to generate *dansō*, *josō*, and *otoko no ko* and potentially surpass existing categories—albeit with certain material costs.

Through a discussion of queer- and trans-materialist approaches to labor, I demonstrate how *onabe*'s labor in the documentary *Shinjuku Boys* enables us to reconfigure social reproduction. Marxist feminists have defined social reproduction as encompassing "various kinds of work—mental, manual, and emotional—aimed at providing the historically and socially, as well as biologically, defined care necessary to maintain existing life and to reproduce the next generation."[7] This allows us to understand how trans and nonbinary employees at Garçon and Paradise perceive work as arduous but also something that affirms their sense of self, being more than just work. Situating Garçon and Paradise within the urban landscape of Tokyo's Japanese (nighttime) entertainment, I chart the classed, gendered, and racialized labor of host and hostess clubs, snack bars, sex work, and maid cafés, particularly in relation to capitalist structures of success and cis-heteronormative models of relationships, to consider the place of trans, queer, and nonbinary employees and the way their labor potentially enables us to rethink social reproduction.

I also delve into employees' motivations to work at Garçon and Paradise, which can be described as fitting into pericapitalist dimensions; despite the (lower than) average pay, the main reasons employees cited were the ability to practice *josō* and *dansō*, a match between the job and their goals and interests, and meaningful interactions with customers and colleagues. In the 2010s the popularity and uptake of the LGBT boom and contemporary *josō* and *dansō* cultures in Japanese mainstream media enabled heightened visibility of trans and nonbinary people. Alongside visibility came workplace inclusion of trans and nonbinary individuals, who have become increasingly valued for their ability to engage in self-promotion and self-commodification, though they also continue to face employment harassment and discrimination. Under pericapitalist modes, while trans and nonbinary employees at Garçon and Paradise were hired to persuasively promote *josō*, *dansō*, and *otoko no ko* for consumption, they strategically used these same categories to position themselves and negotiate their relationships with other (like-minded) people.

### Queer- and Trans-Materialist Approaches to Labor

In the film *Shinjuku Boys*, the scenes set in the *onabe* bar Marilyn often depict excess and showcase the glamorous lives of *onabe* hosts (figure 1.2). At first glance, it doesn't seem as if they are working; employees drink and laugh merrily with customers. Much of the labor *onabe* hosts provide can be considered emotional or affective labor—that is, employees' manipulation of affects and their ability to generate in their customers feelings of "ease, well-being, satisfaction, excitement, or passion."[8] Perhaps because of this, their labor does not appear like "real" work. However, within trans-political economy (TPE) studies, scholars have recently begun paying attention to trans people's labor, especially the caring and intimate labor that sustains their lives.[9] As Nat Raha argues, these forms of labor by gender and sexual minorities who provide care and intimacy must be considered a part of socially reproductive labor.[10] Raha argues that redefining social reproduction theory would pave the way for understanding trans people's work as a form of "resistance" and also "valuable and *necessary*."[11]

Not only is *onabe*'s work at Marilyn a form of resistance against the gender-normative discourse of gender identity disorder (GID) and common sense–inflected productivity, but it is also vital for "reproduc[ing] queer and trans lives, workers, and worlds."[12] This can be seen in *Shinjuku Boys* when customers lament how their well-meaning friends and family have warned them against cavorting with *onabe* hosts. The sister and mother of one employee, Kazuki, openly object to his working in an *onabe* bar. In these examples, such forms of sociality and employment transcend the gender binary inherent in the GID discourse as well as commonsense notions of productivity tied to cis-heteronormative marriage and family. Within TPE, *onabe*'s labor enables queer and trans social reproduction through making a living and enacting alternative social formations. Granted, as the film's closing sequence illustrates, *onabe*'s labor is hard work: their jobs begin in the evenings when they receive customers; last throughout the night as they attend to them, serving them drinks and conversing and singing karaoke with them; and only end around seven in the morning when they send them off. Of course, as I discuss in the following pages, night work is the mainstay of Japanese sex and night entertainment (*mizu shōbai*) and is in this sense not limited to *onabe* bars. This demands that we think of such businesses as not only contributing to the gross domestic product (GDP) but also reconfiguring the notion of social reproduction.

*Shinjuku Boys* illuminates how employees make a living by appealing to customers. At Marilyn, we witness many transactions between customers and employees, but money is never mentioned explicitly. We know neither how much customers spend nor how much employees get paid at or outside the club. Throughout the film, however, we do see customers entering the club and employees serving customers and, in Gaish's case, spending the night with customers at hotels. *Onabe* hosts may play a variety of roles, including being a customer's "special boyfriend," but to the employees, this is just business.

Among the documentary's three protagonists, Gaish is the most popular employee, receiving multiple calls from customers to go out with them. In one scene Gaish gets a call on their cellular phone—what looks to be an ex-

4.1　Gaish's phone call from a bothersome customer. Still from *Shinjuku Boys*, 1995.

pensive Motorola DynaTAC, one of the first commercially available at the time—while having dinner at Tatsu's place (figure 4.1). On the line is one of Gaish's customers, who in a high-pitched voice complains about missing Gaish and wanting to see them but having no money to patronize Marilyn. She adds that she is serious about their relationship but sometimes feels Gaish's motive for going out with her is to make her spend more money at the club. An expressionless Gaish remains on the line listening but mostly stays silent. As her whining goes on, Gaish starts to look bored, and when she finally pauses, they announce they don't have time for her and hang up abruptly, grumbling about the bother of new customers these days and their lack of manners.

What this faceless customer's complaint makes clear is not only that it costs to patronize Marilyn but also that going on romantic dates with Gaish outside the club is tied to the customer's expenditure at the club. From the customer's perspective, Gaish is not sincere about their relationship and is interested in hanging out with her only for the profit she would bring to the club. She is probably not wrong—for Gaish, being an *onabe* host is primarily an occupation.

At the same time, Gaish's labor enables queer and trans social reproduction to flourish. Clubs like Marilyn are the only places where *onabe* can make a living as themselves, that is, without having to change who they are. As Kazuki argues in another scene on a phone call with his mother, there is no job for him anywhere except in Shinjuku, pointing to the limited employment options for *onabe*, particularly at that time. Following queer-materialist approaches to labor, many LGBTQ people around the world, especially those who are poor and working class, face economic challenges, such as income inequality, job discrimination, and inadequate employment benefits, and remain largely invisible.[13] However, at *onabe* bars, employees like Gaish and Kazuki could develop their subjectivity as neither being GID nor *rezubian* (lesbian) but *onabe*. Of course, queer and trans social reproduction is not stable and is often under threat or subject to change, such as, in the Japanese context, the eventual shift to the GID discourse in a stagnating economy.[14] Drawing on Michel Foucault's notion of biopolitics, scholars have criticized the market's influence on state regulation and normalization of laboring queer subjects, especially during a constant state of crisis.[15] Although not depicted in the film, the 1990s recession and GID discourse would gradually change how *onabe* were perceived and the roles they would occupy in TPE, shifting from an association with occupation to medicalization.

As *Shinjuku Boys* shows us, the ties among labor, gender, and sexual minorities are not entirely new. However, with recent studies on the LGBT market, we are only beginning to understand the economic lives of gender and sexual minorities in Japan.[16] Some of these studies have called for companies to promote inclusivity and support gender- and sexual-minority employees in their career advancement, and for the Japanese government to introduce policy changes at the national and municipal levels to ban LGBT discrimination.[17] Drawing on queer- and trans-materialist approaches to labor is vital not only for theorizing their work experiences but also for reconfiguring notions of social reproduction. Constructions of productivity have not quite evolved, and gender and sexual minorities in Japan are still regarded as either threatening or reinforcing existing structures of productivity. To redefine social reproduction in the way Raha calls for requires a dismantling of hegemonic and monolithic capitalistic discourses.

Merging notions of pericapitalist modes with diverse economies, I regard the work of Garçon and Paradise employees who identify as trans and gender nonconforming as a "struggle that is always challenging, and sometimes pleasurable."[18] Although finding a job and doing the work are arduous, they offer a sense of purpose and affirm one's sense of self through reinvention.

As I show later in this chapter, *onabe* hosts' sentiments toward work resonate with those of the trans and nonbinary employees I have spoken to, whose labor similarly includes the provision of affective or emotional labor at the establishments where they work.

## Japanese (Nighttime) Entertainment in the City

Before I turn to the stories at Garçon and Paradise, some background on the urban landscape of Japanese (nighttime) entertainment in Tokyo— the world's most populated city—is necessary.[19] Scholarship on hostess clubs, sex work, and host clubs has charted how employees' classed, gendered, and racialized labor helped to maintain economic success and the cis-heteronormative family.[20] Studying elite hostess clubs in the 1980s, Anne Allison notes that by performing femininity, hostesses make their customers—mainly *salarymen*—"feel like a man," thereby extending the bonds between men in work and business.[21] These roles are amplified at working-class Filipina hostess clubs, where hostesses' gendered and racialized labor of interacting with customers is considered illegal under their "entertainer visa" status as migrant workers.[22] In Tokyo's sex industry, gendered labor also manifests as "healing" (*iyashi*)—a notion tied to "maternal care with sexual gratification and feelings of 'being a man.'"[23] By performing normative femininity, sex workers perceive themselves as providing male customers with relief (through erotic intimacy) and contributing to *salaryman* productivity by downplaying their own labor.[24] A similar combination of healing and romance operates at host clubs, where male hosts' performances of normative masculinity help women customers—primarily hostesses and sex workers—recover from their own gendered labor and return to work the next day.[25] This role reversal interestingly links men's (im)material labor to that of women, which stimulates work productivity in pink economies. Hosts' gendered labor is also classed; handsome young men usually relocate to Tokyo to work at host clubs because they aspire to upward mobility.[26]

Young Japanese people often leave their rural hometowns to seek jobs in Tokyo—a practice known as *jōkyō suru* (to leave for the capital). Many employees of Japanese (nighttime) entertainment are not originally from Tokyo but have converged in the capital for work and school, among other reasons. This includes my interlocutors, who found their social, spatial, and professional networks in the metropolis. Writing about twentieth-century New York City, George Chauncey posits the city's networks enabled gay men to "construct the multiple public identities necessary for them to participate in the gay world."[27] Yet this urban landscape alone is insufficient to explain the thriving *josō* and *dansō* business circles and more recent explosion of contemporary *josō* and *dansō* cultures. Scholars have objected to "metronormativity," a narrative centered on the metropolis as the site for sexual liberation, particularly for LGBTQ individuals who have migrated from the countryside to the city, and others have argued for a "queer anti-urbanism," the celebration—as opposed to erasure—of rural genders and sexualities.[28] While I recognize the importance of rural and suburban gender and sexual minorities, this book's ability to address these issues is limited by my field sites' location in Tokyo.[29] But rather than privileging Tokyo's urban landscape, I am interested in how its material conditions, along with changes to the labor force and consumption patterns due to economic stagnation, enabled gender categories to emerge.

The aforementioned body of work on hostess clubs, sex work, and host clubs has largely centered on gendered, classed, and racialized labor as a vehicle for preserving cis-heteronormative models of relationships and socioeconomic achievement, leaving out the labor of trans and queer individuals. Filling this research gap is trans activist Mitsuhashi Junko, who has written extensively about *josō* and *new-half* hostesses, drawing on her own experience as an unpaid volunteer hostess at Ju-ne, a *josō* snack bar in Kabukichō throughout the 1990s.[30] Like Filipina hostesses, Mitsuhashi's work consisted of making drinks for predominantly cis-male customers, lighting their cigarettes, helping them relax, and making conversation with them.[31] Curiously, Mitsuhashi describes the relations between *josō* hostesses like herself and patrons—cis men who love *josō* individuals—as "quasi-heterosexual."[32] On the one hand, this places *josō* hostesses, some of whom may identify as trans, in the same category as cis women, but on the other hand, it problematically reinforces the gender binary by equating all *josō* and *new half* individuals with trans women. Mitsuhashi's ethnography complicates our understanding of gendered labor by posing new questions about trans and nonbinary labor, especially that of *onabe* and *dansō* employees, on which very little has been written. I contribute to this scholarship by exploring how *josō* and *dansō* employees' labor at Garçon and Paradise shaped and was shaped by markets through tracing how these employees' labor and practices called into question cis-heteronormative gender and "proper" trans and queer identities.

More recently, Marta Fanasca has examined the female masculinity and emotional labor of *dansō* escorts in Akihabara, drawing on Jack Halberstam and Arlie Hochschild.[33] Based on her own experience as a *dansō* escort in the 2010s, Fanasca identifies such work as engendering a close romantic and intimate relationship with predominantly women clients.[34] Part of this labor incorporates masculine aesthetic ideals and behaviors congruent with beautiful boy (*bishōnen*) characters in Japanese anime and manga and flower pretty boys (*kkonminam*) in South Korean television dramas, which Sun Jung has coined "pan-East Asian soft masculinity" to distinguish them from Western—often North American—hard masculinity.[35] In doing so, Fanasca contends, *dansō* escorts express what Halberstam calls "female masculinity," alternative masculinities that women instead of men embody, but they also reinforce instead of subvert masculine gender norms and stereotypes.[36] Like *josō* hostesses in Mitsuhashi's study and *onabe* hosts in *Shinjuku Boys*, *dansō* escorts' relations with their clients could be described as quasi-heterosexual.

Leaning on Hochschild, Fanasca further describes *dansō* escorts' "performing emotions on demand" as a transactional exchange with clients to satisfy the latter, particularly their commodification of *dansō*.[37] Such emotion work represents the dark side of the business, which costs *dansō* escorts must bear through behaving as if they are in love with clients to express deep consideration for them.[38] *Dansō* escorts' emotional labor, especially the enactment of romance with clients that the business hinges on, strikes me as similar to the work of the *onabe* hosts depicted in *Shinjuku Boys*. While *onabe* employees may opt to engage in sexual acts with their customers, as Gaish does, *dansō* escorts are prohibited from doing so by company rules, and the more popular escorts find different tactics to refuse clients. Building on but also departing from Fanasca's fascinating study in many ways, I analyze the value *josō* and *dansō* café-and-bar employees attribute to their labor at Garçon and Paradise, in order to advance scholarship on trans and queer labor in Japan.

Patrick Galbraith's study of maid cafés in Akihabara in the 2000s, where young women's labor and performances of femininity aren't regarded as bolstering their male customers' masculinity, work productivity, and social responsibilities, helps me rethink social reproduction.[39] Often constructed as "failed" and "weird" otaku, these men aren't restored back to work or the reproductive home by maids' labor but instead "escape from reality" to enact alternative forms of sociality.[40] This illustrates the limits of heteronormative perspectives on maid-otaku relations and suggests how queer critiques of maids' gendered labor may be useful. Drawing on Jack Halberstam and Shaka McGlotten, Galbraith reads maid-otaku relations not in terms of "failure" determined by capitalist structures of success and cis-heteronormative relations but as configuring a loose circular form of support for otaku tied neither to coupledom nor to familyhood.[41]

This advances new ways of thinking about social reproduction, especially in *josō* and *dansō* café-and-bars, where employees' labor is not concerned with sustaining customers' work productivity and social responsibilities nor with establishing sexual and romantic relations with them. Instead, Garçon and Paradise provide avenues for like-minded individuals who practice *josō* and *dansō* to build urban social networks and share information and interact with one another. While these establishments are marketplaces and therefore concerned about profit and leveraging gender-crossing practices and consumption, which play a major role in promoting *josō* and *dansō*, these sites inspire diverse performances of femininity and masculinity, which, rather than reinforcing cis-heteronormative relations, are perceived as building participants' embodied subjectivities.

### The Work of *Josō* and *Dansō*

"In the first place, there aren't many places where one can find employment in *josō*," Tobari, a cis heterosexual employee at Paradise, declared when I asked why he worked there. The light-skinned twenty-two-year-old was slim, wore light makeup, and had long, straight hair fashionably dyed red, which I was told wasn't a wig. For Tobari, who practiced *josō* as *shumi* (hobby; taste), the job at Paradise aligned with his aspirations to become a voice artist. An avid anime and manga fan and cosplayer, Tobari had graduated from a voice acting vocational school a year previously and was a freeter at the time I interviewed him.[42] Tobari also worked part-time at a ramen restaurant for practical reasons. The well-paying night shifts at the ramen restaurant near his residence compensated for Paradise's relatively low wages. Nonetheless, because the job at Paradise was a rare example of getting paid to do what he loved, Tobari had no complaints. On the contrary, he found the work enjoyable.

Tobari's experience reveals many similarities with the classed and gendered labor of maids and hostesses. Like the young women who work at maid cafés to pursue their dream jobs, such as to become a singer, Tobari did not mind being paid less at Paradise if his work contributed to his voice acting skills.[43] Although hostesses were paid more, depending on the class status of the hostess club, they also chose this work because it provided them with economic opportunities.[44] For such employees, despite the average pay, their jobs matched their aspirations. However, like other workers within Tokyo's service industry, where many young Japanese people hold two or more part-time jobs at the same time—a phenomenon known as *kakemochi*—these workers could easily be exploited. Tobari was no different as a freeter, a precarious part-time worker at both Paradise and a ramen restaurant to make ends meet.

Though employees' motivations for taking on the job varied from individual to individual as well as between establishments, three reasons stand out in particular. The job enabled employees to pursue their ambitions and interests, allowed them to engage in *josō* and *dansō* practices, and gave them opportunities to foster intimate bonds with customers and colleagues.

*Pursuing One's Ambitions and Interests*

Working part-time at Paradise, Tobari told me, was a means of honing his skills in "feminine ways of speaking" (*onnarashii shaberikata*) so he could eventually become a voice artist. Most employees were like Tobari. Their part-time jobs at the café-and-bars were considered short-term, en route to securing a more permanent position or future profession elsewhere. Unfortunately for Tobari, the voice acting (*seiyū*) industry is so competitive few can find work; to make ends meet, many do various part-time jobs until they can become "specialist *seiyū*" or are forced to quit.[45] With structural changes due to the economic slowdown, this notion of a "better" job to strive for is increasingly a pipe dream. Although Tobari's work in various part-time jobs is purportedly a means to achieve their dream of becoming a voice artist, this could mean an extended period of jobbing just to make rent. This demonstrates the agency of workers like Tobari under pericapitalist modes to receive (less than) average wages for nonmonetary benefits such as upskilling—augmenting their skills—which complements the café-and-bars' business models. Employees derive more value from working toward their aspirations than from the income earned.

The job at Garçon and Paradise also complemented employees' *shumi* and other interests. The Japanese word *shumi* originally emerged in the late nineteenth century as a translation of the English term *taste* and is often translated as "hobby."[46] If we take *shumi* to mean "hobby," working at the establishments could be said to be an extension of some employees' cosplay activities and consumption of anime, manga, and games. I have observed both employees and customers frequently referencing the aesthetics of cute (*kawaii*), beautiful girls (*bishōjo*), beautiful boys (*bishōnen*), and even Takarazuka as starting points for negotiating their *josō* and *dansō* practices.[47] These references seem to veer toward *shumi* as "taste." According to Pierre Bourdieu, "tastes (i.e., manifested preferences) are the practical affirmation of an inevitable difference."[48] Unlike the English word *hobby*, then, *shumi* appears to encompass broader and more nuanced meanings to include what are judged to be good or bad taste and good or bad investments acquired over time. Millie Creighton describes *shumi* as "dedicated engagement in long-term goals that involve self-education and self-development," which implies distinctions of class or, perhaps more accurately, socioeconomic status.[49]

That said, others have rejected the claim that *josō* and *dansō* practices are a kind of hobby or taste. For instance, Oban, a cool-looking twenty-three-year-old employee at Garçon, explained that instead of originating from popular culture, his own practices hailed from a place of being and expressing himself. The dandy Oban wore the latest androgynous fashion and thought of himself as one of a kind. He declared, "If I don't do *dansō*, I will no longer be myself." This reveals how his attachment to *dansō* ran deeper than any sort of hobby or taste, being inextricably tied to his way of being. Of course, popular culture fans could also be said to connect their fandom to their subjectivities. But for Oban, practicing *dansō* is not a voluntary act—not a choice—in the ways that fans cosplay and consume anime at will but rather reflects who he is.

*Practicing* Josō *and* Dansō

Employees often cited the ability to practice *josō* and *dansō* as a major pull factor to the job. This is significant because it remains difficult for *josō* and *dansō* individuals to find employment in the workplace, particularly, as Tobari's story illustrates, for *josō* individuals. In a tough economy, jobs are few and far between, but *josō* and *dansō* individuals who may identify as trans and gender nonconforming are particularly vulnerable because of social marginalization. For instance, due to employment discrimination, trans hostesses are paid less than their cis women counterparts, and *new half* individuals often end up in the sex industry.[50] This is not too different from their plight in the 1980s, as I discussed earlier. For this reason, *josō* business circles are an important starting point for many *josō* individuals because existing within this larger community are small and close-knit networks of people who know one another.

Although Tobari is cis and heterosexual, his search for a job that specifically hires *josō* individuals places him in a similar—albeit not quite the same—position as trans and nonbinary *josō* individuals. Tobari might be considered what Halberstam calls a "queer subject," someone who "will and do[es] opt to live outside of reproductive and familial time as well as on the edges of logics of labor and production."[51] As a queer subject, Tobari lives in queer time and space: he problematizes gender norms through his *josō* labor and practices, holds irregular employment and lives day to day, and has no definite plans for obtaining stable work, getting married, or starting a family. Under the pericapitalist dynamics of Garçon and Paradise, queer subjects seem to abound, occupying a marginal position in between capitalist and noncapitalist spaces. Although employees perform transactional labor and generate profits for the establishments, they find nonmonetary value in their work. Tobari and other employees expressed this nonmonetary value to me in various ways, such as telling me how much they enjoy their job and how rare it is to get paid doing what they love.

Working at Paradise and Garçon also provided an empowering space for employees' gender presentation through their *josō* and *dansō* practices. At Garçon, employees cited feeling comfortable in a job that sanctioned their masculine or androgynous appearance as one of the main reasons for choosing to work there. From my observations, employees appeared positive overall about their masculine or androgynous uniform—a black vest over a white collared shirt and black pants—and for better fit, they often wore their own shirts and men's dress shoes. During special events, they also donned their own clothes and expressed their personal style. All this shows how the workplace is an important site for Hiyori and their colleagues to negotiate their subjectivity through gender expression. Scholarship in the US context has demonstrated how workspaces can be sites of distress for self-identified masculine and queer women who feel pressured to conform to feminine professional attire. Masculine women often seek work that allows them to appear "androgynous or masculine," such as the generic uniforms worn in many service or blue-collar jobs, even rejecting professionalized occupations with more gendered dress expectations; queer women must find the balance between appearing "too queer" and "not queer enough" at the workplace.[52] These are important concerns that Garçon employees considered when seeking employment.

Employees' *dansō* practices extended beyond appearance to include speech and behavior. I observed that on top of casual speech, Hiyori adopted masculine speech, namely, the strongly and mildly masculine first-person pronouns *ore* and *boku*, which shaped the ways they referred to themselves, performed their labor, and behaved around customers. Thinking about Hiyori's agency is important because it allows us to see employees not as passive workers waiting to be exploited for their labor but as individuals who capitalize on their jobs to actively construct meanings for themselves, such as through new forms of sociality and personhood. Employees' agency and the way they regard their own labor remain vital for understanding the—especially nonmonetary—value they attach to their work experiences, which complicates the exploitation framework.

## Fostering Intimacy with Others

Although the aforementioned reasons—the ability to practice *josō* and *dansō* and a match between the job and employees' goals and interests—may explain why employees were initially attracted to the job, they don't elucidate why they continued to work there for many months and, for some, years. As I illustrated through the example of Hiyori, a major incentive for employees was the close bonds they forged with customers and colleagues. Often facilitated by mutual interests in *josō*, *dansō*, and popular culture, employees found pleasure in culti-vating relationships with like-minded individuals. To describe their proximity to other human beings at Garçon and Paradise, employees used affective terms like *tsunagari* (social connectedness), which Hiyori used; *fureai* (contact); and *kakawaru* (to interact with). *Fureai* stresses "mutual (and emotional) contact between two parties" and has recently been applied to senior citizens, such as advocating services for lonely old people in a "society of touching-together" (*fureai shakai*).[53] *Kakawaru* has a variety of meanings, including "to concern," "to affect," and "to adhere to," involving social interaction as well as the ca-pacity to affect and be affected by other people. The sticky qualities of these terms demonstrate the strong bonds cultivated within the commercial spaces of Garçon and Paradise. Such "contact encounters" or interactions among strangers taking place in public spaces cross not only "class lines," as Samuel Delany argues, but also gender and sexuality lines.[54]

As I discussed earlier, in Tokyo's (nighttime) entertainment scene, strang-ers meet for bonding, healing, intimacy, romance, and pleasure in various forms. Although the services that *onabe*, hosts, hostesses, maids, *dansō* es-corts, and sex workers provide differ, what Nayan Shah calls "stranger inti-macy" is central to these sites as individuals engage in meetings that aren't tied to "family and institutional relationships" but nevertheless generate af-fect.[55] For instance, by suspending their familial obligations of being wives and mothers for a night, women are able to engage with hosts and enjoy their romantic attentions, enabling them to return to their family responsi-bilities the next day. Although these contact encounters take place outside of the cis-heteronormative home and family, they nevertheless enable the continuation of such institutions.

The desire for stranger intimacy should also be understood within the broader context of Tokyo's urban life, where social phenomena involving human disconnections abound, notably "lonely deaths" (*kodokushi*), "so-cial withdrawal" (*hikkikomori*), and young men who are unpopular with women, called *himote*.[56] Particularly since the March 2011 Great East Japan

Earthquake and its ensuing tsunami and nuclear disasters, words referencing forms of belonging like *tsunagari* (social connectedness) and *kizuna* (bonds) have become popular in common parlance in attempts to reestablish human-human connections.[57] As I have shown, Garçon and Paradise offer opportunities for strangers who have interests in *josō* and *dansō* to enact alternative forms of sociality that have nothing to do with their home, family, school, or workplace.[58] Garçon and Paradise employees, too, derive much pleasure from nurturing intimate bonds with customers and colleagues.

## Who Employees Are and the Wage and Labor Systems

Employees at Garçon and Paradise were a diverse group. At the beginning of my long-term fieldwork in mid-2016, Garçon had six part-time employees, but after aggressive recruitment, the fleet grew to eight in mid-2017. Employees were between the ages of twenty-one and twenty-nine and came from different backgrounds. Many were originally from outside the Tokyo metropolitan area and ventured into the capital for (better) job opportunities. About half had attended college or vocational school, whereas the rest had completed high school. They all practiced *dansō* in their everyday lives, not just at work, and most located themselves as nonbinary and gender nonconforming. The new additions were welcomed by the six employees who had been rotating among themselves to fill work shifts of five to ten hours a day: typically two employees working the first shift in the afternoons and another three employees working the second shift in the evenings. No prior work experience was necessary for new employees, and Ikki provided on-the-job training in bartending, self-presentation, and attending to customers. Probably because employees were expected to be able to drink as they (learned how to) bartend, twenty years old—the age of majority and the legal drinking age in Japan—was the minimum hiring age.[59] Training in self-presentation included how employees might present themselves to customers, such as through their *dansō* names, the masculine first-person pronouns *ore* and *boku*, and clothing styles. Employees also learned the techniques of how to greet, serve, and converse with customers.

Similar to at Garçon, many of Paradise's employees were not originally from Tokyo and were drawn to the capital for work or study and a different lifestyle. About half were high school graduates, and the other half either held a degree (advanced or vocational) or were still attending college or graduate school. Unlike at Garçon, Paradise's employees were more diverse in terms of age as well as gender and sexuality. Ranging between twenty and thirty-two years old, half the employees were cis and heterosexual, whereas the other half thought of themselves as non-cisgender and nonheterosexual, including transgender, asexual, and bisexual. At the risk of generalizing, I observed that the trans, asexual, and bisexual employees tended to practice *josō* in their everyday lives, whereas those who were cis and heterosexual did not. Most cis heterosexual employees understood their *josō* practices in terms of *shumi* (hobby; taste), fashion, or occupation, that is, as a part of their job at Paradise. When my long-term fieldwork began, Paradise had fifteen employees, four of whom were full-time (the two owners and two managers) and the rest of whom were part-time employees who clocked in once or twice a week for a five- to six-hour shift. Since Paradise was twice as big as Garçon, around five or more employees could work the same shift per day.

Although the number of employees at Paradise remained the same in mid-2017, there was a high turnover of staff as compared to Garçon. However, according to co-owner Miho, the number of employees who quit every year—an average of eight out of ten—was still lower than at maid cafés. Employees quit for various personal reasons, such as to commence a full-time job elsewhere or to move on after graduating from college. Sora, Paradise's manager and a full-time employee, left due to a skin condition that prevented him from applying makeup, which meant he could not practice *josō*, one of the job's basic duties. A handful of employees have even disappeared despite attempts to contact them—Miho humorously called these ex-employees "the ones who have flown" (*tonchatta*).

Most employees I interviewed were reluctant to discuss their income; some spoke about it in deliberately vague terms. For example, Ikki, Garçon's twenty-seven-year-old manager, told me they were "not earning a whole lot," whereas Oban described their earnings using the English word *peanuts*. Despite getting paid less than minimum wage, however, Ikki maintained he was "not discontented" (*fuman nai*). A glance at Garçon's hiring notice on their website in 2017 revealed the starting hourly wage for new employees was JPY 900 (USD 8.30). This was slightly lower than what Paradise employees received and on par with or lower than what other *dansō* establishments offered based on their hiring advertisements.[60] To put things into perspective, Garçon's employees earn 2.5 percent less than Tokyo's legal minimum hourly wage—JPY 932 (USD 8.50) in 2016—whereas Paradise's employees earn only 8 percent more than the minimum wage.[61] Unsurprisingly, none of the employees indicated that salary was a reason for them to work there.

At Paradise, the hourly starting pay for new employees in 2017 was JPY 1,000 (USD 9), which co-owner Hayashi admitted in an interview with me was "low" (*yasui*). Not all employees found the pay low, however. Madoka, a twenty-year-old trans-identified undergraduate, considered the wages at Paradise high as compared to other part-time jobs she had held. On a typical weekday night at Paradise, she would take home about JPY 8,000 (USD 72.70), which includes the hourly wage and performance bonus, such as a 10 percent commission on the drinks customers buy her. That said, Sora, Paradise's manager, a cis heterosexual individual in his twenties, pointed out he could earn more money working nights at a convenience store, which pays at least JPY 1,200 (USD 10.90) per hour. Despite his status as a full-time employee, Sora's wages may not have been much more than those of part-time employees. Employees could augment their meager salary by investing in and running the weekend late-night shifts, when, as discussed in chapter 2, the owners outsourced the labor to some employees to keep Paradise open from 11 p.m. to 5 a.m. While this aligned with Paradise's business model to maximize profit, it also allowed employees to take home the night's earnings to supplement their low pay.

Although Garçon and Paradise offered similar services, their different wage systems made Garçon's employees more precarious than Paradise's employees. Aside from earning less, Garçon's employees did not have the same opportunities as Paradise's employees simply because the establishment did not operate late into the night. Garçon closed at 10 p.m., which is considered early for a bar. To my knowledge, Garçon's employees also did not earn a commission from drinks, and unlike at Paradise, it was not common practice for customers to buy employees drinks. In addition, the difference in wages was commensurate with customers' expenditures at each café-and-bar: Paradise customers spent more, including on drinks for employees, which translated into employees' higher salary, whereas Garçon customers spent less, lowering employees' earnings by about 10 percent. In contrast, the wages of cis women maid café employees were similar to those of Paradise employees, but the incomes of employees at host and hostess clubs are much higher and fluctuate according to their customers' expenditure. Top-ranking hosts could earn more than JPY 5 million (USD 45,500) per month, which may include charges for companionship and sexual services outside the establishment, known as *after*—similar to what Gaish provided in the documentary *Shinjuku Boys*.[62] As I discussed earlier, sexual services were expressly forbidden at Paradise and Garçon not only because the owners wanted to skirt the Businesses Affecting Public Morals Regulation Law but also because in making themselves easily available to customers, employees would tarnish the establishment's reputation and dissuade future patronage.

Employees' labor primarily centered on attending to customers in conversation, which in turn shaped their relationships with patrons and their incomes. At Garçon and Paradise, employees circulated through the establishment and served everyone instead of specific customers. This is an important distinction between Garçon and Paradise, on one hand, and host and hostess clubs, on the other, where a strict table rotation system is put into place to ensure regular patronage and encourage *shimei*, when a customer monogamously designates one primary host or hostess, as the ultimate goal.[63] In this sense, the employee-customer relations at the café-and-bars I look at were more loosely configured because employees' wages were tied neither to the sponsorship of rich patrons nor to the number of first-time customers they could draw to the establishment. Some employees regarded this more loosely defined relation as advantageous to them because it took away the burden of engendering a romance-like relationship with customers. Employees also did not feel obliged to "heal" customers through restoring them back to work and their social responsibilities outside Garçon and Paradise.

Of course, the more popular employees at Paradise could potentially earn a hefty commission from drinks, as some of them, like Eriko, did, and customers could still be attracted to their favorite employees at Garçon and visit the establishment for the express purpose of seeing them, as we saw earlier with the stories of Hikaru and Sakura. Despite this, however, the labor system at Garçon and Paradise did not endorse a one-to-one relationship with customers; in fact, this was written into the rules printed on the menu and expounded to customers the first time they visited Garçon and Paradise. If found to be breaching the rules, employees faced dismissal, and customers could be banned from the establishment.

### Trans and Nonbinary Labor under Pericapitalist Modes

"It doesn't feel like work" (*shigoto no kanji ja nai*), Eriko replied. I had asked the twenty-eight-year-old *toransujendā* (transgender) employee at Paradise, who practiced *josō* on an everyday basis, if she liked working at Paradise. "I feel free [*jiyū*]. There are few jobs someone like me can feel free in—there's usually no such thing," Eriko explained. Previously, Eriko had held part-time jobs at *girls bars* (*gāruzubā*), Japanese drinking establishments that typically hire attractive young women to chat and drink with male patrons.[64] Being shapely and light-skinned, and wearing her dyed dark brown hair in a bob, Eriko was able to pass, working alongside her cis women colleagues. Despite this, she felt "at ease" (*raku*) working at Paradise because she could be "as she was" (*ari no mama*) and didn't have to drink so much to ring up sales—a custom expected at *girls bars*. This was Eriko's second time working at Paradise; she had first worked there during her college days but left after graduating and finding a full-time advertising job in 2013. By the time I interviewed her in 2016, she had quit that job and returned to Paradise to work part-time while searching for a new full-time job.

To Eriko, the job at Paradise was more than just work because she felt free and comfortable being and working there, which, as she noted, was difficult for someone like her. Eriko's story reveals how, for trans people, jobs are often limited by the kind of work they can do and how satisfied they feel about their work experience. Trans women in Japan as elsewhere are commonly assumed to work in the sex and night entertainment industries due to various push and pull factors, such as employment discrimination in other sectors and the need for funds for sex/gender reassignment surgery (SGRS).[65] Indeed, *new half* individuals are often associated with sexual services like *delivery health* (*deribarī herusu*) and *fashion health* (*fasshon herusu*).[66] However, recent scholarship in the US context has challenged assumptions about trans women's work experiences in this industry, arguing that it is not these push and pull factors that lead them into sex work but rather that sex work "made them feel more sexually attractive and appreciated as women."[67] In other words, we need to listen to trans women workers to understand how they themselves derive meaning from the uneven conditions of their labor.

Despite the growing body of literature examining the workplace experiences of LGBT people in Japan, few studies have yet to focus specifically on trans employees' experiences.[68] In the Filipino context, Emmanuel David has discussed the "trans-specific occupational roles, relations, and expectations" of trans women call center employees in the transnational market economy—what he calls "purple-collar labor."[69] This idea of purple-collar labor helps us understand Eriko's work experience at Paradise as being tied to feelings of ease and freedom. Of course, Eriko's comment that her job at Paradise didn't feel like work (*shigoto*) belies the fact that it is work, but it points to the—often nonmonetary—value she and other employees ascribed to their own labor.

At first glance, and as the co-owners of Paradise would have me believe, Eriko and her cis heterosexual *josō* colleagues appeared to be valued similarly. Regardless of their subjectivity, *josō* employees' bodies and (im)material labor are tapped to churn out profit for Paradise and sustain contemporary *josō* culture. This includes trans individuals like Eriko whose needs, desires, and aspirations could be folded into the fabric of capital without challenging the status quo.[70] Yet it is also true that in Paradise's media coverage, employees are often depicted as indisputably cis and heterosexual. On one occasion, I had the opportunity to observe an on-site filming by an online Japanese television network. Such promotional activities were not unusual at Paradise; what I found interesting was how it was staged. For one, Hayashi, who was rarely seen at Paradise, made a special appearance as one of the employees attending to the program's two cis-male hosts and television personalities (*tarento*), who were in their twenties.[71] Second, for the program's question-and-answer segment, only employees who identified as cis and heterosexual, like Sora and Tobari, were chosen. This choice became apparent when Sora and Tobari were asked to describe their romantic partner, and both promptly announced they were interested in women, not men. When asked if they practiced *josō* on an everyday basis, both answered a definite no. Sora claimed he practiced *josō* only for the job, whereas Tobari maintained that his practices aligned with cosplay. That evening, I came away with strong suspicions about the misrepresentation of Paradise and its employees in the media.

This on-site filming episode reveals a gap between media representation and the realities of employees' everyday life. Sora's and Tobari's answers didn't reflect those of their non-cisgender and nonheterosexual colleagues, who were conveniently absent from the filming. Their answers also contradicted the data I had collected through observations and interviews, particularly how the employees located themselves along a wide spectrum of genders and sexualities. Building on my observations in chapter 2, I believe encouraging this kind of media representation was deliberate on the owners' part to maintain distance from Japanese sex and night entertainment, including gay bars and *new half* clubs in Ni-chōme and Kabukichō. By situating Paradise firmly within Akihabara, they could gain more publicity and promote wider consumption of *josō/otoko no ko*. However, this rendered trans *josō* employees, who formed the minority at Paradise—one in five employees—invisible. Although trans employees like Eriko were valued alongside her cis heterosexual colleagues at Paradise, promoting contemporary *josō* culture fell mainly on the latter.

Instead of resisting such media representations, Eriko appeared to go along with this, capitalizing on these material conditions to provide meaning for her lived experience. For instance, she made ends meet while biding her time as she looked for a full-time job in the media and entertainment industry—not to be confused with Japanese sex and night entertainment—which is one of the few nonstigmatized occupations for trans women in Japan. Trans employment discrimination, especially toward trans women, remains prevalent. This is compounded by socioeconomic status, as a significant number of trans people in Japan have lower education levels (up to high school), are unemployed, and earn less than cis people (for those who are employed).[72] With her college education, Eriko had more job opportunities than other trans individuals and was considered privileged.

At Paradise, on top of serving customers drinks and chatting with them, Eriko tried to make customers laugh, which she told me was her way of caring for them. As I watched Eriko interact smoothly with other customers on various occasions, I could see what she meant by this. Many customers laughed at her jokes; some flirted with her openly. One customer in particular, the twenty-eight-year-old cis heterosexual *salaryman* and *heavy user* called Toyotaro, whom we met in chapter 3, fell in love with Eriko. In our interview he likened his feelings for her to "tugging at his heartstrings" (*kinsen ni fureta*) and described them as a "sphere that couldn't be controlled by reason" (*risei ja kontorōru dekinai hani*). What he felt for her was so strong he felt a constant need to see her. In the few months Eriko worked there, Toyotaro spent a small fortune purchasing numerous drinks for her, sometimes at her behest—all with the hope of receiving her affections. Unfortunately for him, she didn't feel the same way about him. Although she generally got along well with customers, Eriko told me she had never been romantically attracted to them. Well aware of Paradise's rules against dating customers, she deliberately kept a careful distance from them. While conscious of Toyotaro's feelings for her, she regarded him as a regular and kept their relationship strictly professional.

Through her affective labor, Eriko ensured customers' steady consumption, benefiting her own income at the same time. In this sense, her encouragement of Toyotaro's feelings, even when unrequited, could be seen as a transaction. Yet Eriko's attempts to augment her income in this way didn't diminish her attachment to the job. Unlike at *girls bars*, where she was expected to and could pass, she could be who she is—simply someone who practices *josō*—at Paradise. I follow nonbinary trans-identified scholar Saoirse Caitlin O'Shea, who defines *passing* as the physical and emotional work of being "recognized and accepted as a gender other than that to which we were assigned at birth . . . [and] a standard that we are judged by and held accountable to, and ironically one that we are blamed for."[73] O'Shea reinterprets Harold Garfinkel's definition to make clear how passing is contingent on binary notions of gender, which erases gender nonconforming people.[74] Not having to pass at Paradise therefore made Eriko feel comfortable, which may explain why she considered working there not quite like work.

*Josō Employees and Sexual Harassment in the Workplace*

Despite increased visibility and valuation of *josō* employees, they have little to no legal protections from workplace discrimination and harassment. In 2016 the Japanese Equal Employment Opportunity Law (EEOL)—the 1986 labor law prohibiting gender discrimination—was revised to include sexual harassment of individuals based on their "gender identity" (*seijinin*) and "sexual orientation" (*seiteki shikō*).[75] Like the 1986 EEOL, which scholars have criticized as weak and failing to protect women from discrimination, the 2017 revision functions mainly as a guideline and has no sanctions for employers who discriminate against gender and sexual minorities.[76] In 2019 the Comprehensive Labor Policy Promotion Act (CLPPA)—also known as the law to prevent workplace bullying—was revised to obligate the Japanese government and companies to introduce measures preventing power harassment.[77] Implemented for all companies in April 2022, the revised CLPPA provisions are similar to the EEOL revision in that there are no penalties for those who refuse to take up workplace harassment prevention.[78] Since I had to reluctantly conclude my fieldwork due to the pandemic, I have not had the opportunity to determine the effect these revisions may have had on establishments like Paradise (and Garçon).

At Paradise, employees were instructed to keep their relationship with patrons professional and, to a certain degree, to endure harassment, but the unequal customer-employee relationship meant that it usually fell on the more vulnerable employees to look out for themselves. Most employees I interviewed were reluctant to discuss sexual harassment, but a few disclosed having encountered unpleasant customers under the influence of drink. For example, Tobari recounted his experience of deflecting unwanted advances from drunk and wayward cis-male customers by dealing with them quietly, demonstrating how he would firmly remove their wandering hands from his body while gently chiding them "no" (*dame*). If things escalated, Paradise's managers would sometimes step in to defuse the situation. I also observed how customers would casually comment on employees' sexual fantasies or tease them about their sexual life and partners. Although these exchanges were often brushed off as harmless jokes, they remained problematic on many levels.

*Josō* employees' experiences of sexual harassment—both verbal and physical—in the workplace are gendered. This is not unlike the sexual harassment borne by cis and trans women at hostess clubs.[79] *Josō* individuals—be they trans or otherwise—are paradoxically devalued for embracing femininity over masculinity and also hypersexualized for their trans-feminine appearance.[80] Tobari's encounter reveals how customers regard *josō* employees as sexually available in the way cis women are often perceived, which is compounded by stereotypes of trans women working in Japanese sex and night entertainment. These attitudes, coupled with narrow legal definitions of sexual harassment, obscure victim-survivors' and perpetrators' understandings of what sexual harassment means.[81] Once, a middle-aged cis-male customer told me that inappropriate contact and remarks don't count as sexual harassment because *josō* employees aren't assigned female at birth. This thinking seems to follow the gender binary prevalent in the GID discourse, in which preoperative *josō* individuals are listed as "male" on the family registry. It is also based on assumptions about *who* can be sexually harassed, be they *josō* employees who are trans women, cis men, or otherwise. Unfortunately, although Paradise had internal measures, such as giving customers a stern warning and even banishing them from the establishment altogether, there was often little employees could do to counter sexual harassment.

### Making New Worlds: Leaving Home to Seek an At-Home Space

"It's a new world [*atarashii sekai*]," Yuta declared, describing Garçon as a place where one could gain new experiences. I had asked why the five-foot-four willowy twenty-eight-year-old employee, who sported short, floppy dyed-blonde hair, chose to work there. Yuta practiced *dansō* in their everyday life and identified as bisexual and *chūsei* (in between genders) or *x-gender* (neither male nor female, or both). When I interviewed them, Yuta had only been working at the café-and-bar for a few months. Having previously worked in the service, education, and administrative sectors, Yuta knew they wanted a job where employee-customer relationships were more "personal" so they could face customers directly. Yuta lamented how, as a former administrator, they sometimes felt distant from customers on the phone because they didn't even know who they were serving. After leaving their hometown, which was three hours from Tokyo by bullet train, Yuta sought a unique job in the capital that would allow them to personally attend to customers. Calling Garçon an "at-home" space, Yuta found working at the café-and-bar appealing for encouraging close interactions between employees and customers. Moreover, as someone with a "masculine" (*otokoppoi*) appearance for whom *dansō* came naturally, Yuta could just be themselves.

Yuta's portrayal of Garçon as a new world signifies multiple things at once: arriving in an unfamiliar city from their rural hometown, starting anew with a one-of-a-kind job and work experience, and developing their subjectivity and social bonds at a novel site from which different practices and understandings of *dansō* emerge. Yuta's relocation from a rural area to the "modern metropolis," where seemingly "backward" queer subjects can freely express their genders and sexualities, resembles a progress narrative.[82] Yet Inderpal Grewal and Caren Kaplan have criticized such a narrative for idealizing queer identity in terms of resistance and rights-based discourse without taking into account other factors, such as the economy and consumer markets.[83] Yuta's negotiation of this new world was closely tied to their work experience, consumption, and the spread of contemporary *dansō* culture, which calls for different ways of discussing their experience. Yuta's desire for a unique job that enabled them to personally serve customers drew them to Garçon. At the same time, as for Eriko, working at Garçon allowed Yuta to be in *dansō*, which for them is not only an everyday practice and mode of masculine presentation but also an articulation of their subjectivity as bisexual and *chūsei* or *x-gender*.

Later in our interview, Yuta told me they identified less strongly with *x-gender* than *chūsei* as they felt they were more comfortably located in between genders, rather than being neither gender, which was how they defined *x-gender*. Despite these subtle differences, Yuta occupied a queer subject position contesting "hegemonic models of gender conformity."[84] Both *chūsei* and *x-gender* fall under the umbrella term *nonbinary gender*, and it is possible for Yuta to slide from *chūsei* to *x-gender* and vice versa.[85] My aim here is less to pinpoint which category most accurately describes Yuta and more to explore how their nonbinary subjectivity informed their *dansō* practices, labor, and consumption. How might we understand Yuta's work experience and their development of emergent genders under pericapitalist modes?

The lack of research on nonbinary individuals suggests little is known about their work experience vis-à-vis that of trans employees with binary gender identities. Even within TPE studies, nonbinary employees are frequently discussed together with trans employees, which subsumes all nonbinary individuals under the umbrella of *transgender*. This conflation of binary trans and nonbinary employees under the category *transgender* is similar in surveys of gender and sexual minorities in the Japanese workplace.[86] More recent sociological studies in the US context have shown how within a binary gender system at most workplaces, nonbinary employees often have limited work options.[87] Due to their disavowal of the gender binary, nonbinary people face more discrimination than individuals identifying as gay, lesbian, or binary trans.[88] As Skylar Davidson's survey findings illustrate, although nonbinary individuals are able to obtain employment, they are less likely to be promoted, and nonbinary employees of color and nonbinary employees assigned female at birth are more likely to be discriminated against than white nonbinary employees and nonbinary employees assigned male at birth.[89] This suggests the need to look more closely at the kinds of discrimination different nonbinary employees may encounter, especially in the context of Japan, where these issues have rarely been studied.

Between 2018 and 2022, annual surveys of gender and sexual minorities in the Japanese workplace consistently showed that nonbinary employees (i.e., FTX, MTX, and beyond) experienced higher rates of unemployment as compared to their gay, lesbian, bisexual, or binary trans colleagues.[90] It also showed that nonbinary employees assigned female at birth (e.g., FTX) were more likely to be unemployed and, if employed, were more likely to work as irregular employees and get paid below JPY 2 million (USD 18,181) per year—much less than nonbinary employees assigned male at birth (e.g., MTX).[91] Although this outcome is congruent with Davidson's findings, more research needs to be done to understand why nonbinary employees assigned female at birth remain the most vulnerable in the Japanese workplace.

At Garçon, employees appeared to be valued similarly rather than differently. This could be because all employees presented as masculine, adopted masculine speech, and located themselves under the umbrella of nonbinary gender, such as *chūsei*, *x-gender*, *musei* (no sex/gender), and questioning. Like Paradise, Garçon tapped into employees' body work of presenting a masculinized appearance and managing their feelings, which challenges the gender binary and proliferates the category *dansō* for other people's consumption.[92] Despite this, there were subtle differences in their individualistic body work and gender presentation, and this shaped how they were valued at Garçon. For instance, the hairstyles and clothing styles (when not in uniform) of some employees, like Hiyori, were inspired by K-pop, whereas anime, manga, and cosplay informed the masculine presentation of others, like Yuta. These different *kei* (styles) are also adopted by *dansō* escorts to designate their personality when engaging with clients.[93] They fit in with the Akihabara context and tap into pan–East Asian soft masculine ideals and behaviors, as exemplified by aesthetically pleasing characters in anime, manga, and Korean dramas.[94]

A few employees, like Oban, believed they were unique in expressing themselves, that is, not originating from any kind of popular culture. Ikki echoed this sentiment when he told me he was the same person he was before he worked there. In his role as Garçon's manager, Ikki witnessed employees who made drastic changes to their gender expression when they first started out at Garçon, such as cutting their long hair short and wearing men's clothing, but this wasn't the case for him.[95] In this way, Ikki and Oban expressed different female masculinities from their colleagues who drew on pan–East Asian soft masculinity. Although subtle, such differences in *dansō* employees' gender presentation were obvious to customers, who approached them like they were idols.

Employees were not equally popular at Garçon; Oban and Ikki, for example, were more popular than their colleagues, and customers would frequent Garçon just to see them. On his birthday and Valentine's Day, Oban received numerous gifts and chocolates from these customers. During a White Day event celebrating the Japanese commercial holiday at the café-and-bar, customers came to buy chocolates and spend time with their favorite employees.[96] This was curious because White Day, which falls on March 14, is a "gendered gift-giving ritual" when men give chocolates to the women they received Valentine's Day chocolates from if they reciprocate their feelings.[97] At Garçon's three-day event, however, customers arrived not to give chocolates but to buy sets of chocolates, postcards, and photographs adorned with images of the handsome employees posing in their White Day get-ups. Customers could also order from a special White Day menu featuring different flavors of cocktails, each named for the employees. Specially designed and made for the occasion, these products commodified Garçon's *dansō* employees for the purpose of motivating sales and intensifying customers' attachments to their favorite employees.

Unlike hosts, hostesses, and, to some extent, *dansō* escorts, who compete with one another to have clients monogamously designate them, newcomer Yuta didn't seem to mind patrons' preference for their more popular colleagues, Oban and Ikki.[98] Yuta appeared to derive value and meaning from their work through what they called an "at-home" space. An at-home space indexes a sense of belonging in an unfamiliar city where Garçon serves as a site for stranger intimacy. As I discussed in chapter 2, employees and customers develop close bonds with one another, leading some regulars to call Garçon their "second home," a place where they could relax and chat with like-minded people. This resonates in many ways with maid cafés, particularly the aptly named @home café, where employees greet customers with "Welcome home" as if they were coming home.[99]

However, unlike maid cafés, where maids and customers interact "in character" using "routinized" phrases, many Garçon employees and customers insisted to me that they engaged with one another in a more natural (*shizen*) manner.[100] At Garçon, contact encounters often began as a simple conversation that blossomed into a deeper relationship—without the burden of any social obligation. Contact encounters aren't disconnected from contemporary *dansō* culture but in fact thrive on it; they also help to propagate *dansō* in the media, public discourse, and everyday life. Like Eriko, Yuta did not appear to resist this heightened *dansō* visibility and similarly capitalized on it to provide meaning for their lived experience. Similar to Tobari, Yuta can be said to feel at home in queer time—alternative modes of temporality to heteronormative reproductive adulthood and family—and in queer space, settings *dansō* individuals create and occupy through their practices and interactions with other people.[101]

For Yuta, value was largely located not in monetary gain—as being an employee at Garçon came with minimum wage and little job security or potential for career advancement—but rather in nonmonetary incentives of being recognized as a nonbinary *dansō* employee. With limited work options for nonbinary individuals, especially for those assigned female at birth, who are more vulnerable in the Japanese workplace, finding a job that acknowledges them for who they are was meaningful to Yuta. Similarly to Eriko, Yuta felt at ease working at Garçon because they could just be someone who practices *dansō*. If money were their main motivation, perhaps they wouldn't have left their hometown for Tokyo, where living costs are higher. Or after arriving in Tokyo, Yuta could have worked in a higher-paying job, such as in a *dansō* host club, an establishment staffed by *dansō* hosts who attend to cis women customers—a cross between a regular host club and an *onabe* bar like Marilyn. One example is Mistral, a popular *dansō* host club that opened in Kabukichō in 2015 during the second wave of contemporary *dansō* culture. However, Yuta told me they didn't even inquire about the job because they believed working as a *dansō* host didn't suit them.

Like their colleague Hiyori, Yuta located the value of their work in providing customers with a sense of *fureai* (contact) and *tsunagari* (social connectedness)—something they readily did at Garçon. Describing their work to me, Yuta related how when meeting a customer for the first time, they would begin by introducing themselves and peppering them with questions about themselves: My name is Yuta. How should I address you? How did you learn of Garçon? What interests you? What are you into? During subsequent visits, Yuta would at times comfort customers or lend a listening ear, but generally they waited for customers to broach the subject first instead of the other way round. In my later conversations with Yuta and observations of their exchanges with customers, I noticed that the *dansō* employee projected a calming aura. After spending a few hours at Garçon speaking to Yuta, customers often left with a lighter heart. I realized Yuta's technique of asking customers about themselves invited them to unburden themselves by giving them space to talk. This experience differed from the detached customer-employee relationship Yuta encountered in their previous roles in the service industry, rendering their work at Garçon more than just work.

Leaving their rural hometown only to seek an at-home space, Yuta stressed the need to cultivate a sense of belonging in an unfamiliar metropolis. This may appear similar to hosts and hostesses who have relocated from their hometowns or home countries in search of new futures and economic opportunities.[102] As Akiko Takeyama observes, many young Japanese working-class men with limited education were willing to gamble with their future after being lured by the exciting prospects of Tokyo's hosting business, eventually assuming a "commodified yet entrepreneurial subjectivity."[103] Although entrepreneurs of some sort whose bodies were valued and commodified at Garçon and Paradise, employees like Yuta and Eriko seldom experienced the same economic trajectories as hosts. Most of the *josō* and *dansō* employees I spoke to didn't work at the café-and-bars because they were motivated by money. Of course, this could be partly attributed to differences in pay and each establishment's business model. However, Garçon and Paradise employees appeared to gain more pleasure from stranger intimacy and from looking and being looked at. They also strategically used the categories *josō* and *dansō* to express their *shumi*, nonnormative subjectivity, and connections to future professions. In these ways, pericapitalist sites like Garçon and Paradise enable gender innovation.

## Conclusion

Employees at Garçon and Paradise were a diverse group who variously produced and sustained emergent categories of *dansō*, *josō*, and *otoko no ko* and, through such reinvention, pushed at the boundaries of gender and sexuality. Under pericapitalist modes, the affective and emotional labor of *onabe*, trans, and nonbinary individuals enable us to reconfigure social reproduction. For *onabe*, trans, and nonbinary employees, their jobs are more than just work, even though they do entail work; their labor also sustains their lives and affirms their sense of self. Despite the (lower than) average pay, employees were drawn to work at the café-and-bars because they could practice *josō* and *dansō*, the job matched their aspirations, and they could forge close bonds with customers and colleagues. Although this situation is potentially exploitative, employees were strategic in employing the same practices and categories of *dansō, josō,* and *otoko no ko* to position themselves, as we saw with Tobari's pursuit of *shumi* and their dream profession of voice acting, Hiyori's and Yuta's fostering of *fureai* and *tsunagari* with other (like-minded) people, and Eriko's and Yuta's expression of their self-recognition and nonnormative subjectivity amid employment discrimination against trans and nonbinary individuals.

With the increased value and visibility of trans and nonbinary people in the workplace, Garçon and Paradise employees were hired to popularize *dansō, josō,* and *otoko no ko,* and their bodies were commodified to encourage consumption. Under pericapitalist dynamics and drawing on Muñoz's reinterpretation of surplus, the value of these employees must be understood simultaneously in monetary and nonmonetary terms. Just as employees are valued for their ability to bring in profit, employees themselves materialize value in other forms, such as capitalizing on their material conditions to provide meaning for their lived experience. Although trans and nonbinary individuals often experience employment harassment and discrimination in the Japanese workplace, nonbinary employees assigned female at birth, like Yuta, remain the most vulnerable. This would mean not only that Eriko's and Yuta's work experiences are different but also that the value accorded to them is different. I attribute this difference in part to the more visible and commercially viable *josō* business circles in comparison to *dansō* business circles—something I take up again in the next chapter as I explore the second wave of contemporary *josō* and *dansō* cultures.

# 5

## Consuming Genders, Fashioning Bodies

*Thinking Style and Beauty in
Contemporary* Josō *and* Dansō *Cultures*

"I don't consciously do [*dansō*], but I've been told I do it," Saito said wryly in an interview. The twenty-nine-year-old, who was a regular customer of Garçon, identified as FTX and bisexual and was soft-spoken and affable, always appearing interested in what others had to say.[1] Now a temporary employee (*haken shain*) doing office work, they had previously held a job in the Japan Self-Defense Forces for two years after graduating from high school. Saito usually wore their hair short with long sideburns and dressed in a loose shirt, pants, and sturdy boots; due to their androgynous appearance, they have been described by other people as "boyish." They related to me how when visiting maid cafés in Akihabara, they were sometimes asked which *dansō* café they worked at, and though they had never held such a job, the easygoing Saito received these queries good-naturedly. Although their nonfeminine appearance was often read as *dansō*, they insisted to me this was "not consciously done" (*ishiki shitenai*).

Back in the mid-2000s, Saito did not derive inspiration for their appearance from anime, manga, or the early *dansō* establishments but rather from the "cool [*kakkōii*] unisex styles" featured in KERA, a women's trendy and street fashion magazine. These styles are separate from both fashion intended for women and fashion labeled *dansō*, the latter of which was regularly featured in KERA only in the 2010s, when AKIRA, a well-known *dansō* artiste, began modeling for the magazine. The confident Saito never shied away from my inquisitive questions. They shared with me how over the years they had experimented with different styles. Their body work, or the work they did on their own body, consisted of wearing unisex clothing, cutting short and styling their hair, and "binding their breasts" (*mune wo tsubusu*). Eventually, Saito's practices, which they regarded as a form of everyday fashion, led them to frequent Garçon.

Saito's experience reveals how consumption flows enable emergent genders through fashion. By *consumption*, I mean not only the services and commodities people purchase but also—drawing on material culture studies—the ways they in turn shape material worlds.[2] This broader definition better captures the agency of those who consume. Fashion theorists have also defined fashion as encompassing the production, consumption, and circulation of clothing and the discourses surrounding it.[3] Clothing is a site from which new subjectivities surface, develop, and are embodied, allowing the wearer to express their "way of being in the world."[4] Precisely because clothes draw attention to the wearer's gender, clothing is an important site where categories emerge from the contestations of male and female, and femininity and masculinity.[5] Through what they wore, Saito actively engaged in their own subject making by purchasing certain commodities and experimenting with different styles. Through adopting cool unisex styles and rejecting girlish feminine styles, Saito became consumed and read by others as *dansō* and boyish. Drawing on what J. K. Gibson-Graham calls "(re)subjectivation," in which individuals make new subjectivities in diverse economies, we might say Saito developed new ways of being within heterogeneous economies through working on the self and being worked on by other people.[6]

Consumption can also limit emergent genders. Despite the explosion of androgynous fashion Saito alluded to, gender is "more important today and more clearly differentiated" in clothing as compared to class and social status in past traditions.[7] For instance, wearing the kimono in the early Edo period (1603–1867) marked age, class, and gender distinctions, but gender differentiation within (modern) clothing only became more extreme during the Meiji period (1868–1912).[8] In contemporary Japan, fashion's relationship with gender is now much more pronounced than its connection with age, class, or other forms of distinction. Such increased gender differentiation inhibits emergent categories by attempting to keep the gender binary intact through what individuals wear. This manifested in strangers' gender policing and interpretation of Saito's appearance as *dansō* and boyish. Although they strove to be nonbinary or agender (having no or neutral gender), they were nevertheless read as masculine by other people based on binary understandings of gender. From Saito's perspective, their wearing of unisex clothing was both feminine and masculine, in between those genders, or neither gender. This seems to align with their identification as FTX and bisexual, opening up new questions about the relationship among gender expression, gender identity, and sexual orientation.

Building on chapter 3, where I argued for Akihabara as a rich site for nonnormative media and practices that introduced the first wave of contemporary *josō* and *dansō* cultures in the 2000s, this chapter illuminates how these media, cultures, and practices expanded beyond Akihabara. What I call the second wave is characterized by how *josō* and *dansō* practices became mainstream and embedded in beauty and fashion throughout the 2010s. We can see this in the growth of businesses and explosion of idol culture, beauty contests, fashion magazines, and variety television centering on *josō* and *dansō*. How do these modes of consumption in the second wave offer us new ways to think about gender innovation? This is the central question I answer in this chapter, along with how the flourishing of emergent genders may give birth to new forms of capitalism.

Although no longer limited to Akihabara, the categories of *dansō*, *josō*, and *otoko no ko* in the 2010s nevertheless relied on commercialized fashion, beauty, and popular cultures as conduits for them to proliferate throughout Tokyo. I posit that my interlocutors played a large role in this process through their co-consumption, or the act of consuming together, of such fashion, beauty, and popular cultures. Their co-consumption simultaneously sustained and contained the production and circulation of emergent genders. Some customers, like Saito, told me they began visiting Garçon only after they adopted unisex styles from KERA. But for others like Masako, the fashionable fifty-two-year-old longtime customer of Paradise we met in chapter 2, it was the other way round—that is, they began practicing *josō* after frequenting establishments where emergent genders came into being. This demonstrates how my interlocutors may inspire the development of new categories from commercialized venues and, conversely, how categorial innovation might also motivate their co-consumption.

The expansion of contemporary *josō* and *dansō* cultures beyond Akihabara, I contend, manifests how trans, queer, and nonbinary people not only tap into commercialized beauty and fashion cultures to survive but also build a world for those like them to thrive. I lean on madison moore's idea of "fabulousness" as a "queer aesthetic" necessary for the survival of marginalized individuals—especially trans and queer people of color—who create, stage, and improvise their own "eccentric" looks in everyday life.[9] Fabulousness echoes Dorinne Kondo's understanding of style—particularly for people on the margins—as an "arena for the production of potentially oppositional identities. Sometimes the body is the most available surface for inscribing resistance."[10] This applies to my interlocutors like Saito, for whom being stylish and fabulous is a means of resisting and exceeding commonsense notions of norms and appearance. Their trans and queer creativity empowers them to reclaim their visibility and transgress gender norms and boundaries, even as some of these looks and styles inevitably become commodified for mainstream media and popular cultures.

At the same time, there are notable differences in *josō* and *dansō* practices and performances in the second wave. In the case of *josō*, normative feminine ideals are extolled and promoted by idol culture, beauty contests, fashion magazines, and variety television, whereas for *dansō*, boyish and androgynous looks are admired and marketed at similarly commercialized venues. To some extent, these differences reveal a gap between mainstream media and popular culture's insistence on normative gender and sexual ideals and trans, queer, and nonbinary people's desire for gender and sexual fluidity. This demonstrates to me a shift in terms of how trans, queer, and nonbinary people might not only understand productivity differently within a society that continues to police and endorse cis-heteronormativity but also devise new ways to exist by using beauty and fashion as their tools of survival.

One way my interlocutors do this is through their body work. Past scholarship on body work and body labor has discussed the paid, unpaid, and underpaid work performed predominantly by women on their own and other people's bodies.[11] Whereas some scholars have defined *body work* mainly as the work done on one's own body, others have extended it to include labor that involves healing, managing, and gratifying another's body.[12] Depending on the person, I use *body work* to refer to work done on one's own or another's body or both. For Saito and Masako, for example, their body work often entailed fashioning their own body to look fabulous. Closely tied to the meanings these customers make from their own body work, consumption, and continued patronage is the body work employees perform as a part of their labor at Garçon and Paradise. As this chapter makes clear, labor and consumption often go hand in hand. Labor informs consumption and vice versa.

Not all customers engage in gender-crossing practices, but a minority of them (desire to) do so. For such customers, visiting Garçon and Paradise enables them to interact with other people based on their shared tastes in *josō* and *dansō*, whether they actually practice *josō* and *dansō* within the establishments or not. As one interlocutor explained to me, plenty of customers who appeared to be cis men—including *salarymen*—were "B-*men*" (before-transformation) customers who patronized Paradise even when they were not in *josō* because they found much pleasure admiring and conversing with the "A-*men*" (after-transformation) employees.[13] Stylish and fabulous employees who were at Paradise to be seen tended to draw admiration from others or inspire them to create their own looks. At Garçon, where fewer customers practiced *dansō*, employees' styles and fabulousness garnered appreciation from fans who patronized the establishment just to catch a glimpse of their favorite employees. Within these affective spaces of looking and being looked at, my interlocutors negotiated their subjectivity and their bonds with like-minded individuals.

Customers' experiences at Garçon and Paradise are uneven. This follows from employees' varying work experiences, as we have seen in chapter 4, which stem in part from systemic discrimination against *dansō* individuals due to their lower visibility, perceived value, and socioeconomic status. Similarly, customers' consumption of *josō* and consumption of *dansō* are also not parallel. When considering the experiences of gender-crossing customers later in this chapter, I show how *josō* individuals, while having a higher socioeconomic status that lets them consume and support their practices, face more blatant discrimination in public than do *dansō* individuals, who are more economically precarious but less likely to be singled out for being different in a male-dominated society.

## Fashion and Gender in Japan

Despite their longer history in religious rituals and theatrical performances, *josō* and *dansō* as fashion practices—rather than as androgyny or gender crossing—are relatively new phenomena. Masafumi Monden characterizes the relationship between gender and clothing in Japan as "delicate" and "precarious" because boundaries are constantly drawn and redrawn over time.[14] One example of such blurring of gender boundaries in Japanese history is the kimono during the Genroku period, the golden age of the Edo period. As Liza Dalby observes, "A few unmistakable clothing cues signaled masculinity and femininity, but in the fashion arena, men borrowed styles from women just as women copied fads from men."[15] Like Dalby, we might consider this uncertainty about people's gender based on what they wore productive for propagating new styles, as it was in Genroku culture.

In Tokyo's fashion industry today, designers like Yohji Yamamoto and Rei Kawabuko of Comme des Garçons have long embraced "androgynous, boundary-pushing looks" or genderless styles, characterized by the intermingling of feminine and masculine aspects.[16] Since the 1970s these Japanese designers have also influenced global fashion industries, such as the Paris collection, which scholars like Dorinne Kondo and Yuniya Kawamura have written about extensively.[17] Examining Comme des Garçons runway shows, Kondo posits that Japanese avant-garde fashion "enlarg[es] possibilities for enacting gender, and subver[ts] the gender binary."[18] She rethinks the relationship between gender and clothing by showing how Japanese designers' use of different shapes and materials—and not revealing the wearer's silhouette—contests gender categories and reconfigures how we construct gender. Comme des Garçons' birth of boyish and androgynous styles is important to note even though I am less concerned with high fashion than with Tokyo's street fashion, where the *josō* and *dansō* practices I am tracing can be found. Kawabuko's stated aim of creating a "feeling of freedom (*jiyū*)" for her wearers encapsulates many of my interlocutors' desire to practice *josō* and *dansō*.[19] Seeking to be free from gender norms and social expectations, these individuals increasingly express themselves differently through what they wear. We might say then that emergent genders are constantly generated on the streets and runways, in the media, and by agents and institutions of fashion involved in the manufacturing, marketing, and distribution of clothing.

Street fashion, especially that worn by Japanese youths, is an ideal site for tracing *josō* and *dansō* as fashion. As several scholars have noted, young Japanese women often herald street style; instead of imitating Western styles, they engage in "creative mixing and matching of contrasting eclectic styles."[20] In doing so, young women unsettle gender norms and mainstream culture, particularly under Japan's changing social and economic conditions.[21] Some examples of subcultural street fashion throughout the 1990s included the Lolita, *kogyaru* (high school girl), and *ganguro* (black face)—not to be confused with blackface, or staged black impersonation.[22] Various scholars have argued that these subcultural styles were important for young women's identity formation, especially in subverting feminine ideals and social expectations.[23] More recently, since the 2010s, "genderless styles" (*jendāresu-kei*) have become popular among young people—something the Japanese media have eagerly picked up on. *Genderless style* denotes styles that do not distinguish between genders, at least in theory. Despite the moniker, being genderless does not mean the playing field is necessarily leveled; genderless boys (*danshi*) remain more visible in the media than genderless girls (*joshi*).[24] One example I have discussed elsewhere is Nakayama Satsuki, a popular genderless girl model, who attributed her adoption of genderless styles to a sense of freedom (*jiyū*).[25] Similar to 1990s subcultural street fashion, Nakayama's genderless practices appear important for her subject making in asserting a different subjectivity through style.

Although distinct from genderless styles, my interlocutors' *josō* and *dansō* practices are a means of resisting commonsense constructions of gender and sexuality. They do this through promoting the idea of multiple permutations of genders and sexualities in fashion as well as in Japanese popular culture, where depending on how an individual understands their practices, gender presentation may or may not be related to gender identity and sexual orientation.[26] Given Japanese high-fashion designers' invention of such styles since the 1970s, however, we might argue this isn't a new phenomenon per se but a return to genderless style beyond the runway. The articulation of genderless styles, *josō*, and *dansō* as fashion today needs to be placed in a broader context of what scholars have called *queer style*, a "subset of grotesque forms of release . . . [and] perturbation of social moral order."[27] Queer style involves not only queering fashion or transgressing aesthetic forms but also LGBTQ individuals engaging in style production, notably as models, designers, and fashion leaders.[28] What meanings do *josō* and *dansō* have, then, for young people who experiment with these forms? This is complicated by the mainstreaming of contemporary *josō* and *dansō* cultures in the second wave, which I elucidate next.

### Second Wave in the 2010s: Flourishing of Contemporary *Josō* and *Dansō* Cultures

If the first wave of contemporary *josō* and *dansō* cultures was about introducing emergent genders through various sites in Akihabara, the second wave was characterized by the expansion of businesses and the explosion of *josō* and *dansō* in mainstream media and popular culture, notably in fashion, variety television, and idol music and fandom. Alternative worlds in the second wave weren't limited to Akihabara or even confined to physical spaces but had become increasingly digital and accessible to a larger group of consumers who embraced gender crossing. With gender innovation now a given, individuals could openly practice and consume *josō* and *dansō* within a highly visible and commercialized context. For instance, the popularity of *dansō joshi* (female-to-male crossdressing girls), mainly among a niche group of women in their teens and twenties, shifted as it proliferated in mainstream circles as a fashion form and amateur practice. This shift, I argue, is important for intensifying *dansō* and developing new connections with fashion and other not-yet-knowable elements within material worlds, potentially reconfiguring our understandings of existing gender categories.

One prominent example illustrating this shift is AKIRA, a *dansō* model who first appeared in the women's street fashion magazine KERA in late 2009. In a YouTube interview, AKIRA remarked that *dansō* only became a boom six months after her debut because KERA readers responded positively to her.[29] This places the start of the second wave of contemporary *dansō* culture around 2010. In 2011, 2012, and 2013, respectively, KERA's editors released three special issues on *dansō* fashion with AKIRA as cover model, titled *KERA BOKU* (figure 5.1). Riding on the success of *KERA BOKU*, *Garçon Girls*, a "*dansō* culture magazine" (*dansō karuchā shi*), was published in late 2013 (figure 5.2).[30] These magazines and AKIRA were influential for popularizing *dansō* fashion, which denotes a boyish and androgynous appearance. Such fashion galvanized the launch of several new *dansō* idol cafés across Nakano, Ikebukuro, and Akihabara, which adopted different strategies to promote their employees as *dansō* idols and groups and build a fan base among their customers. One example is Vipera, a *dansō* group of four members who got their start by running a *dansō* café on certain weekends in Akihabara and released their first album, *Let's Get Together Now*, in mid-2014. Another is ZAC, a visual *kei* (style) *dansō* idol café-and-bar in Ikebukuro where employees performed live. Two of these employees have since debuted as *dansō* artists and models.[31] One ZAC employee, Chitose, collaborated with Vipera on their live performances and modeled in KERA and *Men's Knuckle*, a men's fashion magazine.[32]

The influence of these *dansō* units, idols, and magazines on their consumers cannot be underestimated. One Garçon customer told me they felt motivated to practice *dansō* after discovering AKIRA in *KERA BOKU*. Once, they even sat me down with their personal copies of *KERA BOKU* and showed me the features offering advice on *dansō* fashion they found useful. Although *KERA BOKU* and *Garçon Girls* both underscored *dansō*, their emphases were slightly different.[33] For instance, the cover of volume 3 of *KERA BOKU* was headlined "I Like Boys' Styles," with a subheading above reading "Even Though I'm a Girl" (figure 5.1). This focus on fashion complemented what was inside all three volumes of *KERA BOKU*, which provided an extensive

**5.1** Volume 3 of *KERA BOKU* (2013), featuring AKIRA on its cover.

showcase of *dansō* clothing, makeup, hairstyles, and matching accessories accompanied by various tips for the fashionista and a business directory listing where they could obtain these goods and services. Volumes 1 and 2 each featured *dansō* café-and-bars and escort services, such as 80 + 1 and W's Collection, and volume 3 incorporated street-style photographs of and brief interviews with *dansō* individuals.

In comparison, the cover headline of *Garçon Girls* read "Cooler than Boys" and, below that, "Within Your Reach" (figure 5.2). Unlike *KERA BOKU*'s attention to boys' styles or fashion, *Garçon Girls* underscored the idea of being "cool" (*kakkōii*). A look at its contents reveals a variety of articles featuring not only fashion, 80 + 1, and W's Collection but also in-depth interviews with ordinary *dansō* individuals, *dansō* idol group Fudanjuku,

5.2 *Garçon Girls*, October 25, 2013, featuring actress Goriki Ayame on its cover.

and SECRET GUYZ, Japan's first FTM (female-to-male) transgender group.[34] Here *Garçon Girls* bridges the gap between *dansō* and gender and sexual minorities—something that is rare in mainstream media and was deliberate on the editorial team's end. In their editor's note, the team wrote that through their coverage of *dansō*, FTM, and FTX in *Garçon Girls*, they hoped to show that "*dansō* is not [only] fashion, but also a means [*shudan*]."[35] As a means or method of survival, *dansō* is particularly important to trans and gender nonconforming individuals as it offers new ways of resisting gender norms and expressions, and reinventing themselves through fashion. We might think of *dansō*, FTM, and FTX as connected through clothing, which is a productive site from which genders and sexualities emerge—something fashion theorists have long observed.[36] Hence, the *Garçon Girls* editorial team conveyed the sense that while *dansō* entails practices of dressing, it is first and foremost a way of life.

Having already cemented their status as leading establishments within *josō* and *dansō* business circles respectively, Paradise and Garçon broke new ground for the second wave of contemporary *josō* and *dansō* cultures. People's practices and consumption of *josō* and *dansō* expanded beyond a small group of fans in the mid-2000s to become a boom that propagated *josō/otoko no ko* and *dansō* in mainstream media and culture in the 2010s. Through Hayashi's celebrity connections (being a full-time model, Hayashi was a bit of a *geinō*, or celebrity, as well), Paradise and its employees were regularly promoted on variety television programs, and through this publicity, *josō*, *josōko*, and *otoko no ko* spread in mainstream media. This growing visibility culminated in the nomination of *josōko* for the 2014 U-CAN Keywords-of-the-Year contest, following that of *otoko no ko* in 2010.[37] Many a customer told me they first learned of Paradise from either television or online videos shared through social media. Even international media outside of Japan picked up these stories, bringing numerous tourists to Paradise.

While Garçon also had a large media presence, Paradise was more aggressive in spreading *josō/otoko no ko*. For instance, throughout the 2010s Miho and Hayashi expanded the business to offer a wide range of media and services, such as DVDs and photo books featuring *josō/otoko no ko* and a fashion website and makeup courses for aspiring *josō/otoko no ko* individuals. Although none of these media and services are now available, they have inspired *josō/otoko no ko* beauty shows, contests, and more bars and salons catering to *josō* individuals—a surge that would characterize the second wave. One notable example of *josō* beauty competitions is the Tokyo Cosme Boy Contest in 2009 and 2010, founded by Inoue Miya.[38] Inoue intended for the Tokyo Cosme Boy Contest to internationally proliferate *keshō danshi*—a term meaning "cosmetic boys" (*cosme boys* for short), or men who wear makeup—which Inoue defines as those who are neither a man nor a woman, or both at once.[39] In the 2010s *josō* beauty contests were also held during school culture festivals.[40] Opening in quick succession were a small bar in Ueno owned by Inoue and staffed by cosmetic boys called Wakashu Bar Keshō Danshi (Cosme Boy Bar) in 2011, a *josō* salon-bar in Ni-chōme called Onna no ko Club (Girls Club) in 2015, and a magic-themed *josō* café-and-bar in Ikebukuro called Mahō-ni-kakerarete (Black Magic) in 2016. It was also in the mid-2010s that Hibari-tei, the *josō/otoko no ko* café I discussed in chapter 3, relocated from Akihabara to Shinjuku. Two salons named Leaf-Style and Milky, which offered full makeover services for *josō* individuals, comprising hair, makeup, manicure, rental and styling of wigs, clothing, shoes and accessories, and indoor and outdoor photography, set up shop in Shinjuku and Akihabara, respectively.

These diverse examples illustrate a shift in the production and consumption of *josō/otoko no ko*. Not only did *josō* and *otoko no ko* move away from the 2-dimensional and 2.5-dimensional—tensions that plagued the first wave—as they proliferated in the mainstream, but they also materialized stronger connections to beauty, fashion, and idol culture through turning bodies into commodities for consumption. One potential influence on *josō* beauty salons like Milky and Leaf-Style is what Claire Maree calls Japanese lifestyle television's "queer turn" in the mid-2000s, when *onē-tarento* (queen personalities) took on roles as makeup, fashion, and hairstyling experts.[41] Although Japanese lifestyle television has long promoted consumption as the means for people to improve all aspects of their lives, particularly their physical appearance, this queer turn made *onē-tarento* experts to whom cis women could turn.[42]

Arguably shaped by such makeover programs, Milky and Leaf-Style offered ordinary individuals the chance to practice *josō* or become just like the *josō* anime characters they admired. In the Japanese context, this trope of self-transformation is epitomized by the Cinderella ideal in which one becomes beautiful through "self-discipline," "represent[ing] the possibility of triumph over adversity."[43] Unlike in Euro-American contexts, this is not a story of passivity and dependence; rather, it's a neoliberal ideology: anybody can be Cinderella, including gay men, middle-aged women, and working-class people, as long as they are willing to try their best and work hard at their "aesthetic progress."[44] From this perspective, we might regard *josō* (and *dansō*) practices as an individual achievement of improving and reinventing the self through beautifying and changing one's body.

This could be seen in Milky's one-year-anniversary event in 2017, which took the form of a pop-up café staffed by *josō* individuals made over at the salon located in Akihabara. Its poster (figure 5.3) illustrated the hyperfeminine physical appearance of the ad hoc workers, who simultaneously resembled cute *josō* characters from anime, manga, and games and cis women maids from maid cafés. All the employees had feminine nicknames (*adana*), which I recognized as operating in a similar style to those at Paradise. I learned from an interview that one of Paradise's longtime customers had been involved in Milky's founding, so that similarity is probably not coincidental. Building on Paradise's popularity and the innovated categories, establishments like Milky provide individuals with the means to turn into *josōko* and *otoko no ko*. One interlocutor told me that Leaf-Style was instrumental in shaping her "*josō* debut," demonstrating the importance of *josō*-friendly salons for

**5.3** Flyer of Milky's pop-up *josō* café, 2017.

introducing consumers to alternative worlds and affirming their interests in *josō/otoko no ko* through self-commodification. This is assuming they can afford the cost of going to such salons in the first place, of course.

Although Garçon also shaped the second wave, its plans to expand might be considered less aggressive but perhaps no less ambitious than those of Paradise. Ikki, Garçon's manager, told me that Yuka constantly thought of new ways to appeal to longtime patrons. For example, in the mid-2010s, when Garçon was doing relatively well, Yuka decided to open Aozora, a pop-up bar, to show her gratitude for the increasing number of regular customers. Aozora was available only on certain evenings to a maximum of five regulars at any one time and therefore required advance reservation.[45] Staffed by the same employees as Garçon, Aozora, which Ikki described as a "VIP room," had a cozy atmosphere. Patrons could hang out at a novel space and get up close and personal with employees. Despite Yuka's intentions to cultivate goodwill among regulars, however, I observed that employees simply didn't have the capacity to run Garçon and Aozora concurrently. Hence, only a few short months after the pop-up bar opened, Aozora was put on hold so employees could focus on Garçon's upcoming events for the rest of the year.

In hindsight, Garçon's brisk business could be due in part to the second wave's explosion of *dansō* idols and fashion, which sustained customers' enthusiasm and patronage. For instance, Hikaru, the twenty-one-year-old cis heterosexual woman we met in chapter 3, began frequenting Garçon in the mid-2010s due to her love for *dansō* idols. Hikaru told me over drinks at Garçon about her long-standing fandom of THE HOOPERS, a "boyish girls' group" who made their major debut in 2015 and led the *ikemen joshi* (handsome girls) boom with their short hair and boyish fashion. THE HOOPERS' seven members were selected from five thousand hopefuls through *dansō* idol group Fudanjuku's "next generation auditions," and although they appeared visually similar to Fudanjuku, they were said to resemble Takarazuka and were arguably more successful under Universal Music Japan.[46] Although Garçon didn't specifically leverage the popularity of idols and figures like AKIRA and THE HOOPERS, it benefited indirectly from the mass circulation and commodification of *dansō*. More individuals like Hikaru were rediscovering Garçon as one site out of many for *dansō* consumption, and within this alternative world, they would meet longtime patrons who were women otaku and *fujoshi* (BL women fans) and bond based on their love of *dansō* characters. Such encounters are vital for producing emergent categories and challenging our understandings of genders and sexualities.

Despite the success of Garçon and Paradise, *josō* and *dansō* establishments were often a gamble. Within Akihabara's pink economies as well as *josō* and *dansō* business circles more generally, such establishments tended to be transient and vulnerable to economic shifts. Both Garçon and Paradise started out as entrepreneurial projects as their owners were uncertain whether they would thrive when many such businesses have failed. For example, B:Lily-rose, a *dansō* café that opened around the same time as Garçon, closed after a few years, and Hibari-tei, a *josō/otoko no ko* café that set up shop when Paradise did, went bust in mid-2017—only months after becoming a regular business.

In other instances, some businesses concluded to make way for new ones. For example, Propaganda, the *josō* event I discussed in chapter 2, ended its run in March 2016, though it has remained influential in *josō* business circles, as many of my interlocutors attested, and only a few months later, Diffusion, a monthly late-night *josō* club party, was launched in Kabukichō.[47] At its height, Diffusion was reportedly well attended by straight men, cis women, heterosexually married *otoko no ko*, and other individuals of diverse genders and sexualities. It was even said to surpass Propaganda's popularity.[48] These examples show the fleeting nature of sites where individuals can openly practice and consume *josō* and *dansō* and what it takes for establishments like Garçon and Paradise to stay afloat. And when these businesses fail, *josō* and *dansō* employees lose their jobs, and they and their customers part with this space for sociality or self-fashioning.

### Bodies as Capital: Fashioning *Josō* and *Dansō*

On a typical workday, Kaori arrives at Paradise as early as one to two hours before it opens to "transform" into a woman. The slim, light-skinned, and slightly built (about five feet, three inches tall) cis heterosexual twenty-year-old employee practices *josō* regularly as a form of fashion and *shumi* (hobby; taste). Applying thick makeup, Kaori takes extra care to accentuate the eyes, lips, and cheeks. Using a hair straightener and hairstyling products, he styles his naturally straight black hair, which sits just above his shoulders, and full bangs. He then changes into a short red plaid dress, the uniform Paradise supplies, with high heels and stockings that complement his slender legs. Kaori adds the finishing touches: black leather bracelets and a tiny purse decorated with several skulls and crossbones. Other employees adorn themselves with hair clips, barrettes, earrings, and even small furry stuffed toys, but Kaori prefers the edginess of punk style. Just before his shift begins, he cleans the space, including the restrooms; sets the tables with menus and chopsticks; and displays Paradise's neon signboard downstairs.

Aside from preparatory tasks before Paradise opens for business, Kaori's labor consists predominantly of the work he undertakes on his own body. It would appear that his body work reinforces normative feminine ideals endorsed by commercialized beauty and fashion cultures. However, as Debra Gimlin reminds us, cis women reconfigure beauty ideals and normative femininity by shaping (perceptions of) their own bodies.[49] Such body work is also informed by postfeminism and neoliberalism, in which predominantly middle-class women become seemingly empowered entrepreneurial subjects who manage their bodies and their sexuality through aesthetic self-making.[50] By aestheticizing their bodies using makeup, wigs, hairstyles, clothing, and accessories to present as feminine, employees at

Paradise are constantly in the process of redrawing gender boundaries and reviving categories.

These self-reinventing practices that regulate bodies are frequently presented as freely chosen—practices that enable them to look good on the outside and feel good on the inside. These practices consist of visible regimes, such as beautified faces and bodies decked out in fashionable clothes and accessories, as well as invisible regimes, including skin care and facial and body hair removal. The effort, time, and cost involved in manipulating their bodies to present a feminized appearance all constitute Kaori's and his colleagues' body work, which we might read as queer and fabulous. Queering fashion and looking fabulous are important means of survival for marginalized individuals, who resourcefully create their own original looks and deliberately transform themselves into spectacles to reclaim their visibility.[51] Ultimately, these employees' body work is about countering commonsense "rules of socially accepted appearance" and "daring to inhabit space on [their] own terms."[52]

Employees at Paradise and Garçon also perform physical and emotional labor on customers' bodies. Miliann Kang's definition of *body labor* as "emphasiz[ing] the management of commercialized *embodied* exchanges" is useful for thinking about work that is done on another body.[53] Body labor aligns with the notions of emotional labor and affective labor defined in chapter 4, as well as what Eileen Boris and Rhacel Parreñas term *intimate labor*, the work of providing physical touch, paying close attention, and having "bodily or emotional closeness or personal familiarity."[54] The body work/labor done by Paradise and Garçon employees encompasses multiple dimensions. On one level, they manage their affects and emotions to entertain and induce in customers certain feelings by telling jokes and lending a listening ear, as Eriko and Yuta do (see chapter 4). On another level, they also carry out physical tasks required for the café-and-bar's day-to-day operations, such as keeping the establishment clean, as Kaori does. On a third level—and this could be the most significant—by dressing and behaving as a different gender, employees transform and fashion their bodies to look fabulous, becoming important sites of resistance and consumption both for themselves and for others. This section focuses on the last level—work on the self—through the examples of Kaori and Yu, a twenty-one-year-old employee at Garçon, especially how they negotiate their beauty, style, and fashion to create pleasurable spaces of looking and being looked at.

To contextualize body work and labor, the notions of body capital and technologies of the self are useful here. Scholars have defined *body capital* as value produced from the commodification of laboring bodies, drawing on Pierre Bourdieu's understanding of capital.[55] While Bourdieu does not emphasize the body, Chris Shilling argues the body is "a form of capital in its own right."[56] What Michel Foucault terms *technologies of the self* are "intentional" and "voluntary" practices individuals enact on themselves and their own bodies to "set themselves rules of conduct" to "change themselves in their singular being, and to make their life into an oeuvre that carries certain aesthetic values and meets certain stylistic criteria."[57] As entrepreneurs of body capital, employees at Paradise and Garçon respectively willingly feminize and masculinize their bodies and as a result become valued by the establishments. Moreover, through embodying technologies of the self, employees become fabulous and resist commonsense notions of gender norms and appearance. Their *josō* and *dansō* practices enable them to acquire body capital and negotiate their individual ways of being and also shape the proliferation of *josō* and *dansō* as emergent genders.

*Body Work at Paradise*

Kaori came to work at Paradise after frequenting the café-and-bar in *josō* as a customer. An employee noticed Kaori and, out of the blue, asked if he wanted to give the job a try. Kaori's experience of becoming an employee wasn't unusual; several of the staff I spoke to were also recruited in this manner. Within an environment where employees and customers obtained pleasure from looking and being looked at, Kaori's fabulousness was appreciated. Kaori's body work created an alternative world for reinvention. Indeed, he relished the ability to "change" (*kawaru*) his body the most.

Other employees have given similar reasons for practicing *josō*. Tobari, a twenty-two-year-old employee, described this feeling as a "strong desire to transform one's appearance" (*henshin ganbō*), whereas Sora, Paradise's twenty-seven-year-old manager, enjoyed the "before" and "after" of practicing *josō*. Sora alludes to the Before-body and After-body in makeovers on variety television, where a conventionally attractive "hyper-gendered" appearance is associated with achieving an empowering "authentic self," as well as the B-*men* (before-transformation) and A-*men* (after-transformation) images and videos *josō* individuals often upload on social media.[58] Before-bodies and B-*men* digital content are often vastly different from After-bodies and A-*men* images and videos: the latter tend to be hyperfeminine, with frilly or lacy dresses and heavy makeup to accentuate big eyes, full lips, and long hair. Such normative feminine ideals are similar to those marketed by idol culture, beauty contests, fashion magazines, and variety television in the second wave, which are admired and even valorized at Paradise, raising questions about whether these ideals transgress or reinforce gender norms and boundaries. Is there even room for fabulousness? Why is transformation important for these individuals in the first place?

This collective desire for transformation must be understood as more than just a passing interest in something; Kaori's, Tobari's, and Sora's *josō* practices are about cultivating taste, a certain aesthetic, and a sense of belonging to Paradise. Scholars have argued that nightlife is not only an affective space for the formation of identities and "ad hoc communities with fluid boundaries" based on shared tastes but also an important site for negotiating politics of the everyday.[59] Taking a cultural studies perspective, I take *politics* here to mean an intervention in everyday life and "critical contestation" for diverse voices to be heard and for such dialogues to be elicited.[60] Following from this, Sora, Kaori, and Tobari can be said to disrupt cis-heteronormativity through their conscious practices of dressing. Although they appear to imitate and extol the highly marketed normative feminine ideals from commercialized beauty and fashion cultures, their practices nevertheless resist hegemonic masculinity and express gender fluidity when they innovate new categories at Paradise. Hence, there remains room for living otherwise through carving out a fabulous existence.

*Body Work at Garçon*

At Garçon, the pleasure of looking and being looked at was similarly created by *dansō* employees who were fabulous in their own ways. As at Paradise, employees' body work at Garçon comprised a fair amount of primping and preening, including regular haircuts and dyeing. On a typical workday, Yu arrives at the café-and-bar about thirty minutes before his shift begins. Changing out of his casual clothing into Garçon's waiter-like uniform—a white dress shirt, black waistcoat, and black pants—the twenty-one-year-old, who identifies as questioning, matches it with his own men's dress shoes. Some employees style their tinted hair with wax and wear a bit of eye makeup—inspired by the stage makeup of Takarazuka's *otokoyaku* (male roles)—but Yu prefers to be au naturel. Wearing black full-rim eyeglasses, with their undyed black hair in a short crop, Yu reminds me of a K-pop boy band member. Like his colleagues, he accessorizes his uniform by pinning several badges bearing his favorite anime and manga onto his waistcoat.

Yu's preparation takes up less time and effort than Kaori's. Perhaps because he engages in these practices on a daily basis, he does not seem to stress over the transformational aspect of *dansō*. This was something I found common to all employees at Garçon, who practiced *dansō* in their everyday lives and located themselves along a continuum of genders and sexualities, including *chūsei* (in between genders), *musei* (no sex/gender), and *x-gender* (neither male nor female, or both). When we met Yu earlier, in chapter 1, I noted that he thought of himself as questioning and nonconsciously doing *dansō*, indicating his ambivalence about labeling himself. Despite this, transformation is key to his *dansō* practices. Much effort is needed to achieve the boyish and androgynous good looks heavily marketed in *dansō* idol culture and fashion magazines in the second wave. Even for Yu, this entails routines that are largely invisible to the public eye. Indeed, much of the employees' body work remains hidden, for instance, dieting and exercising to stay slim; getting regular haircuts, dyeing their hair in multiple colors, and styling it; and learning how to wear *dansō* makeup. This body work sometimes has hidden costs, such as in the case of Hiyori, the handsome nonbinary twenty-five-year-old employee we met in chapter 4, whose hair became so damaged after being bleached and dyed a different color every month they decided to hold off on dyeing for a while. I could tell that this inability to imitate the trendy hairstyles of the *dansō* idols and models and K-pop male idols they admired was a blow to Hiyori.

Similar in some ways to Paradise, Garçon enables self-making and community building for *dansō* individuals through their body work and interactions with other people based on a shared taste and aesthetic. Whereas hyperfemininity appears to be prized at Paradise, at Garçon it is boyishness rather than a normative masculinity that's prized. All employees used masculine speech, particularly the strongly and mildly masculine first-person pronouns *ore* and *boku*, and ensured their behavior, consumption, and management of feelings reflected masculine ideals, but their physical appearance is more accurately described as androgynous, a mixing of feminine and masculine elements, following the highly marketed styles from *dansō* idol culture and fashion magazines in the second wave. This means there are different stakes for *dansō* and *josō* individuals involved in the process of generating and embracing emergent genders. I would even venture to say there is a stronger desire among *dansō* individuals for gender and sexual fluidity.

The departure from cis-heteronormativity and commonsense expectations in contemporary Japan was one of the reasons Yu decided to work at Garçon. After graduating from design school, Yu, who had worked in the service industry, was searching online for a bartending job when he came across Garçon. Although there were numerous bars across Tokyo, Garçon caught Yu's eye because he felt it was "not normal" (*futsū ja nai*). He found the requirement for employees to be in *dansō* novel. He also appreciated the more fluid and lengthy conversations or "contact encounters" among patrons and employees, which are unlike the somewhat scripted customer service conversations at ordinary establishments.[61] At Garçon, he could employ casual speech in his interactions with patrons to foster closer employee-customer relationships.

Yu's description of Garçon as "not normal" is apt: employees reconfigure gender boundaries by willingly aestheticizing their bodies to present as masculine, thereby gaining body capital. Like Paradise, Garçon capitalizes on its employees' *dansō* practices to churn out profits through customers, who flock to the establishment to interact with them. The things that make Garçon "not normal" are precisely the things customers want. Customers are also seeking freedom from social norms through contact encounters with others interested in *dansō* culture. Participation in an environment where employees express themselves through masculinizing speech and androgynous looks allows customers to mold their subjectivities as well. Unlike at Paradise, where there is a significant distance between mainstream media's valorization of normative feminine ideals and (some) employees' desire for gender and sexual fluidity, the boyish and androgynous good looks at Garçon align with those marketed in commercialized beauty and fashion cultures, which demands a rethinking of trans, queer, and nonbinary individuals not in terms of productivity but in terms of survival. Instead of asking how trans, queer, and nonbinary individuals are productive or deliberately nonproductive in a cis-heteronormative society, I ask how they use beauty and fashion as tools for survival.

## Queer Styles and Co-Consumption

Pointing to their simple loose-fitting white long-sleeve shirt and laughing, Saito—the *x-gender* longtime customer I began this chapter with—declared that Oban, an employee at Garçon, possessed an "identical or matching" (*osoroi*) one. Balancing a cool appearance with a warm and friendly personality, Oban sported a unique asymmetrical hairstyle and an open interest in riding motorcycles. The twenty-three-year-old had a large following at Garçon, evident in the way customers who favored him spent generously on gifts and occasional drinks for him. Most of his fans were cis feminine-presenting women, unlike Saito, which was why I found his interactions with Saito refreshing to observe. Saito told me they discovered they had similar "tastes in clothing" (*yōfuku no konomi*) when they happened to chat with Oban on this subject. This co-consumption developed into an occasional gift exchange when Oban would compliment Saito for wearing a cool (*kakkōii*) shirt and half-jokingly suggest Saito buy the same shirt for him, and sometimes Saito would. And when Saito noticed Oban was wearing a nice shirt, Oban would reciprocate by detailing where he bought it and even offer to buy it for Saito.

From observation alone, I would not have imagined Oban and Saito shared similar fashion tastes. Though they often liked and donned the same garment, both approached their body work differently. Being different individuals who worked on the self in distinct ways, Oban and Saito articulated alternative masculinities—what Jack Halberstam calls "female masculinity."[62] This engagement with alternative masculinities can be seen in their differing claims to *dansō*: Saito claimed they weren't consciously trying to practice *dansō*—they were read by others as doing so—whereas Oban had no problem calling his practices *dansō*. By pursuing unisex fashion, Saito neither consciously avoided the feminine styles worn by many Japanese cis heterosexual women nor deliberately adopted the masculine styles of cis men. In contrast, Oban perceived his nonfeminine appearance as "natural"—expressing who he was on the inside—as he practiced *dansō* in his everyday life. Oban sported a unique charismatic punk style that was less clean-cut than that of his colleagues and *dansō* idols like THE HOOPERS. Despite these differences in their (re)subjectivation, where individuals make new subjectivities in diverse economies, emergent genders surface, proliferate, and become embraced through their co-consumption of clothing. This could be seen from their interactions about fashion and occasional gift exchange. Their queer style—the multivalent ways in which dress resists, confounds, and dislocates the social order—potentially revives or gives rise to a variety of genders and sexualities.[63]

In Gimlin's ethnography of how cis women engage in body work, she argues they are "capable (within limits) of transforming cultural meanings" of the normative body and self.[64] Drawing on this, I contend that Saito's body work challenges gendered conceptions of embodiment and clothing as feminine or masculine. For instance, to create a less feminine look, Saito cut their hair short and bound their chest to minimize breasts. Despite the physical and mental health challenges of binding, such as feeling pain, panic, and an inability to breathe, a US study of transmasculine young adults by fashion and health science scholars found that "going without a binder caused great stress or anxiety."[65] The same may be true for Saito.

As Saito's clothes shopping experiences show, they did not confine their practices to either gender. Saito told me they sometimes found the styles in the women's section too limiting and restrictive, and the sleeves too short for their build. Saito was about five feet, three inches tall—an average height

5.4    Magazine spread featuring various unisex brands like Algonquins. From volume 3 of *KERA BOKU* (2013).

in Japan—but had broad shoulders and long arms. Due to this, they often ventured into the men's department for larger sizes or searched for unisex tops with longer sleeves by clothing brands like Evo and Algonquins, advertised in *KERA BOKU* (figure 5.4). This is not to say they never shopped in the women's department; rather, they frequented both departments. At first, Saito felt "extremely nervous" (*sugoi kinchō*) about shopping in the men's section, but after many years of doing so, they felt less self-conscious. In recent years, Saito felt there was less prejudice toward them in Japanese society, especially with the mainstreaming of *dansō* and the embrace of genderless fashion.

Saito's shopping experiences demonstrate how attitudes toward men's and women's clothing, who can wear what kinds of garments, and who can shop and be seen in which departments persist. Such understandings are internalized even by Saito after years of socialization in Japanese society. The lack of styles in the women's section for different body sizes and shapes and for non-cis and nonfeminine individuals reveals an implicit bias about who the target consumers of "ladies' fashion" are and what kinds of bodies they are expected to have. Unable to find clothing there that fits them properly, Saito decided to shop in the men's department, but their initial apprehension about being spotted there and judged by others exposes a gender binary that continues to structure clothing, despite the gender-crossing contours of Japanese street style and high-end fashion. The apparent lack of other gender categories means fashion is inevitably divided into men's and women's, even as it plays with gender.[66] As Llewellyn Negrin puts it, "The more one seeks to blur gender boundaries, the more they keep reasserting themselves."[67] Even when, or precisely because, more androgynous styles are introduced, gender categories do not become obsolete but are simply reconfigured. Unsurprisingly, Saito felt uncomfortable about having to fit into clothing from either the men's or women's department and sought a different way to survive.

Clothing stores, clothing sections, and fitting rooms are sites of anxiety for many individuals, particularly women, but all the more so for trans and gender nonconforming people. Scholars have examined cis women's feelings of fear and embarrassment surrounding what they wear and their clothing shopping experiences, but few have so far discussed those of queer, trans, and nonbinary consumers.[68] One exception is Kelly Reddy-Best and Elaine Pedersen, who found that LGBTQ-identified women in the United States negotiated queerness in their appearance using masculine identifiers—such as men's shirts—and experienced distress, shame, and mistreatment when shopping in the men's department.[69] One of their participants, a masculine-presenting queer woman, shared how she was "corrected" for taking men's garments or being in the men's section but also "corrected" in the women's department for being in the "wrong" place.[70] Such forms of gender policing cause anxiety for individuals like Saito who don't seem to belong to either section and desire a style that is in between. Although Saito did not explicitly mention brushes with salespersons and other shoppers, their feelings of distress about clothing should not be dismissed. From their clothing choice and consumption, specifically their mixing of men's and women's items, Saito developed their queer style and innovated diverse genders as a means of survival.

Saito's process of self-fashioning was extended and sustained by their exchanges with Oban. Compliments from employees about customers' appearance and gift giving between individuals who shared similar tastes and interests were common enough at Garçon, but the camaraderie between Oban and Saito was special in two ways. First, *dansō* and androgynously dressed individuals who frequented Garçon were rare. Most regulars did not share Oban's *dansō* practices and clothing styles. For Saito, being able to converse casually and exchange styles with Oban appeared to assuage their anxieties around purchasing and wearing men's clothing. Perhaps this was less about fashion—even though fashion is integral for inscribing their marginal identities—than about a shared sense of not fitting in. To be fabulous is to resist and surpass commonsense norms and appearance.[71] Oban and Saito therefore bonded over their queer style, felt affirmed in their way of being, and constructed alternative forms of sociality. Despite their claim of not consciously doing *dansō*, Saito found their wearing and consumption of unisex clothing was perceived less negatively during and after the second wave. This was partly because their queer style became subsumed under the sign of *dansō* and was conflated with *dansō* practices. However, Saito's nonbinary way of being also appears to be erased as they come to be read by others as doing *dansō*.

Second, though Oban worked part-time at Garçon and Saito was a temporary employee, and so neither had much disposable income, they were generous about occasionally gifting each other clothes. However, because of their status at Garçon as employee and customer, respectively, this was not an equal relationship; it is likely Saito more frequently presented Oban with gifts. At Garçon, most gifts exchanged between employees and customers were anime-, manga-, and game-related merchandise, not so much clothing. As an arguably more personal gift, then, clothing enables the receiver-wearer's formation of new subjectivity through their body work. Moreover, although done voluntarily, such a gift exchange engenders social bonds between the giver and the recipient.[72] The shirt Saito gifts is a gesture of goodwill with the expectation of fostering a better employee-customer relationship, and, in turn, Oban returns the favor to maintain this relationship. Such close bonds nurtured in the alternative world of Garçon go on to sustain the ways in which Oban and Saito live otherwise.

## Making Over the Trans Body

Visiting Paradise over the weekend one summer, I met Jiji, a *josō* customer in her thirties who identified as "MTF (male-to-female) transgender." Jiji alternately referred to herself as *josōko* and *otoko no ko*, contemporary categories to index someone who practices *josō*. It was only later, in an interview, that Jiji told me she wanted to "become [a] woman" (*onna ni naritai*), although she didn't at the moment intend to undergo sex/gender reassignment surgery (SGRS). She was also romantically interested in women—she counted *josōko/otoko no ko* as women—but not men. That evening, we struck up a conversation when she sat next to me by chance. Employees at Paradise routinely placed complete strangers next to each other to get them to make friends. That day, Jiji wore a dark brown shoulder-length wig with bangs, a cute cream blouse, and a pink

5.5    Magazine page from Liz Lisa × My Melody 2016
       Spring Collection, March 2016.

skirt, which she proudly announced came from Liz Lisa, a young women's fashion brand specializing in girlish trends (figure 5.5). As we chatted, Jiji revealed
her love for cats and said her *josō* name or femme name was derived from
her recently deceased cat. Taking the name was a way of honoring her cat.

Halfway through our exchange, Jiji excused herself to run to the bathroom
to touch up her makeup while I ordered more drinks and spoke to Layla, a daz-
zling twenty-something employee who could pass as a cis woman. When Jiji
came back, Layla greeted her warmly using her *josō* name, and she joined our
conversation. It soon became obvious to me that Layla was Jiji's favorite employee.
Later, Jiji told me she was following Layla on Twitter and had first gone to Paradise to meet Layla in person. Jiji greatly admired Layla's "cute" (*kawaii*) appearance, "slim figure" (*sutairu yoi*), and "feminine abilities" (*joshi ryoku*). Most of all,

Jiji said Layla's hospitality made her feel as if she was a "real girl" (*shin no onna no ko*), which made a good impression on her and encouraged her to return.

Underlying Jiji's subject making and understandings of her trans identity is a strong belief in the "wrong body" discourse, or having mismatched corporeality, which is informed by cultural makeover logics popularized by mainstream media, especially Japanese lifestyle television.[73] This is compounded by the high visibility of *onē-tarento* (queen personalities) during the "queer turn" when they instructed cis women in makeup, fashion, and hairstyling.[74] Jiji's conviction of being in the wrong body and their desire to correct this were heavily influenced by mainstream media, which prescribe normative feminine ideals for both cis and trans women. This can be seen from how Jiji described Layla as slim and *kawaii* (cute) with *joshi ryoku* (feminine abilities), all of which align with normative femininity, which was marketed in commercialized beauty and fashion cultures in the second wave. The relationship among cuteness, femininity, and the eagerness to maintain a slim figure is well established in scholarship on young cis women's fashion, body aesthetics, and eating disorders.[75]

*Joshi ryoku* is a newer word nominated for the 2009 U-CAN Keywords-of-the-Year contest to refer to the forces driving one's life as a girl or woman (*joshi*), often sustained through hard work and a sense of self-worth.[76] Someone who is considered to have high levels of *joshi ryoku* would dress and behave femininely, such as in Layla's case. Unlike the English term *girl power* that characterizes postfeminism, *joshi ryoku* can be applied to older women, such as wives and mothers who dress and wear makeup well.[77] Feminist sociologist Kikuchi Natsuno's survey of 782 undergraduates in Aichi Prefecture reveals how *joshi ryoku* remains tied to heteronormative life goals; a woman who has high levels of *joshi ryoku* would achieve perceived success in (heterosexual) love and marriage.[78] When Jiji applied the term to Layla, she assumed Layla subscribed to these life goals and amplified *joshi ryoku* through making over the self, reflecting Jiji's own aspirations to become a woman.

Jiji's embrace of normative feminine ideals, a renegotiation as a part of her body work and (re)subjectivation, had not been without difficulties. Since "coming out" as trans to her parents and best friend, Jiji had struggled with their strong reactions.[79] Jiji's parents took her to the hospital in a bid to "cure" her, whereas her best friend, a cis man she had known since childhood, told her to "disappear from this world" (*ko no yō ni kierō*). To cope with this, Jiji sought advice and friendship from individuals at commercial establishments catering to *josōko* and *otoko no ko*, including Paradise; Onna no ko Club, a salon-bar in Ni-chōme; and Leaf-Style, a makeover

**5.6** Screenshot of Leaf-Style's home page advertising *josō* makeover services, taken on April 1, 2019. leaf-style.jp.

salon in Shinjuku (figure 5.6). Leaf-Style was instrumental in shaping Jiji's transformation; there she made her "*josō* debut" and subsequently learned how to do her own hair and makeup. These safe spaces allow *josōko* like Jiji to congregate and come into contact (*fureai*) with other *josōko*, enacting affective ties among strangers or stranger intimacy.

Other than enabling *josō* individuals to have "encounters" (*deai*) and a "sense of proximity" (*kyorikan*) with one another, these sites were also a significant "source of information" (*jōhōgen*) for those just starting out. For example, Jiji conversed with others about makeup, fashion, coming out to one's family, and places to obtain *josō*-friendly services. For millennials like Jiji, who easily traversed social media and physical sites in *josō* business circles, such conversations were also held online. Incidentally, this was how Jiji found Layla—through *josōko* and other individuals in the scene who either followed or were followed by Layla on Twitter. After following Layla online for several months, Jiji eventually visited Paradise, and in this way, her co-consumption sustained emergent genders.

Although co-consumption was integral to Jiji's subject-making process through stranger intimacy and contact encounters at these commercial spaces, such opportunities are only open to *josō* individuals who have the disposable income and willingness to spend most of their earnings to finance their practices and consumption. Put differently, the degree to which (re)subjectivation occurs is tied in significant ways to *josō* individuals' expenditure on goods and services to adorn their bodies and frequent establishments. Maintaining such a lifestyle is not affordable to all, but Jiji had the economic means to do so. Although I didn't get the sense that Jiji was wealthy—she worked full-time in the courier industry—Liz Lisa, the midlevel fashion brand Jiji wore (figure 5.5), had shoes, clothes, and accessories in the range of JPY 2,200–16,000 (USD 20–145.50). Sold at Shibuya 109, a shopping mecca that showcases the latest fashion trends, Liz Lisa is particularly well known among young women.[80] Purchasing these commodities is in addition to the costs of receiving makeover services at Leaf-Style and patronizing establishments like Paradise and Onna no ko Club. Even among *josō* individuals, their body work differs widely depending on how much they spend, unevenly shaping how gender categories emerge and are embraced. Commercial sites like Paradise, Leaf-Style, and Onna no ko Club remain aligned with makeover and wrong-body discourses perpetuated in the media, in part because endorsing normative feminine ideals attracts more customers. Hence, while *josōko* may themselves have or desire diverse subjectivities, they are encouraged by such sites to pursue normative feminine embodiments.

After I had known Jiji for several months, she suggested that instead of MTF, MTX (male-to-X) might be a more accurate way of describing herself. Although she still feared cis men and felt more comfortable around women, she also envisioned herself as somewhere in between *josōko* and *new half.* When I asked how she came to think of herself as MTX, Jiji said Layla first brought it up during one of their conversations at Paradise (which I was not privy to), and after thinking it over and doing some online research, she decided it made sense.

Jiji's negotiation of gender as fluid complicates stable and straightforward understandings of existing categories. The shift from MTF to MTX exposes the constructedness of man, woman, or other positions along the spectrum, and by articulating how gender and sexual variance may potentially converge, Jiji gestures toward a complex web of desires. Discussing the relationship between gender and sexuality, trans studies scholars have variously argued that the category *trans* should neither be reduced to a sexual identity "modeled on gay or lesbian experience" nor be constructed as without sexuality.[81] Such understandings of trans also depend on an assumed distinction between gender and sexuality, which, as scholars have observed in Asian contexts, "remain entangled even in the face of globalizing pressure to become separate."[82] This is consistent with Jiji's experience as someone for whom gender and sexuality were not necessarily separate. In the process of forging her own way of being, she found that such categories can and do intersect, moving beyond identitarian models of articulating gender and sexuality.

Although co-consumption advances emergent gender categories and Jiji's subject making in the ways I have discussed, sometimes it can inhibit them. Despite the heightened visibility of trans people in Japanese mainstream media—intensified by the LGBT boom—Jiji continued to encounter verbal abuse and physical assault and harassment from strangers both on the streets and online. For example, Jiji was stared at and called "disgusting" (*kimochi warui*) on the subway. Once, she even had stones thrown at her while walking on a sidewalk, one of which hit her head, causing bodily injury. On Twitter, where Jiji uploaded selfies or digital self-portraits, she received numerous anonymous direct messages, including some which called her "ugly" (*busu*) and "gross" (*kimoi*) or told her to "die" (*shine*) and "rot" (*kusare*). Especially in the beginning, when Jiji had just begun practicing *josō* (which was, incidentally, around the time we first met), she told me she felt so hurt and mortified by these (online) attacks and bullying that she wanted to commit suicide. Over the months, as she learned how to do her own hair and makeup, the number of hate messages gradually decreased.

Jiji's experience is not singular; many gender and sexual minorities have long suffered bullying, LGBT bashing, and sexual, physical, and emotional violence.[83] The transphobic reactions directed at her appear to derive from people's recognition of her gender presentation as not passing or as differing from the normative feminine ideals marketed in commercialized beauty and fashion cultures. Precisely due to increased consumption of hyperfeminine trans personalities like *onē-tarento* on television, individuals like Jiji whose gender expression deviates from these ideals in real life become discriminated against. Passing depends on how other people regard trans and gender nonconforming individuals and "authenticate" their gender identity—what Laurel Westbrook and Kristen Schilt call "determining gender."[84] Based on their consumption of these personalities in mainstream media, people determine whether Jiji can pass, and when she does not adhere to these criteria for passing, strangers on the subway single her out, revealing a correlation among passing, consumption, and harassment. Numerous studies have shown how failing to pass frequently results in anti-trans violence, including verbal, sexual, and physical assault and harassment, and it is interesting that the more Jiji consumed to aestheticize herself and the more successful she was at passing, the less she was harassed.[85] Indeed, Jiji herself attributed the harassment she experienced to her "poor" skills in doing her hair and makeup, particularly in her early days of practicing *josō*—a case of victim blaming. However, these hate messages gradually declined when she acquired skill in beautifying herself. As Jiji's adherence to normative feminine ideals shows, trans people must employ a variety of skills to survive within a cis-heteronormative society.

For Jiji, being online intensified the relationship among passing, consumption, and harassment. She was vulnerable to digital harassment because she was judged by her harassers as not passing and because they were emboldened by the anonymity afforded by social media platforms such as Twitter.[86] Her harassers sent her incessant threats and inflammatory comments, often in reaction to her tweets and selfies, without any fear of repercussion. These forms of digital violence negatively impacted her well-being and nearly led to self-harm. On the other hand, online anonymity on certain platforms, such as Tumblr, can also play a positive role, empowering queer users to interact without the risk of being outed or outing themselves, and trans users to create a "safe space where people could present as their new gender."[87] Twitter's willingness to accommodate pseudonyms and multiple accounts enabled Jiji to explore her identity more fully, including experimenting with her *josō* name and gender presentation. She also shared her story, interacted with fellow *josō* individuals, and, through them, accessed *josō*-friendly resources and information without disclosing personal data. Stranger intimacy and contact encounters in the digital world extended into the physical world, at Paradise, allowing her to practice *josō* and see and be seen by other *josō* individuals without fear of harassment. Of course, the opposite is also true; *josō* individuals can cultivate a sense of belonging within these physical sites before developing these bonds online. Jiji's co-consumption unevenly shaped the contours of her (re)subjectivation, at times enabling and at other times limiting emergent categories.

### Conclusion: Beauty and Fashion as Tools of Survival

Employees' and customers' consumption encouraged them to materialize emergent genders, and, in turn, these same categories sustained their co-consumption. This consumption included their body work or labor, the work they did on their own and/or another's body. For employees like Kaori and Yu, this entailed fashioning their bodies both for their jobs and on an everyday basis. Through their fashion and beauty practices, they resisted and surpassed commonsense notions of norms and appearance, contributing to their survival and subject making. Regular customers like Saito experimented with different forms and established their way of being as FTX, mediated through androgynous fashion at Garçon. Similarly, Jiji forged her subjectivity as *josō* and trans, and subsequently as MTX, through an aesthetic culture informed by normative feminine ideals at Paradise. Yet their (re)subjectivation at Garçon and Paradise was uneven. Jiji exemplifies *josō* individuals' higher visibility, socioeconomic status, and risk of assault and harassment, whereas Saito represents *danso* individuals' relative invisibility, economic precarity, and fewer experiences with discrimination.[88] While this might be partly explained by Japanese society's underlying misogyny, including toward trans women, another explanation might be the more visible and larger scale of consumption within *josō* business circles as compared to *danso* business circles, which promotes unequal configurations of sociality between employees and customers at the two establishments.

Thinking style and beauty is particularly important during the second wave of contemporary *josō* and *danso* cultures, which, unlike the first wave in the 2000s, has become more mainstream and embedded in fashion and aesthetic progress. Despite this expansion of contemporary *josō* and *danso* cultures beyond Akihabara, emergent genders continue to rely on commercialized fashion, beauty, and popular cultures as conduits for their proliferation throughout Tokyo. I argue this is vital for trans, queer, and nonbinary people, who draw on such commercialized spaces to survive and, more important, build a world for them to live in.

One way my interlocutors survive and live otherwise is through clothing, which is an important site for expressing who they are and articulating their *josō* and *danso* practices as fashion. Changing one's appearance on the outside is ultimately about self-transformation on the inside. Being fabulous enables them to resist and exceed commonsense notions of norms and appearance. This circulation of queer style and aesthetic progress offers us new ways to think about how emergent genders come into being and how they may lead to capitalist renewal. While there is a gap between their desire for gender and sexual fluidity and mainstream media and popular culture's insistence on normative feminine and masculine ideals, this gap appears to be smaller for those who practice *danso* as compared to those who practice *josō*, although it may also narrow or broaden depending on the individual. As Jiji's case shows, how we understand gender and sexual variance may be more complicated in reality than what has been marketed in commercialized beauty and fashion cultures. It illuminates a more complex web of desires tied less perhaps to the refusal to be productive within a society structured by cis-heteronormativity than to the need to survive. Trans, queer, and nonbinary people like Jiji seek new ways to live by employing beauty and fashion as their tools of survival.

# Coda

*Living Otherwise in the New Normal*

Since fieldwork for this book was conducted, the coronavirus pandemic has created new ways of living, dubbed the *new normal* in media, public, and scholarly discourses around the world—a term that has long been used to characterize life when, following a crisis, new rules, mindsets, and behaviors become necessary. This could be seen, for example, when weak gross domestic product (GDP) growth and high unemployment befell advanced economies after the late 2000s global financial crisis or when technological innovation and development-model reforms followed on the heels of falling economic growth rates in mainland China in the 2010s.[1] In Japan the phrase *new everyday* (*aratana nichijō*) surfaced at the end of May 2020 when the incumbent prime minister, Abe Shinzo, declared a new normal way of life after lifting the first nationwide state of emergency.[2] This wasn't a lockdown but a recommendation for residents to stay at home and for places where people gather to close or have restricted hours.[3] Following that, *new normal* (*nyū nōmaru; atarashii seikatsu yōshiki*), a term popularized by Tokyo governor Koike Yuriko, was nominated for the 2020 U-CAN Keywords-of-the-Year contest.[4] The new normal is illustrated by the Japanese Ministry of Health's slogan, and the winner of the aforementioned contest, *3Cs* (*san mitsu*), which describes how people should behave in "closed spaces," "crowded places," and "close conversation" to keep themselves safe and prevent the virus from spreading.[5]

What does the new normal mean for emergent genders and the ways of living I discuss in this book? How have temporary closures of restaurants and other hospitality businesses during states of emergency affected the survival of *josō* and *dansō* establishments like Garçon and Paradise and that of my interlocutors, who found themselves unable to travel to work or school, frequent these establishments, or interact with one another in person? With such restrictions on people's mobility and everyday life being lifted in 2022 after two and a half years, what does the future now hold for them? I explore these questions as a way of drawing the book to a close.

Throughout *Emergent Genders*, I have argued that markets have been an important force for the emergence and embodiment of gender categories in recessionary Tokyo. Though still in relationship with older or existing forms, emergent genders like *otoko no ko*, *josō*, and *dansō* are vernacular innovations by individuals to express who they are and what they do in the process of becoming. Categorial innovation has become possible—even necessary—amid the increasing impossibility of normative ways of being during prolonged economic stagnation. Through an analysis of the documentary *Shinjuku Boys*, I explored how, in the 1990s, constructions of gender roles shifted from those embedded in heteronormative marriage and family to one where young women gained employment and were able to date *onabe* (masculine-presenting individuals assigned female at birth). In precarious times, particularly from the 2000s onward, what has also become apparent is the potential of popular culture to suture emergent genders and the material. For example, fashion and body work enabled individuals' resistance to commonsense constructions of gender and sexuality, whereas anime, manga, and games facilitated the creation of alternative worlds where consumers could engage in deterritorialized forms of social belonging—that is, related to neither the family, the school, nor the workplace. They were able to live otherwise.

One way my interlocutors survive and live otherwise is through clothing, which is an important site for expressing who they are and articulating their *josō* and *dansō* practices as fashion. Changing one's appearance on the outside is ultimately about self-transformation on the inside. Being fabulous enables them to resist and exceed commonsense notions of norms and appearance. This circulation of queer style and aesthetic progress offers us new ways to think about how emergent genders come into being and how they may lead to capitalist renewal. While there is a gap between their desire for gender and sexual fluidity and mainstream media and popular culture's insistence on normative feminine and masculine ideals, this gap appears to be smaller for those who practice dansō as compared to those who practice *josō*, although it may also narrow or broaden depending on the individual. As Jiji's case shows, how we understand gender and sexual variance may be more complicated in reality than what has been marketed in commercialized beauty and fashion cultures. It illuminates a more complex web of desires tied less perhaps to the refusal to be productive within a society structured by cis-heteronormativity than to the need to survive. Trans, queer, and nonbinary people like Jiji seek new ways to live by employing beauty and fashion as their tools of survival.

*Emergent Genders* has also contended that our understandings of productivity need to be reconfigured. As the Japanese case shows us, people's reactions to the LGBT boom and employment discrimination against gender and sexual minorities hinge on assumptions that they are either productive or unproductive. Instead of beginning with this, we might rethink social reproduction, particularly in terms of queer and trans social reproduction within the trans-political economy (TPE). At Garçon and Paradise, the labor of trans and nonbinary employees like Eriko and Yuta might be read as a "work of resistance that enables [their] *being*" as well as "work that is valuable and *necessary*."[6] To make sense of this contradiction, I drew on Anna Tsing's notion of pericapitalism to help me think about the café-and-bars as simultaneously capitalist and noncapitalist. Just as the employees' labor was extracted to popularize *dansō*, *josō*, and *otoko no ko*, their work also sustained their lives and extended meaning to their practices. I connected this to pink economies, tracing the intersections between cis-heteronormative and nonnormative commercial media, sex-related sites, and entertainment sites in Japan and situating Garçon and Paradise within transnational queer economies. As illustrated by Eriko's and Yuta's different economic trajectories and experiences of workplace harassment and discrimination, these spaces contradictorily enable "new modes of inclusion and exclusion."[7]

One of the contentions this book has advanced is the need to move beyond US-centric identitarian models of analyzing gender and sexuality. This is not to invalidate such models, which many people find helpful for articulating their LGBTQ identities and consider important for advocacy efforts and rights-based movements leading to legal recognition, social support, and health care access. However, for some individuals, especially those who do not fit neatly into existing categories and whose experiences are embedded in other cultures and languages, identity-based modes may be limiting. Identitarian models of gender and sexuality may hinder some people's efforts to express who they are, which demands a rethinking of such models. For many of my interlocutors at Garçon and Paradise, for example, their practices often took precedence over their identities. Doing *josō* and *dansō* had more meaning for them than defining who they were. These practices inform their desires, embodiment, and sense of belonging—and they are also where categorial innovations grow. My interlocutors' stories of being and living otherwise are no less significant, but they have been, for the most part, left out of North American anglophone queer and transgender discourses. Part of my effort in *Emergent Genders* is to write them into these narratives.

**Emergent Genders in Crisis?**

As I reflect on the period during which much of the book was written, as well as multiple crises of the present, it seems to me that thinking about emergent genders is even more pressing today. In a (post)pandemic era, marginalized individuals—including gender-variant and sexually variant people—are especially vulnerable to job loss, inadequate health care, and unsafe, abusive, and alienating environments due to lockdowns and school closures.[8] For instance, one study revealed that because many LGBTQ people in Japan already experience housing instability, their living conditions have worsened from income loss or reduction as a result of the emergency measures.[9] An April 2020 study surveying gender and sexual minorities' (*seitekishōsūsha*) anxieties over catching COVID-19 found they were most concerned about being outed during state investigations of infections and about possibly being excluded from hospital notifications or important decision-making about treatment if their partner fell ill.[10] These studies demonstrate not only the precariousness of gender and sexual minorities but also the alternative ways of living and working that are made possible by the new normal and can or have to emerge when older ways are no longer possible. Pandemic times have the potential to materialize emergent genders because of people's inclination to seek change when faced with a perpetual state of crisis.

Amid an outbreak of COVID-19 in Japan in March 2020—which saw schools closed and the Tokyo Olympics postponed—Garçon officially shut their business. This announcement on Garçon's blog, which I read before it became defunct, was shocking to me; there was no indication the establishment was going to close when I casually visited while on a short business trip to Tokyo in December 2019. In fact, I had planned to return for a longer field trip the following year and shared my plans with one of the employees, who appeared overjoyed to welcome me back. However, the pandemic swiftly put an end to all travel. It was possibly one of the reasons for Garçon's closure as well, though, according to the announcement, the indoor smoking law that came into effect in April 2020, which would ban smoking on its premises—something many customers loved to do—sounded the death knell for Garçon.[11]

I noticed that even after closing, Garçon tried to initiate an ad hoc in-person event every two months until the end of 2020. From what I could glean from its blog, the ad hoc events were similar to Garçon's special events, with the same employees attending to customers and the one-drink-per-hour system in place, except it had a fixed entrance fee and was held at an undisclosed location. Customers were also required to register for the ad hoc event beforehand with their personal information to gain entry, and they were asked to take certain precautions to prevent spread of the coronavirus, such as adhering to the 3Cs, refraining from visiting if they felt ill, and wearing a mask to and inside the establishment. In 2021, however, all activity petered out, including updates, until, eventually, Garçon's blog was taken down.

Paradise's tale, however, was one of survival. To abide by the state(s) of emergency, Paradise reduced their business hours, notably closing early at 8 p.m.—the recommended policy for bars and restaurants.[12] A quick glance at the websites and social media accounts of other *josō* and *dansō* establishments revealed that most—if not all—followed suit to either shift or shorten their opening hours. Despite these limitations Paradise's owners introduced other creative ways to keep the business alive and accommodate customers who were working from and staying at home. For instance, in 2020 Paradise held online drinking parties via Zoom, a video communications platform, and sold entry tickets and other goods such as alcohol and Polaroids on their website. Online drinking parties (*nomikai*) consisted mainly of chatting and drinking with employees. Essentially, they were an online version of the in-person services provided at Paradise. During these drinking parties, the customer was able to treat the employee they were meeting on Zoom to a drink, purchase a Polaroid of them, or buy alcohol for themselves, which would be obtained via home delivery. Customers could also purchase discount coupons to be used the next time they physically visited Paradise—a way of encouraging reluctant customers to return.

At the beginning of 2021, Paradise announced the start of a hybrid format: customers could visit the establishment until its early closure at 8 p.m., after which they could go online and interact with employees via TwitCasting, a live streaming application popular in Japan that allows users to tweet at the same time. Now stylized in Japanese katakana as Tsuikyasu, the platform, operated by Moi Corporation since 2010, purportedly has over thirty million users.[13] Paradise promoted this paid online service as a means of making the establishment accessible to customers who were unable or unwilling to go out as well as extending the in-person experiences of regular customers who patronized the establishment but could not get enough. For instance, on TwitCasting/Tsuikyasu, customers could watch a live video of employees and react through tweets. They could also buy Polaroids and alcohol, including drinks for employees, on Paradise's website. By experimenting with various ways of simulating the face-to-face experience for customers, Paradise's owners sustained the business.

Garçon's and Paradise's stories demonstrate how, when faced with new-normal conditions, the two establishments sought different survival strategies, resulting in different outcomes. In part because Paradise's owners were able to reimagine spaces of work and consumption as not necessarily confined to the physical establishment, they were able to keep the interest of some—especially digitally inclined—customers. As I discussed in chapter 5, community building in *josō* business circles often transcended the digital and physical worlds because many (*josō*) individuals were comfortable interacting with each other across online and offline spaces. Garçon's owner, on the other hand, was less able or willing to respond to the seemingly insurmountable challenges posed by the pandemic and antismoking legislation and thus, after more than a decade of being a leading *dansō* establishment, ceased all operations. As I have shown throughout this book, such businesses are already precarious to begin with, and many have gone under due to stiff competition. But in the new normal, prepandemic ways of living that would normally include large numbers of people eating, drinking, and conversing in close proximity late into the night were rendered unsafe, at least until restrictions were lifted in late 2022. In this context, Paradise's attempts to extend these activities to the online sphere were ingenious because they encouraged customers who hungered for a kind of normalcy to participate in them.

Another survival strategy, employed by the *josō* salon-bar Onna no ko Club in May 2020, was an online fundraising project, exhorting patrons, "Let's protect" (*mamorō*) the establishment against conditions arising from the pandemic by donating money. According to its crowdfunding website, the collected funds would ensure a place of work for employees as well as a "hometown" for everyone to return to at any time (*jikka ni itsudemo kaereru*).[14] Within a month, Onna no ko Club successfully raised nearly JPY 2.5 million (USD 22,727)—more than twice the targeted amount. Today Onna no ko Club remains in business, having returned to welcoming customers.

Could Garçon have survived this crisis if it had just stuck it out? This hypothetical question is difficult to answer, but I read the small masked ad hoc sessions they hosted postclosure as a last-ditch effort to figure out if the business could bounce back. As the termination of all activities indicates, perhaps Garçon has finally thrown in the towel. I was also curious to observe the case of Dracula, a vampire-themed *dansō* café, which, instead of shutting its doors like Garçon, worked around the indoor smoking ban by installing nonsmoking rooms. During the first state of emergency in 2020, Dracula also announced on Twitter that they would take precautions against the coronavirus, such as sanitizing the space and mandating mask wearing for employees and customers.[15] Although Dracula did not go the online route like other businesses, its ability to quickly adapt to numerous obstacles might explain why it was able to remain open. Other establishments, like Mistral, the *dansō* host club I introduced in chapter 4, weren't so fortunate. In early May 2020, Mistral tried to introduce paid online *dansō* host sessions via Zoom where customers could chat with employees—an extension of their weekly TwitCasting/Tsuikyasu sessions.[16] Although Mistral appeared well placed to shift to remote sessions, the lack of in-person interactions must have taken a toll on the business; the club permanently shuttered only two months later. As the examples of Mistral and Dracula show us, switching to paid online socialization does not necessarily guarantee survival for the business.

I also wonder about Garçon's employees, whom I have no way of contacting now, who suddenly found themselves out of a job in a tough job market, having to also cope with the pandemic on their own. For regulars, I imagine the unexpected loss of a support system and social network provided by establishments like Garçon must have been devastating. Although

Paradise was able to survive the pandemic, I wondered how limited opening hours and the shift to online or hybrid formats affected employees during that time, such as less pay, reduced working hours, and the need to learn how to use new digital technologies. Were their customers willing to pay for an online service in lieu of or following a physical service?

And what of the customers? The customers who are irregular and part-time workers were likely the first to be laid off or, if they were unable to work from home, may have (temporarily) lost their income under states of emergency. For those who are gender and sexual minorities, staying at home may mean living in hostile family environments or, if living alone, increased social isolation, which could lead to depression, the exacerbation of existing mental health concerns, or worse.[17] In addition to the worsening living and working conditions gender and sexual minorities face, they also have to worry about catching the coronavirus—and the possibility of being outed against their will.[18] Although the various *josō* and *dansō* establishments tried to introduce alternative ways for customers to interact with employees and one another safely, this continues to be a challenge for most hospitality businesses. Even if they managed to figure out a way to operate safely and stay afloat, customers may be unable or unwilling to frequent these establishments as much as they did during prepandemic times.

## Innovating All the Time

In the new normal, what emergent genders and ways of living can potentially come into being? Some important developments so far are virtual (re)imaginings of non-cisgender and nonheterosexual ways of being and of LGBTQ nightlife and communities arising from increased digitalization of people's everyday lives. In pandemic times, many have had to engage in online learning at school, use digital technologies to work from home, and socialize with family, friends, and strangers from a safe distance. When people's self-expression, interactions with other individuals, and spaces of queer leisure shift online, they become, on the one hand, more accessible to diverse gender-variant and sexually variant individuals, but on the other hand, they also become exposed to safety and privacy issues, such as homophobic and transphobic attacks by users infiltrating online queer spaces. As we know from the transphobic assault and harassment of Jiji, whom we met in chapter 5, these are hardly new concerns. However, they have intensified during the pandemic due to people's increased use of digital technologies.[19]

The same digital technologies also offer "new creative freedoms" and "creativity from the margins" where individuals can carve out alternative spaces for themselves and challenge such technologies' heteronormative structures.[20] For instance, responding to the need for social connectedness, LGBTQ people reinvented digital dance parties.[21] At Club Q, a virtual series of club nights in Canada, participants "appropriate[d] Zoom in ways that redefined, adapted, and reinvented the platform's business-oriented purpose for queer nightlife."[22] This was no different in Japan, where gay bars and *josō* and *dansō* establishments ingeniously held events and peddled their goods and services online until they could reopen.[23] Perhaps immersing oneself in such online connections only shows how in-person interactions still matter and might even be more meaningful in a pandemic since physical intimacy remains desired.[24]

At the same time, these changes point to a hybridization of online and offline spaces long after the pandemic has ended, in which LGBTQ people's lived experience will transcend "different spatial and conceptual configurations . . . remixed and reformulated."[25] Of course, hybridization is already a reality for young gender and sexual minorities in Japan who are digital natives—those who grew up with social media and other modern technologies—and who have now turned to these platforms to survive in a difficult time. A quick glance at Twitter, TikTok, and YouTube reveals the rise of vloggers (video bloggers) like genderless *joshi* (girl) Ayase Rinte and *otoko no ko* duo Unlink Cherry as well as *josō* VTubers (virtual YouTubers) known as *babiniku*, who have debuted, uploaded more videos, and garnered more followers during the pandemic.[26] In the digital sphere, these young individuals actively build connections as content producers, consumers, and members of certain platforms. Through their consumption of videos, images, and tweets, young followers—especially gender and sexual minorities who may feel distressed or isolated at home—can feel supported and maintain social connectedness with like-minded individuals. In turn, they support and keep these vloggers and VTubers afloat through their likes, comments, and subscriptions.

Young gender and sexual minorities who have taken to social media platforms to express who they are and what they do are innovating all the time. They are always in the process of becoming when seeking ways of living and surviving in the new normal, often drawing on popular categories to market themselves, thereby driving boom-based cultures. Instead of seeing such booms as merely fads, we might regard them as vital for reimagining these same categories in precarious times. Moving in and out of *dansō* and *josō/otoko no ko* café-and-bars, my interlocutors continue to negotiate ways of being, living, and becoming otherwise, creating categorial innovations that are not outside of capitalist logics but that, rather, shape and are shaped by capitalist logics. As pericapitalist endeavors, these innovations have the potential to both inhibit and motivate capitalist renewal.

Introduction

1    All translations are the author's unless otherwise stated. See chapter 1 for a discussion of *otoko no ko.*

2    For all my interlocutors, I follow the pronouns they gave during interviews, as far as possible given the differences between Japanese and English pronouns. I retain "café-and-bar" (*kafe ando bā*) because it indexes how this genre of restaurant is popularly called in Japanese.

3    Kawamoto, *Otoko no ko tachi* [About boy daughters].

4    High school girl (JK, or *joshi kōsei*) cafés hire teenage girls wearing high school uniforms to chat with and serve drinks to primarily middle-aged male customers.

5    Golden Gai is a small network of bars located near Kabukichō, an entertainment and red-light district located in Shinjuku.

6    Galbraith, "Maid Cafes."

7    Until April 2020, when the Japanese law banning indoor smoking in Tokyo kicked in, customers could smoke next to nonsmoking patrons within the premises. See Jack Tarrant, "Smoking Diners to Take It Outside as Tokyo Ban Kicks In," Reuters, March 31, 2020, https://www.reuters .com/article/us-health-coronavirus-japan-smoking/smoking-diners-to -take-it-outside-as-tokyo-ban-kicks-in-idUKKBN21I0WC.

8    Originally a derogatory term, *otaku* has been reclaimed by individuals, usually men, who are "engaged in intimate interactions and relations with manga/anime characters, specifically *bishōjo*, or cute girl characters." As I discuss in chapter 3, discourses of otaku are deeply contested and contradictory. See Kam, "Common Sense," 5; Kam, "Anxieties"; and Galbraith, *Otaku and the Struggle*.

9    Numerous works already discuss gay consumption in Shinjuku Ni-chōme. For some examples, see McLelland, *Queer Japan*; McLelland, "Japan's Original 'Gay Boom'"; Sunagawa, *Shinjuku ni-chōme no bunka-jinruigaku* [A cultural anthropology of Shinjuku Ni-chōme]; and Baudinette, *Regimes of Desire*.

10   Adair, Awkward-Rich, and Marvin, "Before Trans Studies," 317. As I discuss later in the introduction, trans studies and queer theory are distinct but share a close relationship. Some scholars like Cáel Keegan have also argued how trans studies "must remain in the position of against" queer theory and its disciplinary boundaries, being "invited and disinvited at the same time." Keegan, "Against Queer Theory," 352.

11   This question is adapted from one asked by the editors of *Transgender Marxism*. See Gleeson and O'Rourke, "Introduction," in *Transgender Marxism*, 2.

12   I discuss the relationship between neoliberal regimes and consumption later in the introduction.

13   To be clear, Gibson-Graham does not necessarily view capitalism as hegemonic but criticizes how various discourses in scholarship or otherwise have "sustained a vision of capitalism as the dominant form of economy." As J. K. Gibson-Graham is the pen name of feminist economic geographers Julie Graham and Katherine Gibson, I will refer to "Gibson-Graham" as one entity in the singular. See Gibson-Graham, *End of Capitalism*, 3–8.

14   Reading an early iteration of this book, Jack Halberstam called these forms my interlocutors generate "vernacular innovations."

15   Gleeson and O'Rourke, "Introduction," 14.

16   Gleeson and O'Rourke, "Introduction," 17.

17   There is vast scholarship on gender and sexual variance in Japan. See, for example, Chalmers, *Emerging Lesbian Voices*; McLelland, *Queer Japan*; Mitsuhashi, "Transgender World"; McLelland, Suganuma, and Welker, *Queer Voices from Japan*; and Dale, "Transgender, Non-Binary Genders."

18   Saeki, *Josō to dansō no bunkashi* [The cultural history of male-to-female and female-to-male cross-dressing].

19   See Leupp, *Male Colors*, 46; and Mitsuhashi, *Josō to nihonjin* [Japanese people and male-to-female cross-dressing].

20  See, for instance, Isaka, *Onnagata*; Leiter, "From Gay to Gei"; Robertson, *Takarazuka*; and Stickland, *Gender Gymnastics*.

21  Williams, *Marxism and Literature*, 123.

22  De Lauretis, *Technologies of Gender*.

23  Peletz defines *gender pluralism* as "pluralistic sensibilities and dispositions regarding bodily practices (adornment, attire, mannerisms) and embodied desires, as well as social roles, sexual relationships, and overall ways of being that bear on or are otherwise linked with local conceptions of femininity, masculinity, androgyny, hermaphroditism, and so on." Peletz, *Gender Pluralism*, 10.

24  J. Nakamura and Fukuda, "'Zombie' Firms in Japan."

25  For works on Japan Inc. (*kigyōka shakai*), see Borovoy, "Japan as Mirror"; and Allison, *Precarious Japan*.

26  Gleeson and O'Rourke, "Introduction," 26.

27  Liu, *Specter of Materialism*, 59.

28  Liu, *Specter of Materialism*, 70.

29  M. Ho, "Queer and Normal." This is also what Marta Fanasca found of *dansō* escorts in Tokyo. See Fanasca, *Female Masculinity*.

30  As Jules Joanne Gleeson and Elle O'Rourke remind us, the theories that are deemed "scholarly" in academia may not reflect the realities of trans lives. See Gleeson and O'Rourke, "Introduction," 3.

31  See, for instance, Gluckman and Reed, *Homo Economics*; Jacobsen and Zeller, *Queer Economics*; Floyd, *Reification of Desire*; Rosenberg and Villarejo, "Introduction"; Chitty, *Sexual Hegemony*; and Gleeson and O'Rourke, *Transgender Marxism*.

32  Liu, *Specter of Materialism*, 58.

33  See some of the discussion in queer-materialist and trans-materialist scholarship, for instance, Lewis and Irving, "Strange Alchemies"; Eng and Puar, "Introduction"; and Puar, *Right to Maim*.

34  On queer theory's anticapitalist ethos see, for instance, Drucker, *Warped*; and Sears, "Queer Anti-Capitalism."

35  This approach underscores the social while not reducing it to a singular hegemonic capitalism. See S. Jackson, "Why a Materialist Feminism."

36  Raha, "Queer Marxist Transfeminism."

37  Tsing, "Sorting Out Commodities," 38; and Tsing, *Mushroom*, 296.

38  Tsing, *Mushroom*, 65.

39  Here I draw on Gibson-Graham's discussion of capitalist hegemony and economic diversity. See Gibson-Graham, *End of Capitalism*.

40 M. Ho, "Categories That Bind."

41 See, for example, Rosenberg and Villarejo, "Introduction"; Floyd, *Reification of Desire*; Ferguson, *Aberrations in Black*; Muñoz, *Disidentifications*; Hollibaugh and Weiss, "Queer Precarity"; Brim, *Poor Queer Studies*; Gluckman and Reed, *Homo Economics*; and Jacobsen and Zeller, *Queer Economics*.

42 Liu identifies five queer-materialist approaches, which I shall not reprise here. For a succinct summary, see Liu, *Specter of Materialism*.

43 Jacobsen and Zeller, *Queer Economics*; and Gluckman and Reed, *Homo Economics*.

44 Binnie, *Globalization of Sexuality*; Ramírez, "Gay Latino Cultural Citizenship"; and Lim, *Brown Boys*.

45 Duggan argues that homonormativity depends on "a privatized, depoliticized gay culture anchored in domesticity and consumption." Duggan, *Twilight of Equality?*, 50.

46 As I discuss in chapter 1, "lesbian" spaces are those shared by women-loving women before the term *rezubian* (a transliteration of *lesbian*) was coined. See Sugiura, "Lesbian Discourses."

47 The Japanese word *sei* can refer to sex, gender, or both. This boom was preceded by the spread of "LGBT" in local activism in the 2010s. See Horie, *Rezubian aidentitī* [Lesbian identities]; Sunagawa, "Tayō na shihai, tayō na teikō" [Diverse rule, diverse resistance]; and Fotache, "Subculture and Social Movement."

48 After Tokyo's Shibuya ward became one of the first to offer same-sex partnership certificates in 2015, 372 other municipalities swiftly followed suit by January 2024. See Marriage for All Japan, "Nihon no pātonāshippu seido" [Japan's partnership system], accessed January 14, 2024, https://www.marriageforall.jp/marriage-equality/japan/. Scholars have criticized how these same-sex partnership certificates not only have no legal standing, and their terms and benefits vary from district to district, but also create the image of a progressive Japan. See Shimizu, "Yōkoso, gei furendorī na machi e" [Welcome to the gay-friendly city]; and Dale, "Same-Sex Marriage." On nondiscrimination laws, see Kyle Knight, "Tokyo's 'Olympic' LGBT Non-Discrimination Law," Human Rights Watch, October 11, 2018, https://www.hrw.org/news/2018/10/11/tokyos-olympic -lgbt-non-discrimination-law.

49 At the time of my fieldwork, JPY 110 equaled approximately USD 1. See Dentsū, "Dentsū daibāshiti rabo ga LGBT chōsa 2015 wo jisshi—LGBT ichiba kibo wo yaku 5.9 chō-en to sanshutsu" [Dentsū Diversity Lab conducts LGBT survey 2015—LGBT market size is estimated to be about

5.9 trillion yen], April 23, 2015, https://www.dentsu.co.jp/news/release
/pdf-cms/2015041-0423.pdf.

50    For instance, Tokyo pledged to incorporate "Diversity & Inclusion" "in
all aspects" of the Games, which entails recognition of people's differences, including their gender identity and sexual orientation. This is
due in part to changes to the International Olympic Committee (IOC)
Charter in 2015 to include sexual orientation. See Tokyo 2020, "Diversity
and Inclusion," accessed May 28, 2021, https://tokyo2020.org/en/games
/diversity-inclusion/ (no longer available).

51    Wallace, "Stepping-Up."

52    Maree, "'LGBT Issues.'"

53    See Tomohiro Osaki, "LDP Lawmaker Mio Sugita Faces Backlash after
Describing LGBT People as 'Unproductive,'" *Japan Times*, July 24, 2018.
Japanese names are rendered surname first. However, depending on the
preference of the individual, such as when they publish in English using
Western ordering, I follow that order.

54    Tomohiro Osaki, "Thousands Rally to Protest LDP Lawmaker Mio Sugita's Remark Calling LGBT People 'Unproductive,'" *Japan Times*, July 27,
2018.

55    D'Emilio, "Capitalism and Gay Identity." See also Hennessy, *Profit and
Pleasure*; Joseph, *Against the Romance*; and Sender, *Business, Not Politics*.

56    Chitty, *Sexual Hegemony*, 35. See also Foucault, *History of Sexuality*,
vol. 1.

57    Grewal and Kaplan, "Global Identities"; Cruz-Malavé and Manalansan,
*Queer Globalizations*; Gopinath, *Impossible Desires*; Liu, *Queer Marxism*;
and Wei, *Queer Chinese Cultures*.

58    Champagne, "Transnationally Queer?"; and Cruz-Malavé and Manalansan, *Queer Globalizations*.

59    On sexual and gender minorities' class and labor issues, see, for instance,
Kawaguchi, "Neoriberarizumu" [Neoliberalism]; Hiramori, "Shokuba
ni okeru seitekimainoriti no kon'nan" [Challenges of sexual and gender
minorities in the workplace]; Hiramori, "Seitekimainoriti ga hataraki
yasui shokuba to wa?" [What is a workplace in which sexual minorities can work comfortably?]; Hattori, "LGBT seisaku no dōkō" [Trends
in LGBT policy]; Nagao, "Seiteki mainoriti (LGBTQ) gakusei no shien"
[Supporting sexual minority (LGBTQ) students]; and J. Anderson, "Invisible Diversity in Companies."
        For workplace surveys see, for instance, Dentsu, "Dentsū daibāshiti
rabo ga LGBT chōsa 2015 wo jisshi—LGBT ichiba kibo wo yaku 5.9 chō-en
to sanshutsu"; Nijiiro Diversity and Center for Gender Studies (CGS) at

International Christian University, *Niji* VOICE *2018 Report*, *Niji* VOICE *2019 Report*, and *Niji* VOICE *2020 Report*.

60     See J. Anderson, "Invisible Diversity in Companies"; Hiramori, "Shokuba ni okeru seitekimainoriti no kon'nan"; and Hiramori, "Seiteikimainoriti ga hataraki yasui shokuba to wa?" I also give an overview of the relation between productivity and heteronormative family and marriage in chapter 2

61     See, for instance, Hattori, "LGBT seisaku no dōkō." It should also be noted that gender and sexual minorities may experience discrimination differently depending on their gender identity and sexual orientation.

62     Lewis and Irving first coined TPE *studies*, and TPE follows feminist political economy, which is grounded in materialist feminist approaches. Feminist political economy is defined as "gendered production, distribution, and consumption of goods and resources and the examination of how ideology is used to stabilize the unequal relations." See Lewis and Irving, "Strange Alchemies"; and Lee, "Feminist Political Economy," 83. On TPE, see also Spade, "Compliance Is Gendered"; Schilt, *One of the Guys?*; and Namaste, *Sex Change, Social Change*.

63     Irving, "Normalized Transgressions," 39–40; and Gleeson and O'Rourke, *Transgender Marxism*.

64     See Lewis and Irving, "Strange Alchemies."

65     A. Wilson, *Intimate Economies of Bangkok*; P. Jackson, *Queer Bangkok*; P. Jackson, *First Queer Voices*; David, "Purple-Collar Labor"; Hegarty, "Value of Transgender"; and Aizura, *Mobile Subjects*.

66     Previously, scholars refuted Dennis Altman's well-known notion of "global queering," the globalizing spread of homosexuality from the West to the rest, arguing for the importance of locally specific modern expressions of genders and sexualities as opposed to having derived from US-centric queer cultures. See Altman, "On Global Queering"; Altman, "Global Gaze/Global Gays"; Halperin, "Response from David Halperin"; Puar, "Global Circuits"; P. Jackson, "Explosion of Thai Identities"; and A. Wilson, "Queering Asia."

67     See P. Jackson, "Capitalism and Global Queering," 360. While *bakla*, *kathoey*, and *waria* have commonly been translated as "trans women," it should be noted that these terms are specific to each cultural context and have multiple definitions.

68     A. Wilson, *Intimate Economies of Bangkok*.

69     Gibson-Graham also criticizes capitalism for being unnamed, "phallic," and contiguous with the social. See Gibson-Graham, "Ethics of the Local"; and Gibson-Graham, *End of Capitalism*, 6–8, 35.

70 Although some have also translated *new half* as "trans women," I retain the term's original meaning as not all *new half* individuals identify as trans. See chapter 1 for a discussion of *new half*.

71 Cat cafés are establishments where cats provide labor for their human customers. Host clubs are establishments where cis men or masculine-presenting employees provide conversation for mostly women.

72 Galbraith, *Otaku and the Struggle*; Plourde, "Cat Cafes"; and Takeyama, *Staged Seduction*.

73 Anagnost, "Introduction."

74 Borovoy, "Japan as Mirror."

75 Unlike flexible work, lifetime employment often hinges on gendered social roles and division of labor in heteronormative family and marriage. See my discussion in chapter 2. See also Matanle, *Japanese Capitalism*; and Lam, *Women and Japanese Management*.

76 Takeyama, *Staged Seduction*; Galbraith, *Otaku and the Struggle*; and Plourde, "Cat Cafes."

77 Takeda, "Structural Reform."

78 I follow Gibson-Graham, who decenters a monolithic Marxian political economy. See Gibson-Graham, *End of Capitalism*.

79 Illouz, *Cold Intimacies*; and Zelizer, *Purchase of Intimacy*. Illouz uses *emotional capitalism* to refer to "a culture in which emotional and economic discourses and practices mutually shape each other" (5). Intimacy might be understood as being physically and emotionally attached to or in proximity to another person or entity. Although, in theory, affect has been defined as pre-emotion, whereas emotion indexes our response when affect is triggered, I follow scholars like Sara Ahmed in thinking of them together as they are embodied and experienced by people in everyday life. See Ahmed, *Cultural Politics of Emotion*.

80 Berlant, *Cruel Optimism*.

81 T. Yamada, "Japanese Capitalism"; Matanle, *Japanese Capitalism*; Takeda, "Structural Reform"; Lechevaliar, *Great Transformation*; and Wakatabe, "Cultural Difference in Economics."

82 See a fuller discussion of *onabe* in chapter 1.

83 M. Yoshimoto, "Postmodern," 9.

84 I was inspired by Claire Maree, who first discussed this connection in her book. See Maree, *Queerqueen*.

85 *Gei* indexes *geinōjin* (entertainer) and predates the use of the English term *gay* in the 1970s United States. "Gay boy" (*gei bōi*) was regarded as an occupational category in mainstream Japanese media, referring

to effeminate gay men who have skills in entertaining. See McLelland, *Queer Japan*; and McLelland, "Japan's Original 'Gay Boom.'"

86    Hebdige, *Subculture*. For works on girls' subcultures that I discuss in chapter 5, see Kawamura, *Fashioning Japanese Subcultures*; Kinsella, *Schoolgirls*; and Winge, "Tokyo Subcultural Street Styles."

87    Galbraith, *Otaku and the Struggle*, 182.

88    McGray, "Japan's Gross National Cool," 47.

89    Nye, *Soft Power*.

90    Allison, "Cool Brand," 93.

91    Maree, "'LGBT Issues.'"

92    Galbraith, *Otaku and the Struggle*, 5.

93    As I discuss in chapter 2, this fandom is known as *moe*, a term originating from the Japanese verb *moeru* (to bud or sprout), a homophone of *moeru* (to burn), and referring to "a euphoric response to fantasy characters or representations of them." Galbraith, "Moe," para. 1.

94    McLelland, "(A)cute Confusion"; and McLelland, "Introduction."

95    Miller, "Cute Masquerade," 19; and Miller, "Taking Girls Seriously."

96    *Josōko* is a category of self-identification for young male-to-female cross-dressing individuals, regardless of their gender identity and sexual orientation.

97    Valentine, *Imagining Transgender*; and Aizura, *Mobile Subjects*.

98    Sedgwick defines *queer* as "the open mesh of possibilities, gaps, overlaps, dissonances and resonances, lapses and excesses of meaning when the constituent elements of anyone's gender, of anyone's sexuality aren't made (or *can't be* made) to signify monolithically." Sedgwick, *Tendencies*, 7.

99    Dale, "Introduction to X-Jendā."

100   Wallace, "Stepping-Up."

101   Fushimi et al., "Sekushuaru mainoritī no 'rentai' to wa" ["Solidarity" of sexual minorities].

102   *Sex/gender reassignment surgery* (SGRS) refers to a range of aesthetic or cosmetic surgeries, genital modifications and reconstructions, and medical procedures to remove or transform genitals and reproductive body parts. Although there are more politically correct terms, such as *gender confirmation surgery* and *gender affirmation surgery*, I retain SGRS because it is still used in the Japanese context. See Itani, "Sick but Legitimate?"

103   Stryker, *Transgender History*, 1.

104   Lovelock, "Call Me Caitlyn," 676.

105   These criteria, which I also discuss in chapter 1, are being over twenty years of age, unmarried, childless, and having undergone "full" SGRS.

See Taniguchi, "Japan's 2003 Gender Identity Disorder Act." In 2023 Japan's Supreme Court ruled that the SGRS requirement for people to legally change their gender is unconstitutional, but it remains to be seen how the government will follow up on this. See Francis Tang and Sakura Murakami, "Japan Court Deems Gender Change Rule Invalid in Landmark Case," Reuters, October 26, 2023, https://www.reuters.com/world /asia-pacific/japans-top-court-set-rule-sterilisation-requirement-gender -change-2023-10-24/.

106  As I discuss elsewhere, while GID is a diagnosis and is no longer used in the *Diagnostic and Statistical Manual of Mental Disorders, Fifth Edition* (*DSM-5*), many Japanese people continue to self-identify as GID. See M. Ho, "Affect"; and M. Ho, "Transgender Celebrity."

107  Dale, "Transgender, Non-Binary Genders."

108  Dale, "Introduction to X-Jendā," para. 1.

109  Dale, "X-Jendā."

110  Dale, "Introduction to X-Jendā." Dana Stachowiak defines *genderqueer* as individuals who "*queer* gender constructs and activate new social relations" when they dismantle the gender binary and create new spaces for self-expression. Stachowiak, "Queering It Up," 534.

111  Other scholars writing about contemporary *josō* and *dansō* cultures have similarly noted the use of *josō*, *dansō*, and *otoko no ko* as "self-chosen" and a "self-label" to express their "doing" and "being." See Fanasca, *Female Masculinity*; Kinsella, "Cuteness, Josō"; and Kinsella, "Otoko no ko Manga."

112  M. Ho, "Queer and Normal."

113  *Josō danshi* is a contemporary term emphasizing *josō* individuals' status as boys, which Yoshimoto Taimatsu observes has since 2009 replaced *otoko no ko* in media coverage. See Yoshimoto T., "Shota josōshōnen" [Shota cross-dressing boys].

114  For studies discussing these issues in Japan, see Itani, "Sick but Legitimate?"; Dale, "Introduction to X-Jendā"; and Lunsing, "LGBT Rights in Japan."

115  Chiang, Henry, and Leung, "Trans-in-Asia, Asia-in-Trans."

116  See chapter 1 for a discussion of otoko no ko.

117  Chiang, Henry, and Leung, "Trans-in-Asia, Asia-in-Trans."

118  McLelland, *Queer Japan*.

119  In the past, Japanese Buddhism even celebrated the *josō* practices of adolescent acolytes in monasteries (*chigo*) and ritualized a pederastic tradition of sexual relationships between these acolytes and adult monks. *Chigo* (infant) were highborn adolescents between twelve and sixteen years old, many of whom adopted appearances that were indistinguishable from maidens (*shōjo*) and were treated as women (*josei*) within a

male-only community. See Faure, *Red Thread*; and Mitsuhashi, *Josō to nihonjin*, 54–60.

120 Lunsing draws on Clifford Geertz's definition of *common sense* as a "cultural phenomenon" that is "liable to change" and located in a specific sociocultural context. Lunsing, *Beyond Common Sense*, 2.

121 Lunsing, *Beyond Common Sense*.

122 For a discussion of this in Britain and the United States, see Weeks, *Sexuality and Its Discontents*.

123 P. Jackson, "Capitalism and Global Queering," 366.

124 Chiang and Wong, "Asia Is Burning"; and Yue, "Trans-Singapore."

125 Chen, *Asia as Method*.

126 Chiang and Wong, "Asia Is Burning"; and Yue, "Trans-Singapore."

127 Valentine, *Imagining Transgender*; Nagar and Swarr, "Introduction"; and Tracy, *Qualitative Research Methods*, 15.

128 My time and spending were on par with regular customers' visits and expenditures, as I discuss in chapters 3 and 5.

129 Ashikari, "Cultivating Japanese Whiteness."

130 As observed by ethnographers in other cultural contexts, foreigners associated with the United States and Europe are often regarded as more open-minded and less discriminatory than local individuals who harbor existing beliefs and attitudes about trans people. See Kulick, *Travesti*; and Swarr, *Sex in Transition*.

131 There is little information on how many *dansō* and *josō/otoko no ko* establishments there are. This estimate is based on my observation as well as numbers during the 2007 maid boom, when there were almost fifty maid cafés in Akihabara, and during the 2009 cat café boom, when the number of cat cafés peaked in Japan. Marta Fanasca also notes there were a total of thirteen *dansō* host clubs, café-and-bars, and escort companies in 2015–16. See Galbraith, "Maid in Japan"; Plourde, "Cat Cafes"; and Fanasca, *Female Masculinity*.

132 One example was Diffusion, a late-night *josō* event in Kabukichō, located in the Shinjuku area of Tokyo, which I discuss in chapter 5.

133 This genealogical approach follows from Foucault, as I discuss in chapter 1. Foucault, *Language, Counter-Memory, Practice*.

134 Although *pink economy* is not a neologism and has been criticized for its hegemonic discourses of constructing all gay and lesbian people as wealthy, passive consumers, I reconfigure it in the Japanese context, in which *pink* more broadly denotes sex and eroticism. See my discussion in chapter 1. For criticisms of the pink economy, see Badgett, *Money, Myths, and Change*; and Binnie, *Globalization of Sexuality*.

135     Gimlin, *Body Work*.

136     This is what Gibson-Graham calls "(re)subjectivation," which I discuss more in chapter 5. See Gibson-Graham, "Ethics of the Local"; and Gibson-Graham, *End of Capitalism*, xxxix.

137     These crises include health and mortality risks, rising unemployment rates, the worst recession since the 1930s Great Depression, and major disruptions to travel, tourism, hospitality, and entertainment industries. See Gita Gopinath, "The Great Lockdown: Worst Economic Downturn since the Great Depression," IMF Blog, April 14, 2020, https://www.imf.org/en/Blogs/Articles/2020/04/14/blog-weo-the-great-lockdown-worst-economic-downturn-since-the-great-depression; and Lora Jones, Daniele Palumbo, and David Brown, "Coronavirus: How the Pandemic Has Changed the World Economy," BBC News, January 24, 2021, https://www.bbc.com/news/business-51706225.

## 1. Categories That Bind

Parts of chapter 1 in its earlier version were published in *Asian Anthropology* in 2020 and in *Sexualities* in 2024. See M. Ho, "Categories That Bind"; and M. Ho, "Queer and Normal."

1     All dialogue from the film *Shinjuku Boys* (1995), which is in Japanese, has been translated to English by the author.

2     Maree, "Ore wa ore dakara," para. 2; and Sugiura, "Lesbian Discourses."

3     Halberstam, *Female Masculinity*.

4     Foucault, *Language, Counter-Memory, Practice*, 144.

5     This aligns with Marta Fanasca's characterization of *dansō* escorts in twenty-first-century Tokyo. See Fanasca, *Female Masculinity*.

6     Illouz, *Cold Intimacies*.

7     Ahmed, *Cultural Politics of Emotion*, 91.

8     Saeki, *Josō to dansō no bunkashi*, 12, 118.

9     Mitsuhashi, *Josō to nihonjin*, 31 35.

10     Saeki, *Josō to dansō no bunkashi*, 13–14.

11     *Warawa* also means "child" in Japanese. See Mitsuhashi, *Josō to nihonjin*, 53–54.

12     *Warawa* in *josō* were also called *chigo*, a word meaning "infant" and used to refer to high-born adolescents between twelve and sixteen years old. Scholars observed that despite wearing makeup and women's clothing, *chigo* remained masculine in other aspects and may therefore be considered androgynous instead of feminine. See Leupp, *Male Colors*, 46; and Mitsuhashi, *Josō to nihonjin*, 54–60.

13    Saeki, *Josō to dansō no bunkashi*, 119.

14    Those who performed "male dancing" (*otoko odori*) were called *shirabyōshi* (white tunic dancers). See Leupp, *Male Colors*, 175.

15    Mitsuhashi, *Josō to nihonjin*, 70–71.

16    Robertson, *Takarazuka*, 51.

17    This relationship stems from a well-established Japanese tradition, "The Way of *wakashu*" (*wakashudō*), in which, perhaps not unlike pederasty in ancient Greece, young boys were initiated into adulthood. See Isaka, *Onnagata*, 16.

18    Men who were sexually attracted to *onnagata* made up the majority of early theater audiences. See Leupp, *Male Colors*, 130; and Mitsuhashi, *Josō to nihonjin*, 87.

19    Despite the ban, women persisted in performing, albeit on a smaller scale, such as in small troupes or in the mansions of feudal lords. See Kawasaki, *Takarazuka*, 166; and Kano, *Acting like a Woman*, 31.

20    For instance, women engaged in a new genre of modern theater called Shingeki (new drama; new theater). For scholarship on Shingeki, see Kano, *Acting like a Woman*; and Stickland, *Gender Gymnastics*.

21    Stickland, *Gender Gymnastics*, 29.

22    "Female" roles are the *onnayaku* (female roles) and *musumeyaku* (daughter roles). For a discussion of their femininities, see Robertson, *Takarazuka*.

23    Stickland, *Gender Gymnastics*, 26.

24    Under the slogan "civilization and enlightenment" (*bunmei kaika*), *josō* and *dansō* were considered "corrupt customs" (*heifū*). Passed in 1872, the new law reinforced the gender binary by controlling men's and women's bodies. See Kano, *Acting like a Woman*, 29; and Pflugfelder, *Cartographies of Desire*, 151–52.

25    Kano, *Acting like a Woman*, 29.

26    For a discussion of such criminal cases, including the "*josō* thief" (*josō no zoku*) case, see Mitsuhashi, *Josō to nihonjin*, 142–45.

27    One such expert who led Japan in sexology (*seigaku*) was Yamamoto Senji. See Frühstück, *Colonizing Sex*, 84.

28    Examples of media published on "homosexuals" (*dōseiaisha*) and "cross-dressers" (*iseisōsha*) include sexological journals, such as *Popular Medicine* (*Tsūzoku Igaku*) and *Popular Hygiene* (*Tsūzoku Eisei*); the daily newspaper *Asahi Shimbun*; and "high-class women's magazines" (*kōkyū fujin zasshi*) like *Women's Review* (*Fujin Kōron*). See Frühstück, *Colonizing Sex*, 112–14; and Mitsuhashi, *Josō to nihonjin*, 152.

29 Mitsuhashi, *Josō to nihonjin*, 157–58.

30 This is similar perhaps to *wakashu* and not unlike pederasty in ancient Greece, as I note in note 17 earlier in this chapter. For a discussion of *nanshoku*, see Reichert, *Company of Men*, 2.

31 Ishida, McLelland, and Murakami, "Origins of 'Queer Studies,'" 36–37.

32 During this time, it was unsurprising for women sex workers (*gaishō*) and *josō* sex workers (*josō no danshō*) to coexist in the same space. Apparently, this was a business strategy to widen their clientele to both groups as customers would otherwise be hesitant to approach *josō* sex workers. The ratio of *josō* sex workers to women sex workers was estimated to be 1:20. See Mitsuhashi, *Josō to nihonjin*, 179–80, 86–87.

33 Mitsuhashi, *Josō to nihonjin*, 182–83.

34 Examples of perverse magazines (*hentai zasshi*) include *Fūzoku Kitan* (Mysterious stories about sexual customs) and *Fūzoku Kagaku* (The science of sexual customs). See Ishida, McLelland, and Murakami, "Origins of 'Queer Studies,'" 38.

35 The regular column in *Fūzoku Kitan* was called "Josō aikō no heya" (A room for lovers of male-to-female cross-dressing), and the club it inspired was called Fūki (Wealth and honor). See McLelland, "From the Stage," 4.

36 McLelland, *Queer Japan*, 117–18.

37 The way I use *female-to-male (FTM) transgender* here reflects how it is used in the Japanese context.

38 T. Aoyama, "Transgendering Shōjo Shōsetsu," 53.

39 Boys Love (BL) first emerged as *shōnen ai* (boys love) in the 1970s and overlapped with and influenced the publication of subsequent genres, such as *JUNE*, *yaoi*, and *bōizu rabu* (boys love). See Welker, "Lilies of the Margin," 48; and McLelland and Welker, "Introduction to 'Boys Love,'" 5.

40 Mitsuhashi, *Josō to nihonjin*, 213. *New half* is an English word coined in Japan (*wasei eigo*), made up of *new* and *half*.

41 Mitsuhashi, *Josō to nihonjin*.

42 Mitsuhashi, *Josō to nihonjin*.

43 For a discussion of the first modern-style *josō* bars opening in Kabukichō in the late 1960s, see Mitsuhashi, *Josō to nihonjin*.

44 Mackie, "How to Be a Girl"; and Koch, *Healing Labor*.

45 Lewis and Irving, "Strange Alchemies"; and Haritaworn, Kuntsman, and Posocco, Introduction.

46 For a discussion of "proper" trans social subjects in the US context, see Irving, "Normalized Transgressions."

47 McLelland, "From the Stage," 8.

48 Toyama, *Miss Dandy*, 222.

49 Toyama, *Miss Dandy*.

50 I follow Toyama's use of masculine pronouns, like *kare* (he/him), for Mizuno. See Toyama, *Miss Dandy*. Mizuno's story has been translated into English. See Toyama, "Era of Dandy Beauties."

51 For a discussion of S, or the relationship between "older sisters" (*onēsama*) and "younger sisters" (*imōto*), see Shamoon, *Passionate Friendship*.

52 Roppongi is well known as an affluent area in Tokyo but also for its late-night bars and clubs. For a discussion of Kikōshi, see Welker, "Telling Her Story."

53 I take this translation from the chapter on Mizuno. See Toyama, "Era of Dandy Beauties."

54 Dale, "Gender Identity, Desire," 168–69.

55 Robertson, *Takarazuka*, 143. In *Shinjuku Boys*, the club is known simply as Marilyn, which I am assuming is short for New Marilyn, as discussed by Robertson.

56 Maree, "Ore wa ore dakara"; and Welker, "Telling Her Story."

57 Robertson, *Takarazuka*, 144. On *Miss Dandy* as a term for *onabe* in Japanese magazines, see Sugiura, "Lesbian Discourses," 139.

58 These *dansō* establishments (*dansō no mise*) flourished in cities like Tokyo, Osaka, Kyoto, and Nagoya during the same period. See McLelland, *Queer Japan*, 119.

59 P. Jackson, "Capitalism and Global Queering," 360–61.

60 *Freeter* is an amalgamation of *free* and the German term *Arbeiter* (worker) and refers to freelance, part-time, and temporary workers between fifteen and thirty-four years old who are neither students nor married (in the case of women). See Obinger, "Working on the Margins"; and Cook, "Intimate Expectations and Practices."

61 Mitsuhashi, "Nihon toranjendā ryakushi" [Brief history of transgender]; and Dale, "Transgender, Non-Binary Genders."

62 While *gei* and *rezubian* are the Japanese terms for "gay" and "lesbian" respectively, I use them to signal different categories than in the US context. Although contemporary scholarship on gay and lesbian individuals and historical works on same-gender eroticism, such as *nanshoku*, were also published in English and Japanese at this time by academics and nonacademics alike, they did not develop evenly, and fewer studies have paid attention to women-loving women. See Suganuma, "Sexual Minority Studies."

63 Suganuma, "Sexual Minority Studies."

64    Despite its name, OCCUR focuses mainly on the issues of gay men, not lesbian women. See Lunsing, "LGBT Rights in Japan."

65    Dale, "Transgender, Non-Binary Genders."

66    On the gay boom and high growth noted in passing, see, for example, Maree, "Queer Women's Culture."

67    Sedgwick, *Tendencies*.

68    Sugiura, "Lesbian Discourses."

69    Despite GID being a medical diagnosis and being depathologized by the World Health Organization (WHO) and in the *Diagnostic and Statistical Manual of Mental Disorders, Fifth Edition* (DSM-5), many Japanese individuals continue to self-identify as *seidōitsuseishōgai* (GID). I discuss this elsewhere. See M. Ho, "Categories That Bind."

70    *Mini communications* (*mini-komi*) refers to alternative media that are "informal networks of communication between members of specialized political groups." See Mackie, "Feminism and the Media," 23; and Oe et al., "Dialogue."

71    Ako et al., "Sex Reassignment Surgery."

72    Torai, *Kataritsugu toransujendā-shi* [Transgender history to be handed down].

73    See Taniguchi, "Japan's 2003 Gender Identity Disorder Act."

74    Yonezawa, "Media to toranjendā" [Media and transgender], 81.

75    See Tsuruta, *Seidōitsuseishougai no esunogurafi* [An ethnography of Gender Identity Disorder].

76    Scholars have long criticized the family registry (*koseki*) as a tool for the state's surveillance and social control of its people and a means of inclusion and exclusion through the documentation of nationality. See Chapman, "Geographies of Self"; and Mori, "Modern Koseki."

77    Dale, "Introduction to X-Jendā"; and Foucault, *History of Sexuality*, vol. 1.

78    Mackie, "How to Be a Girl."

79    Oe et al., "Dialogue."

80    Oe et al., "Dialogue."

81    Dale, "Transgender, Non-Binary Genders." See also the introduction, note 105, for a discussion of the new Supreme Court ruling in 2023.

82    Lewis and Irving, "Strange Alchemies."

83    Tanaka, *Toransujendā feminizumu* [Transgender feminism], 41; and Dale, "Transgender, Non-Binary Genders," 64.

84    For an analysis of these texts, see Dale, "Introduction to X-Jendā."

85    Ahmed, *Cultural Politics of Emotion*.

86    Berlant, *Cruel Optimism*, 1–2.

87    Konings, *Emotional Logic of Capitalism*, 2.

88    Dale, "Introduction to X-Jendā."

89    Dale, "Transgender, Non-Binary Genders," 65.

90    Robertson, *Takarazuka*, 50; and Dale, "Introduction to X-Jendā," para. 4.

91    Dale, "Introduction to X-Jendā."

92    M. Ho, "Categories That Bind."

93    Miho, interview with the author, October 10, 2016.

94    M. Ho, "Categories That Bind." I thank James Welker for first bringing this to my attention.

95    See chapter 2 for a discussion of *moe*.

96    Another example of this niche fandom is *fudanshi* (rotten boys), male fans of BL media. The term *fudanshi* comes from *fujoshi*, meaning "rotten girls," and refers to women BL fans. See Nagaike, *Fantasies of Cross-Dressing*; and Kinsella, "Otoko no ko Manga."

97    Kawamoto, *Otoko no ko tachi*.

98    Kinsella, "Otoko no ko Manga."

99    M. Ho, "From Dansō to Genderless."

100   *Graduating* (*sotsugyō suru*) is a euphemism for employees' resignation from the café-and-bar. As I discuss in later chapters, Paradise's rules prohibit *new half* individuals or those who have begun SGRS from working there. These individuals are expected to work in *new half* establishments, which are considered separate from those like Paradise.

101   M. Ho, "Categories That Bind."

102   Dale, "Introduction to X-Jendā," para. 4.

103   Huegel, GLBTQ.

104   I have written elsewhere about *dansō* individuals' politics and rejection of LGBT. See M. Ho, "Queer and Normal."

105   Feminist politics stems from the systemic exclusion of women in everyday life within a patriarchal society. See Smith, *Everyday World as Problematic*.

## 2. Doing Business in Japan's Pink Economies

1    Prior to employees' departure from the café-and-bar, they often hold a "graduation" (*sotsugyō*) event to bid customers goodbye.

2    Japan passed a new bill in December 2016 to allow for casinos, which are projected to open by the end of the 2020s. See Naoko Takiguchi and

Yuko Kawanishi, "Japan Gambles on Casinos to Fix Its Economic Woes," *East Asia Forum*, February 12, 2020, https://www.eastasiaforum.org/2020/02/12/japan-gambles-on-casinos-to-fix-its-economic-woes/.

3     In Japanese, cheongsams are called *chaina doresu* (China dress), which was how my interlocutors referred to them.

4     Last trains for customers who reside in suburban areas in Tokyo, such as Chiba, can be as early as 11 p.m., whereas those for patrons living downtown are around midnight. First trains usually begin after 5 a.m. Paradise's opening and closing times aligned with the train schedule.

5     Tsing, "Sorting Out Commodities," 38.

6     Gluck, *Japan's Modern Myths*; and Aoki, "Toward a Critical Understanding."

7     Ou-Byung Chae aptly describes Japanese colonialism as the "coworking of attraction/imitation and repulsion/rejection." Chae, "Japanese Colonial Structure," 402.

8     Aoki, "Marxism," 18.

9     The household system (*ie seido*) ensured patrilineal inheritance and relegated women to the home and family, whereas the family registry (*koseki*) ensured every person's family affiliation was registered with the government, functioning as a form of social control. See Frühstück, *Gender and Sexuality*, 3–4.

10    Feminist scholar Ueno Chizuko also observes that "housewife" (*shufu*) was introduced to Japanese people as a "Western concept" during the Meiji period. See Ueno, *Nationalism and Gender*; and Ueno, *Modern Family in Japan*, 100.

11    Ueno, *Nationalism and Gender*.

12    Gottfried and Fasenfest, "Trajectory of Japanese Capitalism."

13    Gottfried, *Reproductive Bargain*.

14    Gottfried and Fasenfest, "Trajectory of Japanese Capitalism."

15    For examples of such works by economists and political scientists that valorize the Japanese political economy, see T. Yamada, "Japanese Capitalism"; Lechevaliar, *Great Transformation*; and Wakatabe, "Cultural Difference in Economics."

16    Kitagawa, "Homeless Policy."

17    Gottfried and Fasenfest, "Trajectory of Japanese Capitalism."

18    Various scholars have since refuted or complicated Yamada's claim about parasite singles (*parasaito shinguru*). Yamada M., *Parasaito shinguru no jidai* [The age of parasite singles].

19    Genda, "Youth Employment," 16.

20      See, for instance, Genda, "Youth Employment"; and Nakano, "Working and Waiting."

21      See chapter 1, note 60, for a definition of *freeter*. See Gottfried and Fasenfest, "Trajectory of Japanese Capitalism"; Obinger, "Working on the Margins"; and Cook, "Intimate Expectations and Practices."

22      In Japan homeless people are narrowly defined as those who live on the streets. See Kitagawa, "Homeless Policy"; and Gottfried, *Reproductive Bargain*.

23      Amamiya characterizes this disconnection using the term *ikizurasa* (hardship of life). Aside from labor and poverty issues, difficult relationships with other people, including those at home, also count as one of the hardships of life. See Amamiya and Beck, "Suffering Forces Us" and Amamiya and Kayano, *"Ikizurasa" nitsuite* [Concerning "hardship of life"].

24      The Japanese term *ibasho* refers to a "space where one feels comfortable and at home." Allison, *Precarious Japan*, 65, 174.

25      Longinotto and Williams, *Shinjuku Boys*.

26      Becker, *Treatise on the Family*.

27      Since the Meiji period, marriage has served as an economic institution. See Ueno, *Modern Family in Japan*.

28      For example, between 1985 and 1990, the number of women who have never married increased by 5 percent for the 20–24 age group, by 10 percent for the 25–29 age group, and by 5 percent for the 30–34 age group. These numbers continued to increase in the next five years between 1990 and 1995, by approximately 2 percent for women in the 20–24 age group and by 10 percent for those in the 25–29 and 30–34 age ranges. See Tokuhiro, *Marriage in Contemporary Japan*, 5, 23.

29      Tokuhiro, *Marriage in Contemporary Japan*.

30      For a discussion of the reproductive bargain, see Gottfried, *Reproductive Bargain*.

31      Chasin, *Selling Out*; and Field, *Over the Rainbow*.

32      Miller, "Wasei Eigo," 127; and Domenig, "Market of Flesh."

33      Pink salons (*pinku saron*) or pink cabarets (*pinku kyabare*) were popular in the 1990s due to their lower prices as compared to "fashion health" (*fasshon herusu*) parlors. See Kadokura, "Japan's Underground Economy."

34      Pink films are distinct from soft-core and hard-core adult videos. For a discussion of these differences, see Domenig, "Market of Flesh," 3; and Nornes, introduction.

35      Nornes, "Introduction," 13–14. Although there are many explanations for the naming of *pink film*, such as the association of pink with erotic

media, one explanation is that it derived from pink salons. See Zahlten, *End of Japanese Cinema*.

36    See, for example, Robertson, *Takarazuka*; Maree, "Ore wa ore dakara"; Abe, *Queer Japanese*; Sugiura, "Increasing Lesbian Visibility"; Kovner, *Occupying Power*; and Koch, *Healing Labor*.

37    See McLelland, *Male Homosexuality*; and Mitsuhashi, *Josō to nihonjin*.

38    Altman, "Global Gaze/Global Gays."

39    Cruz-Malavé and Manalansan, "Introduction."

40    Sears, "Queer Anti-Capitalism"; and Hollibaugh and Weiss, "Queer Precarity," 23.

41    Nagai, *Teihon fūzoku eigyō toshimari fūeihō* [Standard edition management of Adult Entertainment Law].

42    K. Aoyama, "Sex Industry in Japan."

43    For discussions of hostess clubs and corporate entertainment (*settai*), see Allison, *Nightwork*; Matsuda, "Hosutesu-tachi wa nani wo uru no ka" [What hostesses sell]; and Gagné, "Business of Leisure."

44    For example, Akiko Takeyama has discussed the blurring of boundaries between companionship and sex work in host clubs. See Takeyama, *Staged Seduction*.

45    Faier, *Intimate Encounters*; Norma, "Prostitution"; and Parreñas, *Illicit Flirtations*.

46    For a discussion of the shifts in how sex work was perceived and the public morals it was thought to threaten that led to the Prostitution Prevention Law, see Kovner, *Occupying Power*; and K. Aoyama, "Sex Industry in Japan."

47    Article 2 of Prostitution Prevention Law (*Baishun bōshi hō*) of 1956, Pub. L. No. 118, last amended April 1, 2016, https://elaws.e-gov.go.jp/document ?law_unique_id=331AC0000000118_20170401_428AC0000000063.

48    Soaplands (*sōpurando*) were previously called "Turkish baths" (*toruko furo*) and were considered the "best organized and managed of the unofficially sanctioned sex businesses." Kanematsu, "Women of Kabukichō," 86.

49    Jun Hongo, "Law Bends Over Backward to Allow 'Fuzoku,'" *Japan Times*, May 27, 2008.

50    Although it has similar meanings to contemporary terms like *josōko* and *otoko no ko*, *josōsha* is historically specific to individuals in the 1950s. See Mitsuhashi, *Josō to nihonjin*.

51    Mitsuhashi, *Josō to nihonjin*, 209–10.

52    See chapter 1, note 70, for a definition of *mini communications*. Also see Horie, *Rezubian aidentitī*.

53 Although these terms have different meanings, *dansō*, *onabe*, and *rezubian* tended to be conflated during this period. See Sugiura, "Lesbian Discourses."

54 Butch/femme (*tachi/neko*) roles were used to categorize those meeting in lesbian bars in the 1970s. For instance, the *neko* (femme) stereotype corresponded with "heterosexual feminine dress and appearance codes," whereas the *tachi* (butch) stereotype inhabited "a more autonomous powerful and visible role." Chalmers, *Emerging Lesbian Voices*, 27–28.

55 Welker, "'Lesbian History' in Japan."

56 For works on the women's liberation movement (*ūman ribu*) and queer and trans activism in Japan, see, for example, Oe et al., "Dialogue"; Shigematsu, *Scream from the Shadows*; Maree, "Queer Women's Culture"; Suganuma, "Sexual Minority Studies"; and Bullock, Kano, and Welker, *Rethinking Japanese Feminisms*.

57 Some examples of works on homo, queer, and trans economies include Gluckman and Reed, *Homo Economics*; Jacobsen and Zeller, *Queer Economics*; Lewis and Irving, "Strange Alchemies"; and Rosenberg and Villarejo, "Introduction."

58 A portmanteau of *costume* and *play*, cosplay refers to the practice of dressing up as a fictional character from a favorite anime or manga.

59 *Evangelion*, a highly popular anime released after the 1995 Aum Shinrikyō sarin gas attacks, augmented Akihabara's positive image. See Galbraith, "Maid in Japan." See also chapter 3, note 80.

60 I discuss this background in which Akihabara became saturated with maid cafés, which then declined in numbers, in chapter 3.

61 I refrain from citing the interview with Yuka as pseudonyms were not used. Not all higher education institutions in Japan require ethics approval for nonbiomedical research involving human participants, which was likely the case for this study. For more on *moe*, see Galbraith, *Otaku and the Struggle*, 80.

62 One such example of *moe* for women fans lies in the Boys Love (BL) genre in anime and manga, as introduced in chapter 1.

63 As I discussed earlier in the chapter, the expansive Shinjuku area comprises a red-light and nighttime entertainment district (Kabukichō) and gay and lesbian neighborhood (Ni-chōme).

64 See Fanasca, *Female Masculinity*, 38.

65 Josō nyūhāfu puropaganda [Male-to-female cross-dressing *new half* propaganda], accessed May 28, 2021, http://propaganda-party.com (no longer available).

66    Suzuki Atsuki, "Joshika suru otokotachi 'otokorashisa' kimetsuke rare teikō" [Men who are femininized: Resistance against "masculinity"], *Mainichi Shimbun*, February 17, 2013.

67    As the name implies, an irregular business (*futeiki eigyō*) operates with undetermined opening hours instead of regular hours.

68    Although Paradise was not the first to come up with idea of a *josō/otoko no ko* café, it was the first to permanently establish such a restaurant in Akihabara. Hibari-tei remained an irregular business until September 2016 when it eventually secured a brick-and-mortar shop space and relocated to Shinjuku. See "Ganzo otoko no ko kafe 'Hibari-tei' jōsetsu-ten ga honjitsu (16.9.2) ni Kabukichō ni ōpun!! @josō nyūsu 24" [Original otoko no ko café 'Hibari-tei' opened a permanent store in Kabukichō today (2/9/16)!! @Josō news 24" *Josō wārudo* GEEK *josō no nabigētā* [Josō world GEEK josō navigator], last modified September 2, 2016, https://josou.josou-world.jp/blog-entry-900.html.

69    Some examples of anime and manga featuring *josō* characters are discussed by Sharon Kinsella, including *Otome wa boku ni koishiteru* (The maidens are falling for me, 2005) and Miyano Tomochika's *Yubisaki miruku tī* (Fingertip milk tea, 2003–10). See Kinsella, "Cuteness, Josō"; and Kinsella, "Otoko no ko Manga."

70    Morinaga, *Moe keizaigaku* [The study of *moe* economics]; and Morinaga, *Nenshūbōei* [Annual defense].

71    Businesses Affecting Public Morals Regulation Law (*Fūzoku eigyō torishimari hō*) of 1948, Pub. L. No. 122, last amended December 14, 2019, https://elaws.e-gov.go.jp/search/elawsSearch/elaws_search/lsg0500/detail?lawId=323AC0000000122.

72    For more on *shimei*, see Parreñas, *Illicit Flirtations*; and Takeyama, *Staged Seduction*.

73    It is hard to say why this system was adopted without more evidence and with 80 + 1 now having gone under. My guess is that 80 + 1 was likely imitating an idol-fan type of relationship common in many maid cafés.

74    Rice balls could be purchased at restaurants and convenience stores for JPY 100–200 (USD 0.90–1.80) each.

75    Allison, *Precarious Japan*, 65.

76    Daniels, "Feeling at Home."

77    Hayashida et al., "'Ibasho' no yōtai hyōgen" [Fundamental analysis on place-expressions]; Nishikawa, "'Igokochi' to 'ibasho' no gainen no kentō" [Examination of the concepts "igokochi" and "ibasho"]; and Okano, *Young Women in Japan*.

78    *My-homeism* (*mai homu shūgi*) refers literally to a home, "ideally located in a residential neighborhood, stocked with the newest domestic electronics"; at the same time, it also embodies "the attachments (of men at the workplace, women to the household, children to school) that fueled fast-growth economics and rising consumerism." Allison, "Sociality," 95–96. See also Ronald and Alexy, *Home and Family*

79    On otaku's "inappropriate consumption," see Kam, "Common Sense," 163.

80    See chapter 3 for a discussion of the *iyashi* (healing) boom.

81    Eng and Hom, "Introduction"; and Cruz-Malavé and Manalansan, "Introduction."

82    Fortier, "'Coming Home,'" 407; and Gopinath, *Impossible Desires*.

83    *Hegemonic masculinity* refers to ideal forms of being a man legitimated by a dominant minority of men, who prevail over women and other men. See Connell and Messerschmidt, "Hegemonic Masculinity."

84    Roberson and Suzuki, introduction; and T. Hidaka, *Salaryman Masculinity*.

85    Dasgupta, *Salaryman in Japan*.

86    Bakhtin, *Rabelais and His World*, 10.

87    Davis, *Society and Culture*, 131.

88    I decided to use the gender-neutral pronoun *they* as Masako self-identifies as LGBT and, in our interview, appeared uncomfortable with the idea of personal pronouns as they have no awareness of using them.

89    Gimlin, *Body Work*. I discuss my interlocutors' body work in chapter 5.

90    For an in-depth discussion of the masculinity crisis (*otokorashisa no kiki*), see Itō, *Otokorashisa no yukue* [The whereabouts of masculinity], 8. See also Frühstück and Walthall, *Recreating Japanese Men*.

91    Connell and Messerschmidt, "Hegemonic Masculinity."

92    Galbraith, *Otaku and the Struggle*; and Takeyama, *Staged Seduction*.

93    Takeyama, *Staged Seduction*, 102.

94    This was probably due to widespread acceptance of men's extramarital affairs in Japan. Since 2000 women have also engaged in extramarital affairs, and the number of men who have extramarital affairs has increased. See S. Ho, "'Playing like Men'"; and Araki et al., *Sekkusuresu jidai* [Sexless era].

## 3. Alternative Worlds in Akihabara

1    Concept cafés (*konseputo kissa*) are also known as "cosplay" (*kosupure*) or "cosplay-style" (*kosupure-kei*) cafés and restaurants. For a definition of *cosplay*, see chapter 2, note 58.

2   This maid café was Cure Maid café. See Galbraith, *Otaku and the Struggle for Imagination*, 205.

3   Galbraith, "Maid in Japan."

4   See the introduction, note 4, for a definition of *joshi kōsei*, or JK (high school girl), cafés.

5   For a discussion of butler (*shitsuji*) cafés, see Chang, "'Shitsuji kissa' ni okeru 'BL-teki mōsō' to sekushuariti" [The sexuality of "BL fantasy" in Taiwan].

6   *Fujoshi* (rotten girls), originally a derogatory term, has been reclaimed by fans and refers to "women who fantasize about male-male eroticism." See Nagaike, *Fantasies of Cross-Dressing*, 133; and McLelland and Welker, "Introduction to 'Boys Love.'"

7   The first cat (*neko*) café opened in Taiwan in 1998, and soon after, cat cafés became established in other East Asian countries, including in Osaka in 2004 and Tokyo in 2005. See Plourde, "Cat Cafes." Other than cat cafés, a variety of other kinds of animal cafés are concentrated in Tokyo, such as rabbit cafés, owl and other bird cafés, and hedgehog and chinchilla cafés. See Robinson, "Paid Companions"; and Robinson, "Finding Healing."

8   For works introducing Akihabara, see, for instance, Galbraith, "Akihabara"; and Miyake, *Akihabara wa ima* [Akihabara forever].

9   For studies on Akihabara, see, for example, Galbraith, "Akihabara"; Miyake, *Akihabara wa ima*. For studies on Shinjuku, see Sunagawa, *Shinjuku ni-chōme no bunka-jinruigaku*; and Takeyama, *Staged Seduction*.

10  Galbraith, *Otaku and the Struggle*.

11  Although *otaku* usually refers to men, some women and nonbinary individuals may also use the term to refer to themselves as anime, manga, and game fans.

12  Christine Yano complicates the meanings of pink as simultaneously connoting sexiness, cuteness, and femininity, drawing on the consumption of cute objects and postfeminist associations of pink as "feminized" in industrial societies, particularly in the West. See Yano, *Pink Globalization*.

13  For a discussion on "three sacred treasures" (*sanshu no jingi*), see Yoshimi, "'Made in Japan.'"

14  Yoshimi, "'Made in Japan,'" 158–60.

15  For a discussion of "good wife, wise mother" (*ryōsai kenbo*), see Fujimura-Fanselow, "Japanese Ideology"; and Uno, "'Good Wife, Wise Mother.'"

16  Uno, "'Good Wife, Wise Mother.'"

17  Miyake, *Akihabara wa ima*.

18  Miyake, *Akihabara wa ima*, 49–50.

19    Sakurai, "Generation Gap."

20    Miyake, *Akihabara wa ima.*

21    Galbraith, "'"Otaku" Research.'"

22    Poitras, "Contemporary Anime."

23    Galbraith, "Akihabara," 215.

24    A notable example of BL manga—a subgenre called *shōnen-ai* (love be-
      tween adolescent boys)—featuring *bishōnen* characters was Hagio Moto's
      *Tōma no shinzō* (The heart of Thomas, 1974–75). See Fujimoto, *Watashi
      no ibasho wa doko ni aru no?* [Where do I belong?]; and McLelland and
      Welker, "Introduction to 'Boys Love.'"

25    Fujimoto, "Evolution of BL," 77.

26    Fujimoto, "Transgender," 86; see also Fujimoto, "Evolution of BL," 79.

27    Welker, "Beautiful, Borrowed, and Bent."

28    For literature on *otome* (maiden) games, see E. Taylor, "Dating-Simulation
      Games"; and Galbraith, "Bishōjo Games."

29    Examples of *josō* manga include Kishi Yūko's Tamasaburō's *Love Capric-
      cio* (*Tamasaburō koi no kyōsōkyoku*, 1972–79) and Naka Tomoko's *The
      Beautiful Flower Princess* (*Hana no bijo hime*, 1974–80).

30    Fujimoto, *Watashi no ibasho wa doko ni aru no?*

31    Fujimoto, *Watashi no ibasho wa doko ni aru no?*; McLelland, "Japanese
      Girls' Comics"; Mizoguchi, "Male-Male Romance"; and Nagaike, *Fan-
      tasies of Cross-Dressing.*

32    Welker, "Beautiful, Borrowed, and Bent"; Wood, "'Straight' Women,
      Queer Texts"; and Wood, "Boys' Love Anime."

33    Creekmur and Doty, *Out in Culture*; Peele, *Queer Popular Culture*;
      Halberstam, *Female Masculinity*; and Halberstam, *Queer Art of
      Failure.*

34    Nakamori Akio, "'Otaku' mo hitonami ni koi wo suru?" [Do "otaku" love
      like normal people?], *Manga Burikko*, July 1983, last modified Decem-
      ber 16, 2013, http://www.burikko.net/people/otaku02.html. "*Burikko*" is a
      "derogatory Japanese label used to describe women who exhibit feigned
      naivete." For more on the translation of *burikko*, see Miller, "You Are
      Doing Burikko!" 148.

35    Valentine, "Pots and Pans."

36    Kam, "Common Sense," 163.

37    Roberson and Suzuki, introduction; Slater and Galbraith, "Re-Narrating
      Social Class"; Galbraith, *Otaku and the Struggle*; Kam, "Common Sense";
      and Kam, "Anxieties."

38    LaMarre, "Otaku Movement"; and Galbraith, *Otaku and the Struggle.*

39    Galbraith, "Otaku Sexuality in Japan," 206.

40    Kinsella, *Adult Manga*.

41    Galbraith, *Otaku and the Struggle*.

42    Azuma, *Otaku*; and Galbraith, "Akihabara."

43    For an in-depth discussion of *onabe* and *x-gender*, see chapter 1.

44    Miyake, *Akihabara wa ima*.

45    As I discussed in the introduction, Cool Japan is a state-driven ideology akin to soft power as well as a marketing strategy by content industries and a sensibility and orientation rooted in postwar conditions of gloom and disjunction and in Japanese consumer and entertainment style. See McGray, "Japan's Gross National Cool"; Allison, *Millennial Monsters*; and McLelland, "Introduction."

46    Subsequently, many shiny megabuildings were also inaugurated, such as UDX (Urban Development X) in 2006.

47    Galbraith, *Otaku and the Struggle*, 130.

48    In addition to intensified media attention, the Akihabara boom (*akihabara būmu*) was also characterized by a "surge in domestic tourism" and otaku performances. See Galbraith, *Otaku and the Struggle*, 147–49.

49    Nomura Research Institute, *Otaku shijō* [Otaku market]; and Morinaga, *Moe keizaigaku*.

50    Newitz, "Anime Otaku"; and Hills, "Transcultural Otaku."

51    McLelland, "Introduction."

52    Like Akihabara, Nakano and Ikebukuro are areas in central Tokyo well known for anime, manga, and game consumption.

53    See Higo Seishi, "Tokyo hatsu sayonara zeronendai 2000–2009 iyashi airashisa de kokoro risetto" [Leaving Tokyo goodbye zero generation 2000–2009: Resetting one's heart with healing and loveliness], *Tokyo Shimbun*, December 30, 2009.

54    See Chang, "'Shitsuji kissa' ni okeru 'BL-teki mōsō' to sekushuariti."

55    See Iino, "Sekushuaritihyōgen no tayōka" [Diverse expressions of sexuality].

56    "'Josō danshi' fuetemasu fasshon kankaku, seken no teikōheru?" [The number of "boys dressed as women" is increasing: A sense of fashion, a decrease in public resistance?], *Akita Sakigake Shimpo*, December 24, 2009.

57    See "Bijin no dansei meido ga 'okaerinasaimase' 'seishintekiburakura kissa' ni sennyūshita" [A beautiful male maid says "welcome home": Infiltrated a "browser crasher café"], ITmedia News, last modified July 4, 2008, https://www.itmedia.co.jp/news/articles/0807/04/news036.html.

58   Managed by the company Moe Japan, Dear Stage rents out space for various cafés, bars, and live events, especially concerts for rookie idols. A famous example is Denpagumi.inc, an all-female idol group who started out as *chika aidoru* (underground idols) performing at Dear Stage before they achieved success in Japan and abroad.

59   Takagi Rie, "Geinō fūkōkei dansō ni tokimeku otomegokoro būmu tōrai ugokitsugitsugi" [Celebrity wind vane: Has the boom arrived for *dansō* to make maidens' hearts flutter? Moving one at a time], *Chūnichi Shimbun*, February 17, 2014.

60   Kinsella, "Cuteness, Josō"; and Kinsella, "Otoko no ko Manga."

61   One example discussed by Kinsella is *Kids Are Alright: Groovy after School* (*Gakko e ikkō!*, 1997–2005, 2015–2021), a variety program broadcast by Tokyo Broadcasting System (TBS). See Kinsella, "Cuteness, Josō."

62   For a discussion of this, see Galbraith, "Maid in Japan"; and Plourde, "Cat Cafes."

63   Other establishments in Akihabara have similar settings but perhaps for different reasons, such as to construct a "contained fantasy space" in maid cafés. Galbraith, "Maid Cafes," 112.

64   Until Tokyo's antismoking legislation was implemented in April 2020, smoking was allowed on Garçon's premises. See Tarrant, "Tokyo Ban Kicks In."

65   Honda, *Moeru otoko* [Man bursting into blossom]; and Galbraith, "Maid Cafes."

66   Honda, *Moeru otoko*; and Galbraith, *Otaku and the Struggle*.

67   Halberstam, *Queer Art of Failure*, 2.

68   Halberstam, *Queer Art of Failure*.

69   Allison, *Nightwork*; and Borovoy, *Too-Good Wife*.

70   Kinsella, "Otoko no ko Manga."

71   Galbraith, "Otaku Sexuality in Japan"; Galbraith, "Moe"; and Kinsella, "Otoko no ko Manga."

72   *Visual kei* refers to a "Japanese music subculture known for flamboyant theatrics, a woman-dominated fanbase, and its performers' nonnormative, often playfully queer gender expressions." Johnson, "Josō or 'Gender Free'?," 119.

73   Allison, *Precarious Japan*, 120.

74   As I discuss in chapter 4 with the example of Tobari, cosplayers are individuals who do costume play or dress as a fictional character.

75   McConnell-Ginet, "'What's in a Name?'"; Gatson, "Self-Naming Practices"; and Aldrin, "Names and Identity."

76 Crenshaw and Nardi, "What's in a Name?"

77 R. Kang, Brown, and Kiesler, "Why Do People Seek Anonymity"; and Rainie et al., *Anonymity, Privacy, and Security Online.*

78 Ahmed, *Cultural Politics of Emotion*, 45.

79 Roquet, *Ambient Media*, 152.

80 The Kobe earthquake, which killed, injured, and displaced thousands, and the apocalyptic cult Aum Shinrikyō's release of poisonous sarin gas in the Tokyo commuter trains were "episodes of national trauma." Roquet, *Ambient Media*, 153, 214.

81 Fanasca, *Female Masculinity*; Plourde, "Cat Cafes"; Robinson, "Finding Healing"; Robinson, "Paid Companions"; Yamagishi, "Promised Land for Men"; and Koch, *Healing Labor.*

82 Robinson, "Paid Companions," 345.

83 Fanasca, *Female Masculinity*, 108. Although Fanasca proposes *iyashi* (healing) as a point of difference between *dansō* escorts and *dansō* café-and-bars, I make a more nuanced argument here in that there are some differences between the two kinds of establishments but also some similarities.

84 Fanasca, *Female Masculinity*, 108.

85 Stewart, *Ordinary Affects*, 1–2.

86 B. Anderson, *Encountering Affect*, 149.

87 Galbraith and Karlin, "Introduction."

88 Tsing, *Mushroom*, 65.

89 For more on *neko-kei*, see an article on dating in the women's magazine *Ray*: "Neko mitaina kanojo no tokuchō yattsu: Otosu hōhō to jōzuna atsukai-kata wo go shōkai" [Eight features of a girlfriend who is like a cat: Recommendations on how to handle her well], *Ray*, last modified April 1, 2022, https://ray-web.jp/193304.

90 Fanasca, *Female Masculinity*, 76.

91 Hall, "Deconstructing 'the Popular,'" 228.

92 Hall, "Deconstructing 'the Popular,'" 228.

93 Halberstam, *Queer Art of Failure.*

### 4. More than Just Work

1 Assigning pronouns to my interlocutors when writing in English is complicated. Although Marta Fanasca has strongly argued for the use of *he/him* pronouns to refer to *dansō* individuals, this also runs the risk of misgendering my interlocutors, who locate themselves in the middle

of a continuum of genders and sexualities, as S. P. F. Dale once pointed out to me. Elsewhere I have also discussed how gender-neutral pronouns reflect the politics of Garçon employees like Hiyori as not aligning with media and state-driven discourses of LGBT. See Fanasca, *Female Masculinity*; and M. Ho, "Queer and Normal."

2    Tsing, *Mushroom*, 63.

3    Scholars have defined *work* as tasks performed for a job, whereas *labor* has multiple meanings and may refer to "work itself" or its larger context, including the production process, employee-employer relations, and job alienation, exploitation, and devaluation. See Crain, Poster, and Cherry, "Introduction," 6.

4    Parreñas, *Illicit Flirtations*.

5    Muñoz, *Cruising Utopia*.

6    Muñoz, *Cruising Utopia*, 147.

7    Laslett and Brenner, "Gender and Social Reproduction," 383. Yet, even within Marxist feminism, LGBTQ lives continue to be overlooked. Longinotto and Williams, *Shinjuku Boys*.

8    Hardt and Negri, *Multitude*, 108. See also Hochschild, *Managed Heart*.

9    Ward, "Gender Labor"; and Raha, "Queer Marxist Transfeminism."

10   Raha, "Queer Marxist Transfeminism."

11   Raha, "Queer Marxist Transfeminism," 105.

12   Raha, "Queer Marxist Transfeminism," 94.

13   This status is of course compounded by race and ethnicity, which queer-of-color scholars have responded to by proposing that we rethink the marketization of LGBTQ across the axes of class, race, ethnicity, gender, and sexuality as they are located in multiple social and economic formations. See Hollibaugh and Weiss, "Queer Precarity"; Brim, *Poor Queer Studies*; Ferguson, *Aberrations in Black*; and Muñoz, *Disidentifications*.

14   Raha, "Queer Marxist Transfeminism," 95.

15   Rosenberg and Villarejo, "Introduction." See also Floyd, *Reification of Desire*. Biopolitics, or what Foucault calls *biopower*, refers to state management of life and population through political structures, institutions, and disciplinary practices. See Foucault, *History of Sexuality*, vol. 1.

16   See, for instance, Kawaguchi, "Neoriberarizumu"; Hiramori, "Shokuba ni okeru seitekimainoriti no kon'nan"; Hiramori, "Seiteikimainoriti ga hataraki yasui shokuba to wa?"; Hattori, "LGBT seisaku no dōkō"; Nagao, "Seiteki mainoriti (LGBTQ) gakusei no shien"; and J. Anderson, "Invisible Diversity in Companies."

17   Hattori, "LGBT seisaku no dōkō."

18  Raha, "Queer Marxist Transfeminism," 105.

19  In a 2018 United Nations report, Tokyo is listed as the world's largest city, with a population of over thirty-seven million. See United Nations, *World's Cities in 2018*, 4.

20  See, for example, Allison, *Nightwork*; Parreñas, *Illicit Flirtations*; Takeyama, *Staged Seduction*; and Koch, *Healing Labor*. This is not to say that such entertainment is absent outside Tokyo as cities like Osaka and Nagoya have a vibrant nightlife, but much less has been written about them, e.g., Faier, *Intimate Encounters*; Chung, "Gender and Ethnicity"; and Chung, "Transnational Labor Migration."

21  Allison, *Nightwork*, 7–9.

22  Parreñas, *Illicit Flirtations*.

23  Koch, *Healing Labor*, 101.

24  Koch, *Healing Labor*.

25  Yamagishi, "Promised Land for Men."

26  Takeyama, *Staged Seduction*.

27  Chauncey, *Gay New York*, 133–34.

28  See, for instance, Halberstam, *Queer Time and Place*; Herring, *Another Country*; Tongson, *Relocations*; and Podmore, "Disaggregating Sexual Metronormativities."

29  This is unfortunately an underwritten subject in Japan as elsewhere. For a discussion on gay communities in rural Japan, see Benkhart, "Rural Queer Associations."

30  Although Mitsuhashi's work coincided with the 1990s queer movement and gay boom in the mass media, *josō* and *new half* bars and clubs had already become widespread in the 1980s, during the bubble economy. See Mitsuhashi, "Transgender World"; Mitsuhashi, "My Life as a 'Woman'"; and Mitsuhashi, *Josō to nihonjin*.

31  Parreñas, *Illicit Flirtations*.

32  The term used to denote *josō* individuals at the time was *josōsha*, and their lovers were called *josōsha aikō dansei* (men who love *josōsha*). Mitsuhashi, "My Life as a 'Woman,'" 301; and Mitsuhashi, *Josō to nihonjin*.

33  See Halberstam, *Female Masculinity*; and Hochschild, *Managed Heart*.

34  Fanasca, *Female Masculinity*.

35  Jung, *Korean Masculinities*.

36  Fanasca, *Female Masculinity*, 22; and Halberstam, *Female Masculinity*.

37  Fanasca, *Female Masculinity*, 128.

38  Fanasca, *Female Masculinity*, 129.

39    Galbraith, *Otaku and the Struggle.*

40    Galbraith, *Otaku and the Struggle*, 201–2.

41    Galbraith, *Otaku and the Struggle.* See also McGlotten, *Virtual Intimacies.*

42    For a definition of *cosplay*, see chapter 2, note 58. For a definition of *freeter*, see chapter 1, note 60.

43    Galbraith, "Maid Cafes."

44    Parreñas, *Illicit Flirtations.*

45    Ōtsuka, *Seiyūdamashī* [A voice artist's soul].

46    Her, "Concept of Gong-Ye."

47    See chapter 3 for a discussion of *kawaii*, *bishōjo*, and *bishōnen*.

48    Bourdieu, *Distinction*, 56.

49    Creighton, "Japanese Craft Tourism," 470.

50    Parreñas, *Illicit Flirtations*, 86; and Koch, *Healing Labor.*

51    Halberstam, *Queer Time and Place*, 10.

52    Dozier, "Female Masculinity at Work," 201; and Reddy-Best and Pedersen, "Relationship of Gender Expression," 61.

53    Plourde, "Cat Cafes," 118; and Nozawa, "Phatic Traces."

54    Delany, *Times Square Red*, 129.

55    Shah, *Stranger Intimacy*, 55.

56    *Himote* is a composite word made up of *hi* (negative or "un-") and *mote*, from *moteru* (popular or well liked in the romantic sense), indexing young men who do not seem attractive to women. See E. Miles, "Manhood." For a discussion of *kodokushi* and *hikkikomori*, see Allison, *Precarious Japan.*

57    Allison, *Precarious Japan.*

58    See my earlier discussion of alternative socialities in chapter 2.

59    The enactment of a bill to be implemented from 2022 onward will lower the age of majority to eighteen years old, but the legal drinking age will remain at twenty years old. See "Coming of Age: Why Adults in Japan Are Getting Younger," BBC News, June 13, 2018.

60    In 2017 the starting hourly wage for Prince was JPY 900 (USD 8.30), whereas that for Teikoku Geihin was JPY 1,000 (USD 9). This has increased in recent years to JPY 1,000 (USD 9) for Garçon in 2019 and JPY 1,050–2,000 (USD 9.50–18.20) for ZAC and Dracula in 2020. See a recruiting website for concept café employees: Caferun, "Dansō Café-and-Bars Nationwide: Part-Time Jobs and Job Information," accessed January 14, 2024, https://caferun.jp/shoplist/all/dansocafe/. These hourly wages are also much lower than those of *dansō* escorts, who earn JPY 1,650 to 3,300 (USD 15 to 30) depending on their rank. See Fanasca, *Female Masculinity.*

61  It is likely that Garçon provided in-kind benefits such as meals to make up for the difference, which is allowable under the Minimum Wage Act. The country's average minimum hourly wage is much lower, at JPY 823 (USD 7.50), in 2016. See Japanese Law Translation, "Minimum Wage Act (Act No. 137 of 1959)," accessed June 6, 2024, https://www.japaneselawtranslation.go.jp/en/laws/view/3937/en. Also see Japan International Labour Foundation 2017, "Prefectural Minimum Wages for FY 2017 Rise to National Average of 848 Yen," accessed May 29, 2021 https://www.jilaf.or.jp/eng/mbn/2017/245.html (no longer available).

62  *After (afutā)* is short for after-hours activities. See Takeyama, *Staged Seduction.*

63  For more on *shimei*, see Parreñas, *Illicit Flirtations*; and Takeyama, *Staged Seduction.*

64  While *girls bars* share many similarities with hostess clubs, the main difference is that employees at *girls bars* work from behind a counter instead of sitting next to the customer, which is standard practice in hostess clubs.

65  J. Taylor, Lewis, and Haider-Markel, *Rise of Transgender Rights*; and Koch, *Healing Labor.*

66  *Delivery health* typically involves dispatching sex workers to customers' homes or hotel rooms, whereas *fashion health* operates out of massage parlors. See Koch, *Healing Labor.*

67  Nadal et al., "Transgender Female Sex Workers."

68  J. Anderson, "Invisible Diversity in Companies."

69  David, "Purple-Collar Labor," 170.

70  Aizura, "Trans Feminine Value"; and David, "Capital T."

71  Despite the moniker, *tarento* (talent) have no special talent; they are known for being ordinary next-door individuals who appear on television. See Lukács, *Scripted Affects, Branded Selves.*

72  For instance, in 2019 one in five trans people were unemployed, and trans women earned 17.1 percent less than their cisgender peers. See Nijiiro Diversity and CGS, *Niji VOICE 2019 Report.*

73  O'Shea, "I Am Not That Caitlin," 208.

74  Garfinkel defines *passing* as "the work of achieving and making secure their rights to live in the elected sex status while providing for the possibility of detection and ruin carried out within the socially structured conditions in which this work occurred." Garfinkel, *Studies in Ethnomethodology,* 118.

75  See Ministry of Health, Labour, and Welfare, "Kaisei koyō no bun'ya ni okeru danjo no kintōna kikai oyobi taigū no kakuho-tō ni kansuru hōritsu no shikō ni tsuite' no ichibu kaisei ni tsuite" [Partial amendment

of the Ordinance for the Enforcement of the Act on Ensuring Equal Opportunities for and Treatment of Men and Women in Employment], accessed January 14, 2024, https://www.mhlw.go.jp/web/t_doc?dataId =00tc2038&dataType=1&pageNo=1.

76 Fan, "From Office Ladies"; Gelb, "Equal Employment Opportunity Law"; Barrett, "Women in the Workplace"; and Assmann, "25 Years After."

77 Obata, "'Power Harassment' in Japan"; and Satoko Nakagawa, "News Navigator: What's New about Japan's Law to Prevent Workplace Harassment?," *Mainichi* (Tokyo), March 30, 2022, https://mainichi.jp/english /articles/20220329/p2a/00m/0op/013000c.

78 The revised CLPPA provisions are "not prohibitive provisions that can serve as grounds for civil claims for damages." Obata, "'Power Harassment' in Japan," 23.

79 Allison, *Nightwork*; and Parreñas, *Illicit Flirtations*.

80 Trans-femininity might be understood as a spectrum of typically feminine positions, which are related to but distinct from cis-feminine positions presented by individuals who are assigned male at birth. See Chamberland, "Femininity in Transgender Studies."

81 Although Japanese sexual assault and harassment laws were revised in June 2017 to include "forced anal and oral sex," it is uncertain if these revisions apply to non-cis women. See Tomohiro Osaki, "Diet Makes Historic Revision to Century-Old Sex-Crime Laws," *Japan Times*, June 16, 2017.

82 Grewal and Kaplan, "Global Identities," 670.

83 Grewal and Kaplan, "Global Identities."

84 Halberstam, *Female Masculinity*, 9.

85 Based on this fluidity, my analysis of *dansō* individuals differs from Fanasca's clear separation of *dansō* from *x-gender*. See Fanasca, *Female Masculinity*, 6.

86 See, for example, Nijiiro Diversity and CGS, *Niji VOICE 2018 Report*; Nijiiro Diversity and CGS, *Niji VOICE 2019 Report*; and Nijiiro Diversity and CGS, *Niji VOICE 2020 Report*.

87 Davidson, "Gender Inequality"; and Dray et al., "Beyond the Gender Binary."

88 Matsuno and Budge, "Non-Binary/Genderqueer Identities"; and Vijlbrief, Saharso, and Ghorashi, "Transcending the Gender Binary."

89 Davidson, "Gender Inequality."

90 Nijiiro Diversity and CGS, *Niji VOICE 2018 Report*; Nijiiro Diversity and CGS, *Niji VOICE 2019 Report*; Nijiiro Diversity and CGS, *Niji VOICE 2020 Report*; and Nijiiro Diversity and CGS, *Niji VOICE 2022 Report*.

91 Nijiiro Diversity and CGS, *Niji VOICE 2019 Report*; Nijiiro Diversity and CGS, *Niji VOICE 2020 Report*; and Nijiiro Diversity and CGS, *Niji VOICE 2022 Report*.

92 As I discuss in chapter 5, *body work* refers to the work one does on one's body. See Gimlin, *Body Work*.

93 See chapter 3 for a discussion of *kei*. See also Fanasca, *Female Masculinity*.

94 Jung, *Korean Masculinities*.

95 Fanasca describes this process when she "transformed" into a *dansō* escort. See Fanasca, *Female Masculinity*.

96 White Day is a Japanese commercial holiday invented in the late 1970s by confectioneries to sell chocolates. Creighton, "'Sweet Love.'"

97 Minowa, Belk, and Matsui, "Practicing Masculinity."

98 Parreñas, *Illicit Flirtations*; and Takeyama, *Staged Seduction*. Each regular customer is designated by their affiliation to the *dansō* escort whose services they engage the most, and it is an unspoken rule that other escorts do not "infringe on this [love-like] relationship." Fanasca, *Female Masculinity*, 132.

99 Galbraith, "Maid Cafes."

100 Galbraith, "Maid Cafes," 104.

101 Halberstam, *Queer Time and Place*.

102 Faier, *Intimate Encounters*; and Takeyama, *Staged Seduction*.

103 Takeyama, *Staged Seduction*, 74–75.

## 5. Consuming Genders, Fashioning Bodies

Ideas for chapter 5 grew out of an article that appeared in *Inter-Asia Cultural Studies* in 2021, which was subsequently republished in *Gender in Japanese Popular Culture: Rethinking Masculinities and Femininities* in 2023. See M. Ho, "From Dansō to Genderless."

1 X is derived from *x-gender*, which is defined as neither male nor female, or both. For an in-depth discussion, see chapter 1.

2 *Consumption* is defined as the "social process by which people construct the symbolically laden material worlds they inhabit and which, reciprocally, act back on them in complex ways." Dietler, "Consumption," 209.

3 *Fashion* is different from *dress*, which refers to the act of "clothing the body"—including "dressing up" in the functional or aesthetic sense (i.e., adornment). See Leopold, "Manufacture"; E. Wilson, *Adorned in Dreams*; and Entwistle, *Fashioned Body*.

4 Calefato, "Fashion and Worldliness," 76; see also E. Wilson, *Adorned in Dreams*; Barthes, *Language of Fashion*; and Entwistle, *Fashioned Body*.

5 As Elizabeth Wilson puts it, fashion is "obsessed with gender, defines and redefines the gender boundary." E. Wilson, *Adorned in Dreams*, 117.

6 Gibson-Graham, *End of Capitalism*; and Gibson-Graham, "Ethics of the Local."

7 Entwistle, *Fashioned Body*, 119; Slade, *Japanese Fashion*; and Monden, *Japanese Fashion Cultures*.

8 Slade, *Japanese Fashion*; and Monden, *Japanese Fashion Cultures*.

9 moore, *Fabulous*, vii, 103.

10 Kondo, *About Face*, 106.

11 Gimlin, *Body Work*; Gimlin, "What Is 'Body Work'?"; Wolkowitz, *Bodies at Work*; M. Kang, *Managed Hand*; and Mears, "Aesthetic Labor."

12 For more on body work done on one's body, see Gimlin, *Body Work*; and Gimlin, "What Is 'Body Work'?" For more on body work done on another's body, see Wolkowitz, *Bodies at Work*; and M. Kang, *Managed Hand*.

13 *Men* means "face" or "side" in Japanese. Prior to its popularization in social media, this practice seems to have derived from the *josō* business circles, in which individuals adopted the beauty terminology "before" and "after" to describe their stages of pre- and post-transformation.

14 Monden, *Japanese Fashion Cultures*.

15 Dalby, *Kimono*, 288–89.

16 Yagi, *Tokyo Street Style*.

17 Kondo, *About Face*; Kawamura, *Japanese Revolution*; and English, *Japanese Fashion Designers*.

18 Kondo, *About Face*, 105.

19 Kondo, *About Face*, 118, 25.

20 Kawamura, *Fashioning Japanese Subcultures*, 785; see also Monden, *Japanese Fashion Cultures*.

21 Kawamura, *Fashioning Japanese Subcultures*; and Winge, "Tokyo Subcultural Street Styles."

22 Young women who embraced the Lolita style "dress[ed] as anachronistic visual representations of Victorian-era dolls, covered from head to toe in lace, ruffles, and bows." Winge, "Undressing and Dressing Loli," 47. The *kogyaru* (high school girl) style is characterized by young women wearing knee-high white socks and short plaid skirts that looked like school uniforms, whereas those in the *ganguro* (black face) style had bright makeup, dyed or bleached hair, artificially tanned skin, bright miniskirts or short pants, and high platform boots. See Kawamura,

"Japan Fashion Subcultures." I have discussed the racial and gender politics of black face and *ganguro* in the Japanese context elsewhere. See M. Ho, "Consuming Women in Blackface."

23 Uema, "Gendai joshi kōkōsei" [Present-day high school girls]; Winge, "Undressing and Dressing Loli"; Kinsella, *Schoolgirls*; and M. Ho, "Consuming Women in Blackface."

24 For a discussion of genderless *joshi* (girls), see M. Ho, "From Dansō to Genderless."

25 M. Ho, "From Dansō to Genderless."

26 K. Nakamura and Matsuo, "Female Masculinity"; Negrin, *Appearance and Identity*; Entwistle, *Fashioned Body*; and Monden, *Japanese Fashion Cultures*.

27 Geczy and Karaminas, *Queer Style*, 22.

28 Steele, "Queer History of Fashion"; and Cole and Lewis, "LGBTQ Fashion and Style."

29 See VICE Japan, "*Dansō* Cross-Dressing," YouTube, uploaded April 8, 2013, https://youtu.be/NmovOYv5KKU. I have analyzed this documentary feature in relation to queer style elsewhere. See M. Ho, "From Dansō to Genderless." Although I use *she/her* pronouns for AKIRA, it is important to note that AKIRA employs *ore*, the masculine first-person pronoun for "I/me," and media narratives variously refer to AKIRA as *he/him* and *she/her*.

30 There was talk of a second volume, but for some reason it did not materialize. See *Dansō Zasshi "Garçon Girls" Henshū-bu no Burogu \*10tsuki 15-nichi sōkan!\** [Editorial Department Blog of "Garçon Girls," Dansō Magazine \* Launched on October 15th!\*], "'Garçon Girls' kōshiki sunappu satsuei-kai no oshirase [Announcement of the official 'Garçon Girls' snap photoshoot]," December 24, 2013, https://ameblo.jp/garcongirls/entry-11735414299.html.

31 See chapter 3, note 73, for a definition of *visual kei*.

32 *Men's Knuckle* is a men's fashion magazine focused on "older brother style" (*onīkei*), a chic and sexy mode popular among men in their twenties.

33 Tianyi Vespera Xie has also underscored the differences between various *dansō* magazines, including *Garçon Girls* and KERA BOKU. See Xie, "Ikemen Dansō Girls."

34 In 2018 SECRET GUYZ disbanded. For an analysis of SECRET GUYZ, see Yuen, "Cultural Citizenship."

35 See Garçon Girls Editorial Team, "From Editors," *Garçon Girls*, October 25, 2013, 5.

36    Calefato, "Fashion and Worldliness"; E. Wilson, *Adorned in Dreams*; and Barthes, *Language of Fashion*.

37    See *'Gendaiyōgo no kisochishiki'-sen yūkyan chingo ryūkōgotaishō* ["Encyclopedia of contemporary words" U-CAN Keywords-of-the-Year Contest], "Dai 40-kai 2023-nen jushō gō [40th contest 2023 words]," accessed January 14, 2024, https://www.jiyu.co.jp/singo/.

38    For more on the Tokyo Cosme Boy Contest (*tōkyō keshō danshi sengen*), see Kinsella, "Cuteness, Josō."

39    This definition appears similar to that of *x-gender*. It is possible that Inoue may have identified as *x-gender* but used the term *keshō danshi* instead. Inoue self-identifies as a *sekusharu mainoritī* (sexual minority). See Inoue, *Kesho danshi* [Cosme boy].

40    For work on university *josō* contests, see Miyazaki, "Hybrid Masculinities?"

41    See Maree, *Queerqueen*. *Onē* are individuals who use *onē-kotoba* (queen or older-sister speech), a type of speech associated with *josō* and "effeminate intonation contours and gestures in various degrees of intensity." Maynard, *Fluid Orality*, 115.

42    Maree has discussed the politics of *onē-tarento* instructing cis women on "feminine" skills. See Maree, *Queerqueen*. Lifestyle television programs, which have emerged since the late 1980s, show consumers how to "reinforce and cultivate their individuality through taste preferences and define their identity through lifestyle choices." Lukács, *Scripted Affects*, 43.

43    Miller, "Japan's Cinderella Motif," 393, 398.

44    See Miller, "Japan's Cinderella Motif," 393–98.

45    According to Ikki, Yuka uses Aozora's site for the other services her company provides, such as staging events.

46    See "'Ikemen joshi' gundan! THE HOOPERS rainen sangatsu debyū" ["Handsome girls" corps! THE HOOPERS debuts in March next year], *Sankei Sports*, December 13, 2014; "Za fūpāzu ga debyūkyoku 'itoshikoishi kimikoishi' no hatsubaikinen ibento" [Sale event for the Hooper's debut song "itoshikoishi kimikoishi"], *Sports Hōchi*, March 5, 2015; and "THE HOOPERS sekai debyū! Shinkyoku 192kakoku chiiki de haishin" [The Hoopers debuts worldwide! New song is delivered to 192 areas and countries], *Sankei Sports*, January 23, 2017.

47    Propaganda ended because its president felt it had accomplished its goal of spreading *josō* culture. See Hayashi, "Heart Net TV (Hātonetto TV)."

48    Kunitomo Kozi, "Kabukichō no josō harowin pātī de jendāfurī na sankasha-tachi no koe wo kiitemita" [At a *josō* Halloween party in

Kabukichō, I listened to the voices of gender-free participants], *Nikkan* SPA! [Daily SPA, October 30, 2017, https://nikkan-spa.jp/1423055.

49   Gimlin, *Body Work.*

50   Gill and Scharff, introduction; and Elias, Gill, and Scharff, "Aesthetic Labour."

51   Geczy and Karaminas, *Queer Style*; and moore, *Fabulous.*

52   moore, *Fabulous*, 8–9.

53   M. Kang, *Managed Hand*, 21.

54   Boris and Parreñas, Introduction, 1.

55   Bourdieu defines *capital* as "accumulated labor (in its materialized form or its 'incorporated,' embodied form) which, when appropriated on a private, i.e., exclusive, basis by agents or groups of agents, enables them to appropriate social energy in the form of reified or living labor." Bourdieu, "Forms of Capital," 241. See also Shilling, "Educating the Body"; Shilling, *Body and Social Theory*; and Wacquant, "Pugs at Work."

56   Shilling, "Educating the Body," 654.

57   Foucault, *History of Sexuality*, 2:10–11.

58   Weber, *Makeover TV.*

59   Thornton, *Club Cultures*, 15; see also moore, *Fabulous*; and Khubchandani, *Ishtyle.*

60   hooks, *Yearning*, 195.

61   As I illustrated in chapter 4, *contact encounters*, a term I take from Samuel Delany, indexes interactions among strangers that often cross class, gender, and sexuality lines. See Delany, *Times Square Red.*

62   Halberstam, *Female Masculinity.*

63   Geczy and Karaminas, *Queer Style.*

64   Gimlin, *Body Work*, 8.

65   Teti et al., "Exploration of Apparel," 63.

66   Entwistle, *Fashioned Body.*

67   Negrin, *Appearance and Identity*, 141.

68   See, for example, Clarke and Miller, "Fashion and Anxiety"; Colls, "Outsize/Outside"; and Kwan, "Navigating Public Spaces."

69   Reddy-Best and Pedersen, "Relationship of Gender Expression"; and Reddy-Best and Pedersen, "Queer Women's Experiences."

70   Reddy-Best and Pedersen, "Queer Women's Experiences," 273.

71   moore, *Fabulous.*

72   Mauss, *Gift.*

73    Lovelock, "Call Me Caitlyn."

74    For an analysis of *onē-tarento* as lifestyle experts, see Maree, *Queerqueen*.

75    See, for example, Kinsella, "Cuties in Japan"; Pike and Borovoy, "Rise of Eating Disorders"; Miller, *Beauty Up*; Hansen, "Eating Disorders and Self-Harm"; and Yano, *Pink Globalization*.

76    Kikuchi, *Nihon no posutofeminizumu* [Japan's postfeminism].

77    *Joshi ryoku* has also been used to describe cis heterosexual men, although few scholars have so far discussed this. I follow Rosalind Gill's definition of *postfeminism* as a sensibility characterized by the "undoing" of feminist gains and perceptions of feminism as redundant while referencing "girl power" and strong and successful young women in media and popular culture. See Gill, "Affective, Cultural and Psychic Life."

78    Kikuchi, *Nihon no posutofeminizumu*.

79    Jiji used the term *kamingu auto* (coming out).

80    LIZ LISA has also been tied to a particular Shibuya subculture group called Lomamba, an amalgamation of Lolita and Mamba styles. Mamba (also *manba*) is a style evolved from *yamamba* (mountain ogress) and *ganguro* (black face) girl subcultures in which young women wore bright makeup on their tanned, dark skin. For a discussion of these styles in relation to race and ethnicity, see Kawamura, "Japan Fashion Subcultures"; and Kinsella, *Schoolgirls*.

81    Stryker and Aizura, "Introduction," 3; see also Stryker, "Transgender Studies," and Whittle, "Where Did We Go Wrong?"

82    Chiang, Henry, and Leung, "Trans-in-Asia," 308; see also Valentine, "'I Went to Bed.'"

83    Although Japan does not have a cultural history of homophobia or transphobia, leading some to think that physical violence against sexual minorities is uncommon, discrimination often abounds in social settings like the family, school, and workplace. See, for instance, Lunsing, "LGBT Rights in Japan"; DiStefano, "Intimate Partner Violence"; Y. Hidaka and Operario, "Attempted Suicide"; and Kasai, "Sexual and Gender Minorities."

84    Westbrook and Schilt, "Doing Gender, Determining Gender."

85    See, for example, Schilt and Westbrook, "Doing Gender, Doing Heteronormativity"; Salamon, *Life and Death*; and Billard, "'Passing.'"

86    Although Twitter is now X, I retain Twitter because my study and data collection preceded this rebranding. Scholars have shown how anonymity "disinhibits" users, who tend to engage more frequently in cyberbullying and harassment due to the lack of accountability. See, for example, Udris, "Cyberbullying"; Barlett, "Anonymously Hurting Others Online"; and Cho and Kwon, "Impacts of Identity Verification."

87 Haimson et al., "Tumblr Was a Trans Technology," 350; see also Cavalcante, *Struggling for Ordinary*.

88 Lunsing, "LGBT Rights in Japan."

## Coda

1 Mohamed A. El-Erian, "Navigating the New Normal in Industrial Countries: Per Jacobsson Foundation Lecture," International Monetary Fund,
October 10, 2010, https://www.imf.org/en/News/Articles/2015/09/28/04
/53/sp101010; and Li, "Understanding and Adapting."

2 Haruka Murayama, "'Kowai,' 'Fuan' and Language in the 'New Normal,'"
*Japan Times*, May 26 2020.

3 Looi, "Covid-19."

4 See '*Gendaiyōgo no kisochishiki'-sen yūkyan chingo ryūkōgotaishō*
["Encyclopedia of contemporary words" U-CAN Keywords-of-the-Year
Contest], "Dai 37-kai 2020-nen jushōgo" [Thirty-seventh contest 2020
words], accessed January 14, 2024, https://www.jiyu.co.jp/singo/index
.php?eid=00037.

5 The Japanese to English translations of "closed spaces" (*mippei*), "crowded
places" (*misshū*), and "close conversation" (*missetsu*) follow those in an
interview with Koike. See Koike Yuriko, "The Mind, Skill and Body of the
New Normal in Tokyo," *Urban Solutions*, no. 18 (October 30, 2020): 6–11,
https://www.clc.gov.sg/docs/default-source/urban-solutions/urbsol18pdf
/1_interview_newnormaltokyo.pdf.

6 Raha, "Queer Marxist Transfeminism," 105.

7 Hollibaugh and Weiss, "Queer Precarity," 23.

8 Salerno, Williams, and Gattamorta, "LGBTQ Populations."

9 Fujita et al., "'Staying at Home.'"

10 Unless they have same-sex partnership certificates in certain districts
that allow medical decision-making and hospital visitation rights, most
same-gender partners are not legally recognized in Japan. This survey
was carried out by Marriage for All Japan, an institution established by
lawyers in Japan to advocate the freedom to marry for all individuals. See
Marriage for All Japan, "LGBTQ tōjisha kara korona wazawai de 'byōin
de kazoku to shite atsukawa reru no ka' kyōsei-tekina kaminguauto ni
tsunagaru'-tō, fuan ya kiki-kan no koe ga atsumaru. Dōsei kon hōsei-ka
o mezasu dantai ga, kinkyū onrain ankēto no sokuhō o happyō" [LGBTQ
individuals react to the coronavirus with anxiety and a sense of crisis,
such as "Will I be treated as family in the hospital?" "It leads to me having to come out." An organization aiming to enact same-sex marriage
legislation has released breaking news on an emergency online survey],

PR *Times*, April 21, 2020, https://prtimes.jp/main/html/rd/p/000000002
.000054117.html. For a discussion of these issues among the Japanese
LGBTQ+ community, see Sunagawa, "Shingata korona uirusu kansenshō
to LGBT" [New coronavirus infections and LGBT]; and Tamagawa,
*Japanese LGBTQ+ Community*.

11  Tarrant, "Tokyo Ban Kicks In."

12  See "Tokyo's COVID-19 State of Emergency Extended 2 Weeks," *Kyodo
News*, March 5, 2021, https://english.kyodonews.net/news/2021/03
/77f840e58454-tokyos-covid-19-state-of-emergency-to-be-extended-2
-weeks.html.

13  This number is accurate as of August 2021. See Moi Corporation, "'Twit-
Casting' kara 'tsuikyasu' ni kawarimasu" [Change from "TwitCasting"
to "Tsuikyasu"], PR *Times*, August 18, 2021, https://prtimes.jp/main/html
/rd/p/000000050.000043237.html.

14  See "Itsudemo kaereru, minna no jikka 'onna no ko kurabu' wo mamorō
purojekuto" [Project to protect Onna no ko Club, everyone's home and
a place to return to anytime], CAMPFIRE, accessed January 14, 2024,
https://camp-fire.jp/projects/view/280481.

15  @dracula_dansou, "Sekai no ko no yōna jōkyō no naka go raijō kudasaru
okyakusama arigatōgozaimasu. Ima made kanki ya jūgyōin, okyakusama
no te no shōdoku, masuku taiō, ten'nai no shōdoku, eigyō jikan tanshuku,
mata 4 tsuki 1-nichi kara hajimarimashita kaisei kenkō zōshin-hō ni yori
tennai ni kitsuen-shitsu o mōkeru-tō taiō shite kimashitaga, konkai no
kyūgyō yōsei gyōshu ni tōten wa fukuma rete orazu kyōryoku-kin mo
nai tame eigyō wa tenpo keizoku ya jūgyōin no seikatsu-tō mo kangae
tsudzuke saseteitadaku ni shite orimasu. Gorikai itadakemasu yō yoroshiku onegaiitashimasu. Mata go raijō sa reru okyakusama wa taichō-tō
kiwotsukete go raijō shite kudasaru yō yoroshiku onegaiitashimasu.
[During this current global situation, thank you to all our customers
who visit us. Until now, we have taken measures such as ventilation,
disinfecting the hands of employees and customers, wearing masks, disinfecting the store, shortening business hours, and setting up smoking
rooms in accordance to the revised Health Promotion Act beginning on
April 1st. However, since our store has not been asked to close and we're
not receiving any financial support, our store will continue to operate,
considering our employees' livelihood. We appreciate your understanding. We also ask that all customers take care of their health when visit-
ing]," Twitter, April 10, 2020, accessed May 31, 2021, https://twitter.com
/dracula_dansou/status/1248512062277308418 (no longer available).

16  @hostmistral, "[Jūdai happyō] zoom ni yoru onrain dansō hosuto
'misutoraru' ga kyō kara kaishi!" [(Important announcement) Mistral's

online dansō hosting begins on Zoom today! Mistral-online.net], Twitter, May 2, 2020, accessed July 29, 2022, https://twitter.com/hostmistral/status/1256505688638943232 (no longer available).

17  For an overview of some of these issues, see Fujita et al., "'Staying at Home.'"

18  See Marriage for All Japan, "LGBTQ tōjisha kara korona wazawai de."

19  Steinfield, "Forced Out of the Closet."

20  moore, *Fabulous*, 18; Brown, "Online Clubbing," 4; and Duguay, Trépanier, and Chartrand, "Hottest IS Queer Club."

21  Spencer Kornhaber, "The Coronavirus Is Testing Queer Culture," *Atlantic*, June 11, 2020, https://www.theatlantic.com/culture/archive/2020/06/how-quarantine-reshaping-queer-nightlife/612865/.

22  Duguay, Trépanier, and Chartrand, "Hottest New Queer Club," 2213.

23  See Elaine Lies, "Battered but Unbowed by Coronavirus, Tokyo's Gay District Forges Stronger Ties," Reuters, December 3, 2020, https://www.reuters.com/article/us-health-coronavirus-japan-lgbt-idUSKBN28D03I. For a glimpse into how the closure of gay bars affected some members of the LGBTQ+ community in Japan, see Tamagawa, *Japanese LGBTQ+ Community*.

24  A. Anderson and Knee, "Queer Isolation."

25  S. Miles, "Let's (Not) Go Outside."

26  *Genderless* refers to fashion styles that do not distinguish between genders, at least in theory. See chapter 5 for a discussion. @rinsta_xd., TikTok, accessed January 14, 2024, https://www.tiktok.com/@rinsta_xd. The duo Unlink Cherry was previously known as MM (pronounced as *meimei*) and debuted in September 2020 but later changed their name. See @unlinkcherry, "[Jūdai happyō] konotabi, MM (meimei) aratame Unlink Cherry (anrinkucherī)" to shite katsudō shite iku koto ni narimashita! 🍒 " [(Important announcement) MM (meimei) will now be active as 'Unlink Cherry' 🍒], Twitter, April 27, 2023, https://twitter.com/unlinkcherry/status/1651540471674720256?s=20. *Babiniku* is short for *bācharu bishōjo juniku* (virtual beautiful girl incarnation). As of 2021 there were sixty-two registered *babiniku*. See Bredikhina and Giard, "Becoming a Virtual Cutie."

Abe, Hideko. *Queer Japanese: Gender and Sexual Identities through Linguistic Practices.* New York: Palgrave Macmillan, 2010.

Adair, Cassius, Cameron Awkward-Rich, and Amy Marvin. "Before Trans Studies." *TSQ: Transgender Studies Quarterly* 7, no. 3 (2020): 306–20.

Ahmed, Sara. *The Cultural Politics of Emotion.* Edinburgh: Edinburgh University Press, 2004.

Aizura, Aren Z. *Mobile Subjects: Transnational Imaginaries of Gender Reassignment.* Durham, NC: Duke University Press, 2018.

Aizura, Aren Z. "Trans Feminine Value, Racialized Others and the Limits of Necropolitics." In *Queer Necropolitics*, edited by Jin Haritaworn, Adi Kuntsman, and Silvia Posocco, 129–47. New York: Routledge, 2014.

Ako Takamatsu, Harashina Takao, Inoue Yoshiharu, Kinoshita Katsuyuki, Ishihara Osamu, and Uchijima Yutaka. "Beginnings of Sex Reassignment Surgery in Japan." *The International Journal of Transgenderism* 5, no. 1 (2001). https://cdn.atria.nl/ezines/web/IJT/97-03/numbers/symposion/ijtv005n001 _02.htm (no longer available).

Aldrin, Emilia. "Names and Identity." In *The Oxford Handbook of Names and Naming*, edited by Carole Hough, 382–94. Oxford: Oxford University Press, 2016.

Allison, Anne. "The Cool Brand, Affective Activism and Japanese Youth." *Theory, Culture and Society* 26, nos. 2–3 (2009): 89–111.

Allison, Anne. *Millennial Monsters: Japanese Toys and the Global Imagination.* Berkeley: University of California Press, 2006.

Allison, Anne. *Nightwork: Sexuality, Pleasure, and Corporate Masculinity in a Tokyo Hostess Club*. Chicago: University of Chicago Press, 1994.

Allison, Anne. *Precarious Japan*. Durham, NC: Duke University Press, 2013.

Allison, Anne. "A Sociality of, and beyond, 'My-Home' in Post-Corporate Japan." *Cambridge Journal of Anthropology* 30, no. 1 (2012): 95–108.

Altman, Dennis. "Global Gaze/Global Gays." GLQ: *A Journal of Lesbian and Gay Studies* 3, no. 4 (1997): 417–36.

Altman, Dennis. "On Global Queering." *Australian Humanities Review*, no. 2 (1996). http://australianhumanitiesreview.org/1996/07/01/on-global-queering/.

Amamiya Karin, and Jodie Beck. 2010. "Suffering Forces Us to Think beyond the Right–Left Barrier." *Mechademia: Second Arc* 5: 251–65.

Amamiya Karin, and Toshihito Kayano. *"Ikizurasa" nitsuite: Hinkon, aidentitī, nashonarizumu* [Concerning "hardship of life": Poverty, identity, nationalism]. Tokyo: Kobunsha Shinsho, 2008.

Anagnost, Ann. "Introduction: Life-Making in Neoliberal Times." In *Global Futures in East Asia: Youth, Nation, and the New Economy in Uncertain Times*, edited by Ann Anagnost, Andrea Arai, and Hai Ren, 1–18. Stanford, CA: Stanford University Press, 2013.

American Psychiatric Association (APA). 2013. *Diagnostic and Statistical Manual of Mental Disorders, Fifth Edition (DSM-5)*. Washington, DC: APA.

Anderson, Austin R., and Eric Knee. "Queer Isolation or Queering Isolation? Reflecting upon the Ramifications of COVID-19 on the Future of Queer Leisure Spaces." *Leisure Sciences* 43, nos. 1–2 (2021): 118–24.

Anderson, Ben. *Encountering Affect: Capacities, Apparatuses, Conditions*. Burlington, VT: Ashgate, 2014.

Anderson, Joel Daniel. "Invisible Diversity in Companies in Japan: Understanding the Antecedents and Outcomes of Workplace Climates of Exclusion for LGBT Employees." *J. F. Oberlin Journal of Business Management Studies*, no. 10 (2019): 39–64.

Aoki, Hideo. "Marxism and the Debate on the Transition to Capitalism in Prewar Japan." *Critical Sociology* 47, no. 1 (2021): 17–36.

Aoki, Hideo. "Toward a Critical Understanding of the Japanese State and Capitalism." *Critical Sociology* 47, no. 1 (2021): 5–15.

Aoyama, Kaoru. "The Sex Industry in Japan: The Danger of Invisibility." In *Routledge Handbook of Sexuality Studies in East Asia*, edited by Mark McLelland and Vera Mackie, 281–93. New York: Routledge, 2015.

Aoyama, Tomiko. "Transgendering Shōjo Shōsetsu: Girls' Inter-Text/Sex-Uality." In *Genders, Transgenders and Sexualities in Japan*, edited by Mark McLelland and Romit Dasgupta, 49–64. New York: Routledge, 2005.

Araki Chineko, Ishida Masami, Ohkawa Reiko, Kaneko Kazuko, Horiguchi Sadao, and Horiguchi Masako. *Sekkusuresu jidai no chūkōnen "sei"* [Middle-aged people's "sex" in the sexless era]. Tokyo: Harunosora, 2016.

Ashikari, Mikiko. "Cultivating Japanese Whiteness: The 'Whitening' Cosmetics Boom and the Japanese Identity." *Journal of Material Culture* 10, no. 1 (2005): 73–91.

Assmann, Stephanie. "25 Years after the Enactment of the Equal Employment Opportunity Law (EEOL): Online Access to Gender Equality in Japan." *Asian Politics and Policy* 4, no. 2 (2012): 280–85.

Azuma, Hiroki. *Otaku: Japan's Database Animals.* Translated by Jonathan E. Abel and Shion Kono. Minneapolis: University of Minnesota Press, 2009.

Badgett, M. V. Lee. *Money, Myths, and Change: The Economic Lives of Lesbians and Gay Men.* Chicago: University of Chicago Press, 2001.

Bakhtin, Mikhail. *Rabelais and His World.* Translated by Hélène Iswolsky. Bloomington: Indiana University Press, 1984.

Barlett, Christopher P. "Anonymously Hurting Others Online: The Effect of Anonymity on Cyberbullying Frequency." *Psychology of Popular Media Culture* 4, no. 2 (2015): 70–79.

Barrett, Kelly. "Women in the Workplace: Sexual Discrimination in Japan." *Human Rights Brief* 11, no. 2 (2004): 5–8.

Barthes, Roland. *The Language of Fashion.* Edited by Andy Stafford and Michael Carter. London: Bloomsbury, 2013.

Baudinette, Thomas. *Regimes of Desire: Young Gay Men, Media, and Masculinity in Tokyo.* Ann Arbor: University of Michigan Press, 2021.

Becker, Gary S. *A Treatise on the Family.* Cambridge, MA: Harvard University Press, 1993.

Benkhart, Alex. "Rural Queer Associations: Metropolitan Homonormativity and Gay Communities in Rural Japan." *electronic journal of contemporary japanese studies* 14, no. 1 (2014). http://www.japanesestudies.org.uk/ejcjs/vol14/iss1/benkhart.html.

Berlant, Lauren. *Cruel Optimism.* Durham, NC: Duke University Press, 2011.

Billard, Thomas J. "'Passing' and the Politics of Deception: Transgender Bodies, Cisgender Aesthetics, and the Policing of Inconspicuous Marginal Identities." In *The Palgrave Handbook of Deceptive Communication*, edited by Tony Docan-Morgan, 463–77. New York: Palgrave Macmillan, 2019.

Binnie, Jon. *The Globalization of Sexuality.* London: Sage, 2004.

Boris, Eileen, and Rhacel Parreñas. Introduction to *Intimate Labors: Cultures, Technologies, and the Politics of Care*, edited by Eileen Boris and Rhacel Parreñas, 1–12. Stanford, CA: Stanford University Press, 2010.

Borovoy, Amy. "Japan as Mirror: Neoliberalism's Promise and Costs." In *Ethnographies of Neoliberalism*, edited by Carol J. Greenhouse, 60–74. Philadelphia: University of Pennsylvania Press, 2010.

Borovoy, Amy. *The Too-Good Wife: Alcohol, Codependency, and the Politics of Nurturance in Postwar Japan.* Berkeley: University of California Press, 2005.

Bourdieu, Pierre. *Distinction: A Social Critique of the Judgement of Taste.* Translated by Richard Nice. Cambridge, MA: Harvard University Press, 1984.

Bourdieu, Pierre. "The Forms of Capital." In *Handbook of Theory of Research for the Sociology of Education*, edited by John Richardson, 241–58. Westport, CT: Greenwood, 1986.

Bredikhina, Liudmila, and Agnès Giard. "Becoming a Virtual Cutie: Digital Cross-Dressing in Japan." *Convergence: The International Journal of Research into New Media Technologies* 28, no. 6 (2022): 1643–61.

Brim, Matt. *Poor Queer Studies: Confronting Elitism in the University*. Durham, NC: Duke University Press, 2020.

Brown, Hannah M. "Online Clubbing and Digital Drag: Queer Nightlife in Pandemic Times." *Critical Studies in Improvisation* 14, no. 1 (2021): 1–7.

Bullock, Julia C., Ayako Kano, and James Welker, eds. *Rethinking Japanese Feminisms*. Honolulu: University of Hawai'i Press, 2018.

Calefato, Patrizia. "Fashion and Worldliness: Language and Imagery of the Clothed Body." *Fashion Theory: The Journal of Dress, Body and Culture* 1, no. 1 (1997): 69–90.

Cavalcante, Andre. *Struggling for Ordinary: Media and Transgender Belonging in Everyday Life*. New York: New York University Press, 2018.

Chae, Ou-Byung. "Japanese Colonial Structure in Korea in Comparative Perspective." In *Sociology and Empire: The Imperial Entanglements of a Discipline*, edited by George Steinmetz, 396–414. Durham, NC: Duke University Press, 2013.

Chalmers, Sharon. *Emerging Lesbian Voices from Japan*. London: Routledge, 2002.

Chamberland, Alex Alvina. "Femininity in Transgender Studies: Reflections from an Interview Study in New York City." *Lambda Nordica* 21, nos. 1–2 (2016): 107–33.

Champagne, John. "Transnationally Queer? A Prolegomenon." *Socialist Review* 27, nos. 1–2 (1999): 143–64.

Chang, Wei-Jung. "'Shitsuji kissa' ni okeru 'bl-teki mōsō' to sekushuariti: Taiwan hito fujoshi no 'mōsō'jissen' jirei kara" [The sexuality of "BL fantasy" in Taiwan: A case study of Taiwanese fujoshi's fantasy practice]. *Journal of the Graduate School of Humanities and Sciences* 15 (2013): 291–99. http://hdl.handle.net/10083/52848.

Chapman, David. "Geographies of Self and Other: Mapping Japan through the Koseki." *Asia-Pacific Journal: Japan Focus* 9, no. 29 (2011): 1–20. https://apjjf.org/2011/9/29/David-Chapman/3565/article.html.

Chasin, Alexandra. *Selling Out: The Gay and Lesbian Movement Goes to Market*. New York: Palgrave, 2000.

Chauncey, George. *Gay New York: Gender, Urban Culture, and the Making of the Gay Male World, 1890–1940*. New York: Basic Books, 1994.

Chen, Kuan-Hsing. *Asia as Method: Toward Deimperialization*. Durham, NC: Duke University Press, 2010.

Chiang, Howard, Todd A. Henry, and Helen Hok-Sze Leung. "Trans-in-Asia, Asia-in-Trans: An Introduction." *TSQ: Transgender Studies Quarterly* 5, no. 3 (2018): 298–310.

Chiang, Howard, and Alvin K. Wong. "Asia Is Burning: Queer Asia as Critique." *Culture, Theory and Critique* 58, no. 2 (2017): 121–26.

Chitty, Christopher. *Sexual Hegemony: Statecraft, Sodomy, and Capital in the Rise of the World System.* Durham, NC: Duke University Press, 2020.

Cho, Daegon, and K. Hazel Kwon. "The Impacts of Identity Verification and Disclosure of Social Cues on Flaming in Online User Comments." *Computers in Human Behavior* 51 (2015): 363–72.

Chung, Haeng-ja. "Gender and Ethnicity at Work: Korean 'Hostess' Club Rose in Japan." In *Gender and Labour in Korea and Japan: Sexing Class,* edited by Ruth Barraclough and Elyssa Faison, 128–48. New York: Routledge, 2009.

Chung, Haeng-ja. "Transnational Labor Migration in Japan: The Case of Korean Nightclub Hostesses in Osaka." *Bulletin of the National Museum of Ethnology* 40, no. 1 (2015): 101–19.

Clarke, Alison, and Daniel Miller. "Fashion and Anxiety." *Fashion Theory: The Journal of Dress, Body and Culture* 6, no. 2 (2002): 191–213.

Cole, Shaun, and Reina Lewis. "Seeing, Recording and Discussing LGBTQ Fashion and Style." *Fashion, Style and Popular Culture* 3, no. 2 (2016): 149–55.

Colls, Rachel. "Outsize/Outside: Bodily Bignesses and the Emotional Experiences of British Women Shopping for Clothes." *Gender, Place and Culture* 13, no. 5 (2006): 529–45.

Connell, R. W., and James W. Messerschmidt. "Hegemonic Masculinity: Rethinking the Concept." *Gender and Society* 19, no. 6 (2005): 829–59.

Cook, Emma E. "Intimate Expectations and Practices: Freeter Relationships and Marriage in Contemporary Japan." *Asian Anthropology* 13, no. 1 (2014): 36–51.

Crain, Marion, Winifred Poster, and Miriam Cherry. "Introduction: Conceptualizing Invisible Labor." In *Invisible Labor: Hidden Work in the Contemporary World,* edited by Marion Crain, Winifred Poster, and Miriam Cherry, 3–27. Berkeley: University of California Press, 2016.

Creekmur, Corey K., and Alexander Doty, eds. *Out in Culture: Gay, Lesbian, and Queer Essays on Popular Culture.* Durham, NC: Duke University Press, 1995.

Creighton, Millie R. "Japanese Craft Tourism: Liberating the Crane Wife." *Annals of Tourism Research* 22, no. 2 (1995): 463–78.

Creighton, Millie R. "'Sweet Love' and Women's Place: Valentine's Day, Japan Style." *Journal of Popular Culture* 27, no. 3 (1993): 1–19.

Crenshaw, Nicole, and Bonnie Nardi. "What's in a Name? Naming Practices in Online Video Games." *CHI PLAY '14: Proceedings of the First ACM SIGCHI Annual Symposium on Computer-Human Interaction in Play* (2014): 67–76. https://doi.org/10.1145/2658537.2658685.

Cruz-Malavé, Arnaldo, and Martin F. Manalansan IV. "Introduction: Dissident Sexualities/Alternative Globalisms." In *Queer Globalizations: Citizenship and the Afterlife of Colonialism,* edited by Arnaldo Cruz-Malavé and Martin F. Manalansan IV, 1–10. New York: New York University Press 2022.

Cruz-Malavé, Arnaldo, and Martin F. Manalansan IV, eds. *Queer Globalizations: Citizenship and the Afterlife of Colonialism*. New York: New York University Press, 2002.

Dalby, Liza. *Kimono: Fashioning Culture*. London: Vintage, 2001.

Dale, S. P. F. "Gender Identity, Desire, and Intimacy: Sexual Scripts and X-Gender." In *Intimate Japan: Ethnographies of Closeness and Conflict*, edited by Allison Alexy and Emma E. Cook, 164–80. Honolulu: University of Hawai'i Press, 2019.

Dale, S. P. F. "An Introduction to X-Jendā: Examining a New Gender Identity in Japan." *Intersections: Gender and Sexuality in Asia and the Pacific*, no. 31 (2012). http://intersections.anu.edu.au/issue31/dale.htm.

Dale, S. P. F. "Same-Sex Marriage and the Question of Queerness—Institutional Performativity and Marriage in Japan." *Asian Anthropology* 19, no. 2 (2020): 143–59.

Dale, S. P. F. "Transgender, Non-Binary Genders, and Intersex in Japan." In *The Routledge Companion to Gender and Japanese Culture*, edited by Jennifer Coates, Lucy Fraser, and Mark Pendleton, 60–68. London: Routledge, 2020.

Dale, S. P. F. "X-Jendā." *TSQ: Transgender Studies Quarterly* 1, nos. 1–2 (2014): 270–72. http://intersections.anu.edu.au/issue31/dale.htm.

Daniels, Inge. "Feeling at Home in Contemporary Japan: Space, Atmosphere and Intimacy." *Emotion, Space and Society* 15 (2015): 47–55.

Dasgupta, Romit. *Re-Reading the Salaryman in Japan: Crafting Masculinities*. London: Routledge, 2013.

David, Emmanuel. "Capital T: Trans Visibility, Corporate Capitalism, and Commodity Culture." *TSQ: Transgender Studies Quarterly* 4, no. 1 (2017): 28–41.

David, Emmanuel. "Purple-Collar Labor: Transgender Workers and Queer Value at Global Call Centers in the Philippines." *Gender and Society* 29, no. 2 (2015): 169–94.

Davidson, Skylar. "Gender Inequality: Nonbinary Transgender People in the Workplace." *Cogent Social Sciences* 2, no. 1 (2016): 1–12.

Davis, Natalie Zemon. *Society and Culture in Early Modern France*. Stanford, CA: Stanford University Press, 1975.

Delany, Samuel R. *Times Square Red, Times Square Blue*. New York: New York University Press, 1999.

De Lauretis, Teresa. *Technologies of Gender: Essays on Theory, Film, and Fiction*. Bloomington: Indiana University Press, 1987.

D'Emilio, John. "Capitalism and Gay Identity." In *The Lesbian and Gay Studies Reader*, edited by Henry Abelove, Michèle Aina Barale, and David M. Halperin, 467–76. New York: Routledge, 1993.

Dietler, Michael. "Consumption." In *The Oxford Handbook of Material Culture Studies*, edited by Dan Hicks and Mary C. Beaudry, 209–28. Oxford: Oxford University Press, 2010.

DiStefano, Anthony S. "Intimate Partner Violence among Sexual Minorities in Japan: Exploring Perceptions and Experiences." *Journal of Homosexuality* 56, no. 2 (2009): 121–46.

Domenig, Roland. "The Market of Flesh and the Rise of the 'Pink Film.'" In *The Pink Book: The Japanese Eroduction and Its Contents*, edited by Abé Mark Nornes, 17–48. Ann Arbor, MI: Kinema Club, 2014.

Dozier, Raine. "Female Masculinity at Work: Managing Stigma on the Job." *Psychology of Women Quarterly* 41, no. 2 (2017): 197–209.

Dray, Kelly K., Vaughn R. E. Smith, Toni P. Kostecki, Isaac E. Sabat, and Cassidy R. Thomson. "Moving beyond the Gender Binary: Examining Workplace Perceptions of Nonbinary and Transgender Employees." *Gender, Work and Organization* 27, no. 6 (2020): 1181–91.

Drucker, Peter. *Warped: Gay Normality and Queer Anticapitalism*. Chicago: Haymarket Books, 2015.

Duggan, Lisa. *The Twilight of Equality? Neoliberalism, Cultural Politics, and the Attack on Democracy*. Boston: Beacon, 2003.

Duguay, Stefanie, Anne-Marie Trépanier, and Alex Chartrand. "The Hottest New Queer Club: Investigating Club Quarantine's Off-Label Queer Use of Zoom during the COVID-19 Pandemic." *Information, Communication and Society* 26, no. 11 (2023): 2212–28.

Elias, Ana, Rosalind Gill, and Christina Scharff. "Aesthetic Labour: Beauty Politics in Neoliberalism." In *Aesthetic Labour: Rethinking Beauty Politics in Neoliberalism*, edited by Ana Elias, Rosalind Gill, and Christina Scharff, 3–50. London: Palgrave Macmillan, 2017.

Eng, David L., and Alice Y. Hom. "Introduction: Q & A: Notes on a Queer Asian America." In *Q & A: Queer in Asian America*, edited by David L. Eng and Alice Y. Hom, 1–21. Philadelphia: Temple University Press, 1998.

Eng, David L., and Jasbir K. Puar. "Introduction: Left of Queer." *Social Text* 38, no. 4 (2020): 1–23.

English, Bonnie. *Japanese Fashion Designers: The Work and Influence of Issey Miyake, Yohji Yamamotot and Rei Kawakubo*. Oxford: Berg, 2011.

Entwistle, Joanne. *The Fashioned Body: Fashion, Dress and Social Theory*. Cambridge, UK: Polity, 2015.

Faier, Lieba. *Intimate Encounters: Filipina Women and the Remaking of Rural Japan*. Berkeley: University of California Press, 2009.

Fan, Jennifer S. "From Office Ladies to Women Warriors: The Effect of the EEOL on Japanese Women." *UCLA Women's Law Journal* 10, no. 1 (1999): 103–40.

Fanasca, Marta. *Female Masculinity and the Business of Emotions in Tokyo*. London: Routledge, 2024.

Faure, Bernard. *The Red Thread: Buddhist Approaches to Sexuality*. Princeton, NJ: Princeton University Press, 1998.

Ferguson, Roderick. *Aberrations in Black: Toward a Queer of Color Critique*. Minneapolis: University of Minnesota Press, 2003.

Field, Nicola. *Over the Rainbow: Money, Class and Homophobia*. 2nd ed. Manchester, UK: Dog Horn, 2016.

Floyd, Kevin. *The Reification of Desire: Towards a Queer Marxism*. Minneapolis: University of Minnesota Press, 2009.

Fortier, Anne-Marie. "'Coming Home': Queer Migrations and Multiple Evocations of Home." *European Journal of Cultural Studies* 4, no. 4 (2001): 405–24.

Fotache, Ioana. "Subculture and Social Movement in the LGBT Boom: Constructing a Framework for Analysis." *Annals of Dimitrie Cantemir Christian University*, no. 1 (2018): 145–62. https://www.ceeol.com/search/article -detail?id=739853.

Foucault, Michel. *The History of Sexuality*. Vol. 1, *An Introduction*. Translated by Robert Hurley. New York: Vintage Books, 1990.

Foucault, Michel. *The History of Sexuality*. Vol. 2, *The Use of Pleasure*. Translated by Robert Hurley. New York: Vintage Books, 1985.

Foucault, Michel. *Language, Counter-Memory, Practice: Selected Essays and Interviews*. Translated by Donald F. Bouchard and Sherry Simon. Ithaca, NY: Cornell University Press, 1977.

Frühstück, Sabine. *Colonizing Sex: Sexology and Social Control in Modern Japan*. Berkeley: University of California Press, 2003.

Frühstück, Sabine. *Gender and Sexuality in Modern Japan*. Cambridge: Cambridge University Press, 2022.

Frühstück, Sabine, and Anne Walthall, eds. *Recreating Japanese Men*. Berkeley: University of California Press, 2011.

Fujimoto, Yukari. "The Evolution of BL as 'Playing with Gender': Viewing the Genesis and Development of BL from a Contemporary Perspective." In *Boys Love Manga and Beyond: History, Culture, and Community in Japan*, edited by Mark McLelland, Kazumi Nagaike, Katsuhiko Suganuma, and James Welker, 76–92. Jackson: University of Mississippi Press, 2015.

Fujimoto, Yukari. "Transgender: Female Hermaphrodites and Male Androgynes." *U.S.-Japan Women's Journal*, no. 27 (2004): 76–117.

Fujimoto, Yukari. *Watashi no ibasho wa doko ni aru no? Shōjo manga ga utsusu kokoro no katachi* [Where do I belong? The shape of the heart reflected in girls' comics]. Tokyo: Gakuyō shobō, 1998.

Fujimura-Fanselow, Kumiko. "The Japanese Ideology of 'Good Wives and Wise Mothers': Trends in Contemporary Research." *Gender and History* 3, no. 3 (1991): 345–48.

Fujita, Masami, Sadatoshi Matsuoka, Hiroyuki Kiyohara, Yousuke Kumakura, Yuko Takeda, Norimichi Goishi, Masayoshi Tarui, et al. "'Staying at Home' to Tackle COVID-19 Pandemic: Rhetoric or Reality? Cross-Cutting Analysis of Nine Population Groups Vulnerable to Homelessness in Japan." *Tropical Medicine and Health* 48, no. 92 (2020): 1–12.

Fushimi Noriaki, Mitsuhashi Junko, Ooe Chizuka, and Kawabe Kinzo. "Sekushuaru mainoritī no 'rentai' to wa" ["Solidarity" of sexual minorities]. In *Sei toiu "kyōen"—Taiwa-hen* [It's a "banque" what we call sex—A dialogue], edited by Fushimi Noriaki, 463–90. Tokyo: Pot, 2005.

Gagné, Nana Okura. "The Business of Leisure, the Leisure of Business: Rethinking Hegemonic Masculinity through Gendered Service in Tokyo Hostess Clubs." *Asian Anthropology* 9, no. 1 (2010): 29–55.

Galbraith, Patrick W. "Akihabara: Conditioning a Public 'Otaku' Image." *Mechademia: Second Arc* 5 (2010): 210–30.

Galbraith, Patrick W. "Bishōjo Games: 'Techno-Intimacy' and the Virtually Human in Japan." *Games Studies: The International Journal of Computer Game Research* 11, no. 2 (2011). http://gamestudies.org/1102/articles/galbraith.

Galbraith, Patrick W. "Maid Cafes: The Affect of Fictional Characters in Akihabara, Japan." *Asian Anthropology* 12, no. 2 (2013): 104–25.

Galbraith, Patrick W. "Maid in Japan: An Ethnographic Account of Alternative Intimacy." *Intersections: Gender and Sexuality in Asia and the Pacific*, no. 25 (2011). http://intersections.anu.edu.au/issue25/galbraith.htm.

Galbraith, Patrick W. "Moe: Exploring Virtual Potential in Post-Millennial Japan." *electronic journal of contemporary japanese studies* 9, no. 3 (2009). http://www.japanesestudies.org.uk/articles/2009/Galbraith.html.

Galbraith, Patrick W. *Otaku and the Struggle for Imagination in Japan*. Durham, NC: Duke University Press, 2019.

Galbraith, Patrick W. ""Otaku" Research' and Anxiety about Failed Men." In *Debating Otaku in Contemporary Japan: Historical Perspectives and New Horizons*, edited by Patrick W. Galbraith, Thiam Huat Kam, and Björn-Ole Kamm, 21–34. London: Bloomsbury, 2015.

Galbraith, Patrick W. "Otaku Sexuality in Japan." In *Routledge Handbook of Sexuality Studies in East Asia*, edited by Mark McLelland and Vera Mackie, 205–17. New York: Routledge, 2015.

Galbraith, Patrick W., and Jason G. Karlin. "Introduction: The Mirror of Idols and Celebrity." In *Idols and Celebrity in Japanese Media Culture*, edited by Patrick W. Galbraith and Jason G. Karlin, 1–32. New York: Palgrave Macmillan, 2012.

Garfinkel, Harold. *Studies in Ethnomethodology*. Englewood Cliffs, NJ: Prentice-Hall, 1967.

Gatson, Sarah N. "Self-Naming Practices on the Internet: Identity, Authenticity, and Community." *Cultural Studies ↔ Critical Methodologies* 11, no. 3 (2011): 224–35.

Geczy, Adam, and Vicki Karaminas. *Queer Style*. London: Bloomsbury, 2013.

Gelb, Joyce. "The Equal Employment Opportunity Law: A Decade of Change for Japanese Women?" *Law and Policy* 22, nos. 3–4 (2000): 385–407.

Genda, Yuji. "Youth Employment and Parasite Singles." *Japan Labor Bulletin* 39, no. 3 (2000): 9–22.

Gibson-Graham, J. K. *The End of Capitalism (as We Knew It): A Feminist Critique of Political Economy*. Minneapolis: University of Minnesota Press, 2006.

Gibson-Graham, J. K. "An Ethics of the Local." *Rethinking Marxism* 15, no. 1 (2003): 49–74.

Gill, Rosalind. "The Affective, Cultural and Psychic Life of Postfeminism: A Postfeminist Sensibility 10 Years On." *European Journal of Cultural Studies* 20, no. 6 (2017): 606–26.

Gill, Rosalind, and Christina Scharff. Introduction to *New Femininities: Postfeminism, Neoliberalism and Subjectivity*, edited by Rosalind Gill and Christina Scharff, 1–17. London: Palgrave Macmillan, 2011.

Gimlin, Debra L. *Body Work: Beauty and Self-Image in American Culture*. Berkeley: University of California Press, 2002.

Gimlin, Debra L. "What Is 'Body Work'? A Review of the Literature." *Sociology Compass* 1, no. 1 (2007): 353–70.

Gleeson, Jules Joanne, and Elle O'Rourke, eds. *Transgender Marxism*. London: Pluto, 2021.

Gluck, Carol. *Japan's Modern Myths: Ideology in the Late Meiji Period*. Princeton, NJ: Princeton University Press, 1985.

Gluckman, Amy, and Betsy Reed, eds. *Homo Economics: Capitalism, Community and Lesbian and Gay Life*. New York: Routledge, 1997.

Gopinath, Gayatri. *Impossible Desires: Queer Diasporas and South Asian Public Cultures*. Durham, NC: Duke University Press, 2005.

Gottfried, Heidi. *The Reproductive Bargain: Deciphering the Enigma of Japanese Capitalism*. Leiden: Brill, 2016.

Gottfried, Heidi, and David Fasenfest. "Understanding the Trajectory of Japanese Capitalism." *Critical Sociology* 47, no. 1 (2021): 149–61.

Grewal, Inderpal, and Caren Kaplan. "Global Identities: Theorizing Transnational Studies of Sexuality." GLQ: *A Journal of Lesbian and Gay Studies* 7, no. 4 (2001): 663–79.

Haimson, Oliver L., Avery Dame-Griff, Elias Capello, and Zahari Richter. "Tumblr Was a Trans Technology: The Meaning, Importance, History, and Future of Trans Technologies." *Feminist Media Studies* 21, no. 3 (2021): 345–61.

Halberstam, Jack. *Female Masculinity*. Durham, NC: Duke University Press, 1998.

Halberstam, Jack. *In a Queer Time and Place: Transgender Bodies, Subcultural Lives*. New York: New York University Press, 2005.

Halberstam, Jack. *The Queer Art of Failure*. Durham, NC: Duke University Press, 2011.

Hall, Stuart. "Notes on Deconstructing 'the Popular.'" In *People's History and Socialist Theory*, edited by Raphael Samuel, 227–39. London: Routledge, 1981.

Halperin, David. "A Response from David Halperin to Dennis Altman." *Australian Humanities Review* (1996). http://australianhumanitiesreview.org/2008/05/01/a-response-from-david-halperin-to-dennis-altman/.

Hansen, Gitte Marianne. "Eating Disorders and Self-Harm in Japanese Culture and Cultural Expressions." *Contemporary Japan* 23, no. 1 (2011): 49–69.

Hardt, Michael, and Antonio Negri. *Multitude: War and Democracy in the Age of Empire*. New York: Penguin, 2004.

Haritaworn, Jin, Adi Kuntsman, and Silvia Posocco. Introduction to *Queer Necropolitics*, edited by Jin Haritaworn, Adi Kuntsman, and Silvia Posocco, 1–27. New York: Routledge, 2014.

Hattori Yasushi. "LGBT seisaku no dōkō to kigyō no LGBT taiō no jōkyō" [Trends in LGBT policy and corporate responses to LGBT issues]. *Kikan seisaku keiei kenkyū*, no. 4 (2017): 91–101.

Hayashi Atsushi. "Heart Net TV (Hātonetto TV)." In *Ikizurai nara kaechaeba? Toransujendā Satsuki* [If it's hard to live, why not change it? Transgender Satsuki]. Tokyo, Japan: NHK (Nippon Hōsō Kyōkai), May 30, 2016. 29 min.

Hayashida Daisaku, Funahashi Kunio, Suzuki Takeshi, and Kita Michihiro. "'Ibasho' no yōtai hyōgen ni kansuru kiso-teki bunseki: Toshi seikatsu-sha no 'igokochi no yoi basho' ni miru ningen—kankyō kankei no kenkyū" [Fundamental analysis on place-expressions: Person-environment relationship study through workers' expression of comfortable places]. *Journal of Architecture and Planning* 69, no. 579 (2004): 45–52.

Hebdige, Dick. *Subculture: The Meaning of Style*. 1979. London: Routledge, 2002.

Hegarty, Benjamin. "The Value of Transgender: Waria Affective Labor for Transnational Media Markets in Indonesia." *TSQ: Transgender Studies Quarterly* 4, no. 1 (2017): 78–95.

Hennessy, Rosemary. *Profit and Pleasure: Sexual Identities in Late Capitalism*. New York: Routledge, 2000.

Her, Boyoon. "The Formation of the Concept of Gong-Ye in the Korean Modern Age." *Journal of Design History* 27, no. 4 (2014): 335–50.

Herring, Scott. *Another Country: Queer Anti-Urbanism*. New York: New York University Press, 2010.

Hidaka, Tomoko. *Salaryman Masculinity: Continuity and Change in Hegemonic Masculinity in Japan*. Leiden: Brill, 2010.

Hidaka, Yasuharu, and Don Operario. "Attempted Suicide, Psychological Health and Exposure to Harassment among Japanese Homosexual, Bisexual or Other Men Questioning Their Sexual Orientation Recruited via the Internet." *Journal of Epidemiology and Community Health* 60 (2006): 962–67.

Hills, Matt. "Transcultural Otaku: Japanese Representations of Fandom and Representations of Japan in Anime/Manga Fan Cultures." *Media in Transition* 2 (2002): 10–12.

Hiramori Daiki. "Seiteikimainoriti ga hataraki yasui shokuba to wa? 'LGBT ni kansuru shokuba kankyō ankēto' no bunseki kekka kara" [What is a workplace in which sexual minorities can work comfortably? From an analysis of the "workplace climate survey on LGBT"]. *Labor Survey* 561 (2017): 10–14.

Hiramori Daiki. "Shokuba ni okeru seitekimainoriti no kon'nan—Shūnyū oyobi kinzoku iyoku no tahenryōkaiseki" [Challenges of sexual and gender minorities in the workplace: Multivariate analyses of income and willingness to continue working]. *Gender and Sexual Minority* 10 (2015): 91–118.

Ho, Michelle H. S. "Affect: Nishihara Satsuki." In Japanese Media and Popular Culture: An Open-Access Digital Initiative of the University of Tokyo, edited by Patrick W. Galbraith, Jason G. Karlin, and Shunsuke Nozawa. University of Tokyo, 2020. Article published April 13, 2020. https://jmpc-utokyo.com/keyword/affect/.

Ho, Michelle H. S. "Categories That Bind: Transgender, Crossdressing, and Transnational Sexualities in Tokyo." *Sexualities* 27, nos. 1–2 (2024): 94–112.

Ho, Michelle H. S. "Consuming Women in Blackface: Racialized Affect and Transnational Femininity in Japanese Advertising." *Japanese Studies* 37, no. 1 (2017): 46–69.

Ho, Michelle H. S. "A Different Kind of Transgender Celebrity: From Entertainment Narrative to the 'Wrong Body' Discourse in Japanese Media Culture." *Television and New Media* 23, no. 8 (2022): 803–21.

Ho, Michelle H. S. "From Dansō to Genderless: Mediating Queer Styles and Androgynous Bodies in Japan." *Inter-Asia Cultural Studies* 22, no. 2 (2021): 129–38.

Ho, Michelle H. S. "Queer and Normal: Dansō (Female-to-Male Crossdressing) Lives and Politics in Contemporary Tokyo." *Asian Anthropology* 19, no. 2 (2020): 102–18.

Ho, Swee Lin. "'Playing like Men': The Extramarital Experiences of Women in Contemporary Japan." *Ethnos* 77, no. 3 (2012): 321–43.

Hochschild, Arlie Russell. *The Managed Heart: Commercialization of Human Feeling*. Berkeley: University of California Press, 1983.

Hollibaugh, Amber, and Margot Weiss. "Queer Precarity and the Myth of Gay Affluence." *New Labor Forum* 24, no. 3 (2015): 18–27.

Honda Tōru. *Moeru otoko* [Man bursting into blossom]. Tokyo: Chikuma Shobō, 2005.

hooks, bell. *Yearning: Race, Gender, and Cultural Politics*. New York: Routledge, 2015.

Horie Yuri. *Rezubian aidentitī* [Lesbian identities]. Kyoto: Rakuhoku Shuppan, 2015.

Huegel, Kelly. GLBTQ: *The Survival Guide for Gay, Lesbian, Bisexual, Transgender, and Questioning Teens*. Minneapolis: Free Spirit, 2011.

Iino Tomoko. "Sekushuaritihyōgen no tayōka isō no conseputo kafe" [Diverse expressions of sexuality: A study of the concept cafe]. *Jissen joshitankidaigaku kiyo* 37 (2016): 45–62. http://ci.nii.ac.jp/naid/120005760096.

Illouz, Eva. *Cold Intimacies: The Making of Emotional Capitalism*. Cambridge, UK: Polity, 2007.

Inoue Miya. *Kesho danshi: Otoko to onna jinsei wo nibai tanoshimu hōhō* [Cosme boy: How to enjoy life twice as a man and a woman]. Tokyo: Ohta Shuppan, 2012.

Irving, Dan. "Normalized Transgressions: Legitimizing the Transsexual Body as Productive." *Radical History Review*, no. 100 (2008): 38–59.

Isaka, Maki. *Onnagata: A Labyrinth of Gendering in Kabuki Theater*. Seattle: University of Washington Press, 2016.

Ishida, Hitoshi, Mark McLelland, and Takanori Murakami. "The Origins of 'Queer Studies' in Postwar Japan." In *Genders, Transgenders and Sexualities in Japan*, edited by Mark McLelland and Romit Dasgupta, 33–49. New York: Routledge, 2005.

Itani, Satoko. "Sick but Legitimate? Gender Identity Disorder and a New Gender Identity Category in Japan." In *Sociology of Diagnosis*, edited by PJ McGann and David J. Hutson, 281–306. Bingley, UK: Emerald Group, 2011.

Itō Kimio. *Otokorashisa no yukue: Dansei bunka no bunka shakaigaku* [The whereabouts of masculinity: Cultural sociology of men's culture]. Tokyo: Shinyōsha, 1993.

Jackson, Peter A. "Capitalism and Global Queering: National Markets, Parallels among Sexual Cultures, and Multiple Queer Modernities." *GLQ: A Journal of Lesbian and Gay Studies* 15, no. 3 (2009): 357–95.

Jackson, Peter A. "An Explosion of Thai Identities: Global Queering and Re-imagining Queer Theory." *Culture, Health and Sexuality: An International Journal for Research, Intervention and Care* 2, no. 4 (2000): 405–24.

Jackson, Peter A. *First Queer Voices from Thailand: Uncle Go's Advice Columns for Gays, Lesbians and Kathoeys*. Hong Kong: Hong Kong University Press, 2016.

Jackson, Peter A., ed. *Queer Bangkok: 21st Century Markets, Media, and Rights*. Hong Kong: Hong Kong University Press, 2011.

Jackson, Stevi. "Why a Materialist Feminism Is (Still) Possible—And Necessary." *Women's Studies International Forum* 24, nos. 3–4 (2001): 283–93.

Jacobsen, Joyce, and Adam Zeller, eds. *Queer Economics: A Reader*. New York: Routledge, 2008.

Johnson, Adrienne Renee. "Josō or 'Gender Free'? Playfully Queer 'Lives' in Visual Kei." *Asian Anthropology* 19, no. 2 (2020): 119–42.

Joseph, Miranda. *Against the Romance of Community*. Minneapolis: University of Minnesota Press, 2002.

Jung, Sun. *Korean Masculinities and Transcultural Consumption: Yonsama, Rain, Oldboy, K-Pop Idols*. Hong Kong: Hong Kong University Press, 2011.

Kadokura, Takashi. "Chapter 2. Japan's Underground Economy." *Japanese Economy* 34, no. 2 (2007): 20–49.

Kam, Thiam Huat. "The Anxieties That Make the 'Otaku': Capital and the Common Sense of Consumption in Contemporary Japan." *Japanese Studies* 33, no. 1 (2013): 39–61.

Kam, Thiam Huat. "The Common Sense That Makes the 'Otaku': Rules for Consuming Popular Culture in Contemporary Japan." *Japan Forum* 25, no. 2 (2013): 151–73.

Kanematsu, Sachiko. "The Women of Kabukichō." *Japan Quarterly* 35, no. 1 (1988): 84–89.

Kang, Miliann. *The Managed Hand: Race, Gender, and the Body in Beauty Service Work*. Berkeley: University of California Press, 2010.

Kang, Ruogu, Stephanie Brown, and Sara Kiesler. "Why Do People Seek Anonymity on the Internet? Informing Policy and Design." Paper presented at the SIGCHI Conference on Human Factors in Computing Systems (CHI '13), New York, April 27–May 2, 2013.

Kano, Ayako. *Acting like a Woman in Modern Japan: Theatre, Gender, and Nationalism*. New York: Palgrave, 2001.

Kasai, Makiko. "Sexual and Gender Minorities and Bullying in Japan." In *Sexual Orientation, Gender Identity, and Schooling: The Nexus of Research, Practice, and Policy*, edited by Stephen T. Russell and Stacey S. Horn, 185–93. Oxford: Oxford University Press, 2017.

Kawaguchi Kazunari. "Neoriberarizumu taisei to kuia teki shutai: Kajika ni tomonau mujun" [Neoliberalism and queer subjects: Contradictions accompanying visibility]. *Hiroshima Shūdai Ronshū* 54, no. 1 (2013): 151–69.

Kawamoto Nao. *Otoko no ko tachi* [About boy daughters]. Tokyo: Kawade Shobō Shinsha, 2014.

Kawamura, Yuniya. *Fashioning Japanese Subcultures*. London: Berg, 2012.

Kawamura, Yuniya. *The Japanese Revolution in Paris Fashion*. Oxford: Berg, 2004.

Kawamura, Yuniya. "Japan Fashion Subcultures." In *Japan Fashion Now*, edited by Valerie Steele, Patricia Mears, Yuniya Kawamura, and Hiroshi Narumi, 209–28. New Haven, CT: Yale University Press, 2010.

Kawasaki Kenko. *Takarazuka shōhi shakai no supekutakura* [Takarazuka: The consumer society spectacle]. Tokyo: Kōdansha Sensho Mechie, 1999.

Keegan, Cáel. "Against Queer Theory." *TSQ: Transgender Studies Quarterly* 7, no. 3 (2020): 349–53.

Khubchandani, Kareem. *Ishtyle: Accenting Gay Indian Nightlife*. Ann Arbor: University of Michigan Press, 2020.

Kikuchi Natsuno. *Nihon no posutofeminizumu joshi ryoku to neoriberarizumu* [Japan's postfeminism: Women's power and neoliberalism]. Tokyo: Ōtsukishoten, 2019.

Kinsella, Sharon. *Adult Manga: Culture and Power in Contemporary Japanese Society*. Honolulu: University of Hawai'i Press, 2000.

Kinsella, Sharon. "Cuteness, Josō, and the Need to Appeal: Otoko no ko in Male Subculture in 2010s Japan." *Japan Forum* 32, no. 3 (2020): 432–58.

Kinsella, Sharon. "Cuties in Japan." In *Women, Media and Consumption in Japan*, edited by Brian Moeran and Lise Skov, 220–54. Honolulu: University of Hawai'i Press, 1995.

Kinsella, Sharon. "Otoko no ko Manga and New Wave Crossdressing in the 2000s: A Two-Dimensional to Three-Dimensional Male Subculture." *Mechademia: Second Arc* 13, no. 1 (2020): 40–56.

Kinsella, Sharon. *Schoolgirls, Money and Rebellion in Japan*. New York: Routledge, 2013.

Kitagawa, Yukihiko. "Homeless Policy as a Policy for Controlling Poverty in Tokyo: Considering the Relationship between Welfare Measures and Punitive Measures." *Critical Sociology* 47, no. 1 (2021): 91–110.

Koch, Gabriele. *Healing Labor: Japanese Sex Work in the Gendered Economy*. Stanford, CA: Stanford University Press, 2020.

Kondo, Dorinne. *About Face: Performing Race in Fashion and Theater*. New York: Routledge, 1997.

Konings, Martijn. *The Emotional Logic of Capitalism: What Progressives Have Missed*. Stanford, CA: Stanford University Press, 2015.

Kovner, Sarah. *Occupying Power: Sex Workers and Servicemen in Postwar Japan*. Stanford, CA: Stanford University Press, 2012.

Kulick, Don. *Travesti: Sex, Gender, and Culture among Brazilian Transgendered Prostitutes*. Chicago: University of Chicago Press, 1998.

Kwan, Samantha. "Navigating Public Spaces: Gender, Race, and Body Privilege in Everyday Life." *Feminist Formations* 22, no. 2 (2010): 144–66.

Lam, Alice C. L. *Women and Japanese Management: Discrimination and Reform*. New York: Routledge, 1992.

LaMarre, Thomas. "Otaku Movement." In *Japan after Japan: Social and Cultural Life from the Recessionary 1990s to the Present*, edited by Tomiko Yoda and Harry Harootunian, 358–94. Durham, NC: Duke University Press, 2006.

Laslett, Barbara, and Johanna Brenner. "Gender and Social Reproduction: Historical Perspectives." *Annual Review of Sociology* 15 (1989): 381–404.

Lechevaliar, Sébastien. *The Great Transformation of Japanese Capitalism*. New York: Routledge, 2014.

Lee, Micky. "A Feminist Political Economy of Communication." *Feminist Media Studies* 11, no. 1 (2011): 83–87.

Leiter, Samuel L. "From Gay to Gei: The Onnagata and the Creation of Kabuki's Female Characters." *Comparative Drama* 33, no. 4 (1999–2000): 495–514.

Leopold, Ellen. "The Manufacture of the Fashion System." In *Chic Thrills: A Fashion Reader*, edited by Juliet Ash and Elizabeth Wilson, 101–17. London: Pandora, 1992.

Leupp, Gary. *Male Colors: The Construction of Homosexuality in Tokugawa Japan*. Berkeley: University of California Press, 1995.

Lewis, Vek, and Dan Irving. "Strange Alchemies: The Trans-Mutations of Power and Political Economy." *TSQ: Transgender Studies Quarterly* 4, no. 1 (2017): 4–15.

Li, Yang. "Understanding and Adapting to the New Normal." In *China's Economic New Normal: Growth, Structure, and Momentum*, edited by Fang Cai, 5–12. Singapore: Springer, 2020.

Lim, Eng-Beng. *Brown Boys and Rice Queens: Spellbinding Performance in the Asias*. New York: New York University Press, 2014.

Liu, Petrus. *Queer Marxism in Two Chinas.* Durham, NC: Duke University Press, 2015.

Liu, Petrus. *The Specter of Materialism: Queer Theory and Marxism in the Age of the Beijing Consensus.* Durham, NC: Duke University Press, 2023.

Longinotto, Kim, and Jano Williams, dir. *Shinjuku Boys.* 1995. Women Make Movies.

Looi, Mun-Keat. "Covid-19: Japan Declares State of Emergency as Tokyo Cases Soar." *BMJ* 369 (2020): m1447. https://doi.org/10.1136/bmj.m1447.

Lovelock, Michael. "Call Me Caitlyn: Making and Making over the 'Authentic' Transgender Body in Anglo-American Popular Culture." *Journal of Gender Studies* 26, no. 6 (2017): 675–87.

Lukács, Gabriella. *Scripted Affects, Branded Selves: Television, Subjectivity, and Capitalism in 1990s Japan.* Durham, NC: Duke University Press, 2010.

Lunsing, Wim. *Beyond Common Sense: Sexuality and Gender in Contemporary Japan.* London: Kegan Paul International, 2001.

Lunsing, Wim. "LGBT Rights in Japan." *Peace Review: A Journal of Social Justice* 17 (2005): 143–48.

Mackie, Vera. "Feminism and the Media in Japan." *Japanese Studies* 12, no. 2 (1992): 23–31.

Mackie, Vera. "How to Be a Girl: Mainstream Media Portrayals of Transgendered Lives in Japan." *Asian Studies Review* 32, no. 3 (2008): 411–23.

Maree, Claire. "'LGBT Issues' and the 2020 Games." *Asia-Pacific Journal: Japan Focus* 18, no. 4 (2020). https://apjjf.org/2020/4/Maree.html.

Maree, Claire. "Ore wa ore dakara ['Because I'm me']: A Study of Gender and Language in the Documentary *Shinjuku Boys.*" *Intersections: Gender, History and Culture in the Asian Context*, no. 9 (2003). http://intersections.anu.edu.au/issue9/maree.html.

Maree, Claire. *Queerqueen: Linguistic Excess in Japanese Media.* New York: Oxford University Press, 2020.

Maree, Claire. "Queer Women's Culture and History in Japan." In *Routledge Handbook of Sexuality Studies in East Asia*, edited by Mark McLelland and Vera Mackie, 230–43. New York: Routledge, 2015.

Matanle, Peter C. D. *Japanese Capitalism and Modernity in a Global Era: Refabricating Lifetime Employment Relations.* New York: Routledge, 2003.

Matsuda Saori. "Hosutesu-tachi wa nani wo uru no ka 'iro' to 'ningen kankei' no sābisu no bunseki" [What hostesses sell: Analysis of "sex appeal" and "relationship"]. Paper presented at the Japanese Society of Cultural Anthropology (JASCA) 43rd Conference, Osaka, May 29–31, 2009.

Matsuno, Emmie, and Stephanie L. Budge. "Non-Binary/Genderqueer Identities: A Critical Review of the Literature." *Current Sexual Health Reports* 9, no. 3 (2017): 116–20.

Mauss, Marcel. *The Gift: The Form and Reason for Exchange in Archaic Societies.* London: Routledge, 2002.

Maynard, Senko K. *Fluid Orality in the Discourse of Japanese Popular Culture.* Amsterdam: John Benjamins, 2016.

McConnell-Ginet, Sally. "'What's in a Name?' Social Labeling and Gender Practices." In *The Handbook of Language and Gender,* edited by Janet Holmes and Miriam Meyerhoff, 69–97. Hoboken, NJ: Blackwell, 2003.

McGlotten, Shaka. 2013. *Virtual Intimacies: Media, Affect, and Queer Sociality.* Buffalo: State University of New York Press.

McGray, Douglas. "Japan's Gross National Cool." *Foreign Policy,* no. 130 (2002): 44–54.

McLelland, Mark. "(A)cute Confusion: The Unpredictable Journey of Japanese Popular Culture." *Intersections: Gender and Sexuality in Asia and the Pacific,* no. 20 (2009). http://intersections.anu.edu.au/issue20/mclelland.htm.

McLelland, Mark. "From the Stage to the Clinic: Changing Transgender Identities in Post-War Japan." *Japan Forum* 16, no. 1 (2004): 1–20.

McLelland, Mark. "Introduction: Negotiating 'Cool Japan' in Research and Teaching." In *The End of Cool Japan: Ethical, Legal, and Cultural Challenges to Japanese Popular Culture,* edited by Mark McLelland, 1–30. New York: Routledge, 2017.

McLelland, Mark. "Japan's Original 'Gay Boom.'" In *Popular Culture, Globalization and Japan,* edited by Matthew Allen and Rumi Sakamoto, 158–73. New York: Routledge, 2006.

McLelland, Mark. *Male Homosexuality in Modern Japan: Cultural Myths and Social Realities.* London: Curzon, 2005.

McLelland, Mark. *Queer Japan from the Pacific War to the Internet Age.* Lanham, MD: Rowman and Littlefield, 2005.

McLelland, Mark. "Why Are Japanese Girls' Comics Full of Boys Bonking?" *Intensities: The Journal of Cult Media,* no. 1 (2001). https://intensitiescultmedia .files.wordpress.com/2012/12/mclelland.pdf.

McLelland, Mark, Katsuhiko Suganuma, and James Welker, eds. *Queer Voices from Japan: First-Person Narratives from Japan's Sexual Minorities.* Lanham, MD: Lexington Books, 2007.

McLelland, Mark, and James Welker. "An Introduction to 'Boys Love' in Japan." In *Boys Love Manga and Beyond: History, Culture, and Community in Japan,* edited by Mark McLelland, Kazumi Nagaike, Katsuhiko Suganuma, and James Welker, 3–20. Jackson: University of Mississippi Press, 2015.

Mears, Ashley. "Aesthetic Labor for the Sociologies of Work, Gender, and Beauty." *Sociology Compass* 8, no. 12 (2014): 1330–43.

Miles, Elizabeth. "Manhood and the Burdens of Intimacy." In *Intimate Japan: Ethnographies of Closeness and Conflict,* edited by Allison Alexy and Emma Cook, 148–63. Honolulu: University of Hawai'i Press, 2019.

Miles, Sam. "Let's (Not) Go Outside: Grindr, Hybrid Space, and Digital Queer Neighborhoods." In *The Life and Afterlife of Gay Neighborhoods,* edited by Alex Bitterman and Daniel Baldwin Hess, 203–20. New York: Springer, 2020.

Miller, Laura. *Beauty Up: Exploring Contemporary Japanese Body Aesthetics*. Berkeley: University of California Press, 2006.

Miller, Laura. "Cute Masquerade and the Pimping of Japan." *International Journal of Japanese Sociology*, no. 20 (2011): 18–29.

Miller, Laura. "Japan's Cinderella Motif: Beauty Industry and Mass Culture Interpretations of a Popular Icon." *Asian Studies Review* 32, no. 3 (2008): 393–409.

Miller, Laura. "Taking Girls Seriously in 'Cool Japan' Ideology." *Japan Studies Review* 15 (2011): 97–106.

Miller, Laura. "Wasei Eigo: English 'Loanwords' Coined in Japan." In *The Life of Language: Papers in Linguistics in Honor of William Bright*, edited by Jane H. Hill, P. J. Mistry, and Lyle Campbell, 123–40. Berlin: De Gruyter Mouton, 1998.

Miller, Laura. "You Are Doing Burikko! Censoring/Scrutinizing Artificers of Cute Femininity in Japanese." In *Japanese Language, Gender, and Ideology: Cultural Models and Real People*, edited by Shigeko Okamoto and Janet S. Shibamoto Smith, 148–65. Oxford: Oxford University Press, 2004.

Minowa, Yuko, Russell W. Belk, and Takeshi Matsui. "Practicing Masculinity and Reciprocation in Gendered Gift-Giving Rituals: White Day in Japan 1980–2009." In *Gifts, Romance, and Consumer Culture*, edited by Yuko Minowa and Russell W. Belk, 101–25. New York: Routledge, 2019.

Mitsuhashi Junko. *Josō to nihonjin* [Japanese people and male-to-female cross-dressing]. Tokyo: Kodansha Gendai Shinsho, 2008.

Mitsuhashi, Junko. "My Life as a 'Woman.'" Translated by Katsuhiko Suganuma. In *Queer Voices: First-Person Narratives from Japan's Sexual Minorities*, edited by Katsuhiko Suganuma, Mark McLelland, and James Welker, 295–312. Lanham, MD: Lexington, 2007.

Mitsuhashi Junko. "Nihon toranjendā ryakushi (sono 2)—Sengo no shintenkai" [Brief history of transgender in Japan number 2: Postwar new developments]. In *Toransujendarizumu sengen: Seibetsu no jikoketteiken to tayō na sei no kōtei* [Transgenderism declaration: Sex/gender rights and affirmation of diverse genders/sexualities], edited by Izumi Yonezawa, 104–18. Tokyo: Shakaihihyōsha, 2003.

Mitsuhashi, Junko. "The Transgender World in Contemporary Japan: The Male to Female Cross-Dressers' Community in Shinjuku." *Inter-Asia Cultural Studies* 7, no. 2 (2006): 202–27.

Miyake Riichi. *Akihabara wa ima* [Akihabara forever]. Tokyo: Geijutsushinbunsha, 2010.

Miyazaki, Ayumi. "Hybrid Masculinities? Reflexive Accounts of Japanese Youth at University Josō Contests." In *Gender in Japanese Popular Culture: Rethinking Masculinities and Femininities*, edited by Sirpa Salenius, 123–50. Cham, Switzerland: Palgrave Macmillan, 2023.

Mizoguchi, Akiko. "Male-Male Romance by and for Women in Japan: A History and the Subgenres of 'Yaoi' Fictions." *U.S.-Japan Women's Journal*, no. 25 (2003): 49–75.

Monden, Masafumi. *Japanese Fashion Cultures: Dress and Gender in Contemporary Japan*. London: Bloomsbury, 2015.

moore, madison. *Fabulous: The Rise of the Beautiful Eccentric*. New Haven, CT: Yale University Press, 2018.

Mori, Kenji. "The Development of the Modern Koseki." Translated by Karl Jacob Krogness. In *Japan's Household Registration System and Citizenship: Koseki, Identification and Documentation*, edited by David Chapman and Karl Jacob Krogness, 59–75. New York: Routledge, 2014.

Morinaga Takurō. *Moe keizaigaku* [The study of *moe* economics]. Tokyo: Kodansha, 2005.

Morinaga Takurō. *Nenshūbōei daikyōkō jidai ni jibunbōeiryoku* [Annual defense: Self-defense forces in an era of Great Depression]. Tokyo: Kadokawa ssc Shinsho, 2008.

Muñoz, José Esteban. *Cruising Utopia: The Then and There of Queer Futurity*. New York: New York University Press, 2009.

Muñoz, José Esteban. *Disidentifications: Queers of Color and the Performance of Politics*. Minneapolis: University of Minnesota Press, 1999.

Nadal, Kevin L., Vivian H. Vargas, Vanessa Meterko, Sahran Hamit, and Kathryn Mclean. "Transgender Female Sex Workers in New York City: Personal Perspectives, Gender Identity Development, and Psychological Processes." In *Managing Diversity in Today's Workplace: Strategies for Employees and Employers*, vol. 1, *Gender, Race, Sexual Orientation, Ethnicity, and Power*, edited by Michele A. Paludi, 123–53. Santa Barbara, CA: Praeger, 2012.

Nagai Yoshikazu. *Teihon fūzoku eigyō toshimari fūeihō to sei dansu kajino wo kisei suru kono kuni no arikata* [Standard edition management of Adult Entertainment Law: How this country should regulate sex, dance, and casino]. Tokyo: Kawade, 2015.

Nagaike, Kazumi. *Fantasies of Cross-Dressing: Japanese Women Write Male-Male Erotica*. Leiden: Brill, 2012.

Nagao Yukiko. "Shūshoku katsudō ni okeru seiteki mainoriti (LGBTQ) gakusei no shien—Fukusō kihan wo chūshin ni" [Supporting sexual minority (LGBTQ) students during job hunting: Focusing on clothing norms]. *Career Education and Research* 36 (2018): 31–39.

Nagar, Richa, and Amanda Lock Swarr. "Introduction: Theorizing Transnational Feminist Praxis." In *Critical Transnational Feminist Praxis*, edited by Amanda Lock Swarr and Richa Nagar, 1–20. Albany: State University of New York Press, 2010.

Nakamura, Junichi, and Shinichi Fukuda. "What Happened to 'Zombie' Firms in Japan? Reexamination for the Lost Two Decades." *Global Journal of Economics* 2, no. 2 (2013): 1–18.

Nakamura, Karen, and Hisako Matsuo. "Female Masculinity and Fantasy Spaces: Transcending Genders in the Takarazuka Theatre and Japanese Popular Culture." In *Men and Masculinities in Contemporary Japan: Dislocating the*

*Salaryman Doxa*, edited by James E. Roberson and Nobue Suzuki, 59–73. New York: Routledge, 2003.

Nakano, Lynne. "Working and Waiting for an 'Appropriate Person': How Single Women Support and Resist Family in Japan." In *Home and Family in Japan: Continuity and Transformation*, edited by Richard Ronald and Allison Alexy, 131–51. London: Routledge, 2011.

Namaste, Viviane. *Sex Change, Social Change: Reflections on Identity, Institutions, and Imperialism*. Toronto: Women's Press, 2011.

Negrin, Llewellyn. *Appearance and Identity: Fashioning the Body in Postmodernity*. New York: Palgrave Macmillan, 2008.

Newitz, Annalee. "Anime Otaku: Japanese Animation Fans Outside Japan." *Bad Subjects* 13, no. 11 (1994): 1–14.

Nijiiro Diversity and Center for Gender Studies (CGS) at International Christian University. *Niji VOICE 2018 Report*. Tokyo: Nijiiro Diversity and CJS, 2018. https://nijibridge.jp/wp-content/uploads/2020/11/nijiVOICE2018.pdf.

Nijiiro Diversity and Center for Gender Studies (CGS) at International Christian University. *Niji VOICE 2019 Report*. Tokyo: Nijiiro Diversity and CJS, 2019. https://nijibridge.jp/wp-content/uploads/2020/11/20200125nijiVOICE _web.pdf.

Nijiiro Diversity and Center for Gender Studies (CGS) at International Christian University. *Niji VOICE 2020 Report*. Tokyo: Nijiiro Diversity and CJS, 2020. https://nijibridge.jp/wp-content/uploads/2020/12/nijiVOICE2020.pdf.

Nijiiro Diversity and Center for Gender Studies (CGS) at International Christian University. *Niji VOICE 2022 Report*. Tokyo: Nijiiro Diversity and CJS, 2023. https://nijibridge.jp/wp-content/uploads/2023/03/nijiVOICE2022 _report.pdf.

Nishikawa Kinue. "'Igokochi' to 'ibasho' no gainen no kentō" [Examination of the concepts "igokochi" and "ibasho"]. *Journal of the Graduate School of Business Administration*, no. 17 (2021): 1–11.

Nomura Research Institute. *Otaku shijō no kenkyū* [Research on the otaku market]. Tokyo: Tōyō Keizai Shinpōsha, 2005.

Norma, Caroline. "Prostitution and the 1960s' Origins of Corporate Entertaining in Japan." *Women's Studies International Forum* 34, no. 6 (2011): 509–19.

Nornes, Abé Mark. Introduction to *The Pink Book: The Japanese Eroduction and Its Contents*, edited by Abé Mark Nornes, 1–16. Ann Arbor, MI: Kinema Club, 2014.

Nozawa, Shunsuke. "Phatic Traces: Sociality in Contemporary Japan." *Anthropological Quarterly* 88, no. 2 (2015): 373–400.

Nye, Joseph S. *Soft Power: The Means to Success in World Politics*. New York: Public Affairs, 2004.

Obata, Fumiko. "The Law to Prevent 'Power Harassment' in Japan." *Japan Labor Issues* 5, no. 28 (2021): 23–36.

Obinger, Julia. "Working on the Margins: Japan's Precariat and Working Poor." *Electronic Journal of Contemporary Japanese Studies* 9, no. 1 (2009). http://www.japanesestudies.org.uk/discussionpapers/2009/Obinger.html.

Oe, Chizuka, Masae Torai, Aya Kamikawa, and Kumiko Fujimura-Fanselow. "Dialogue: Three Activists on Gender and Sexuality." Translated by Minata Hara. In *Transforming Japan: How Feminism and Diversity Are Making a Difference*, edited by Kumiko Fujimura-Fanselow, 177–96. New York: Feminist Press, 2011.

Okano, Kaori H. *Young Women in Japan: Transitions to Adulthood*. New York: Routledge, 2009.

O'Shea, Saoirse Caitlin. "I Am Not That Caitlin: A Critique of Both the Transphobic Media Reaction to Caitlyn Jenner's *Vanity Fair* Cover Shoot and of Passing." *Culture and Organization* 25, no. 3 (2019): 202–16.

Ōtsuka Akio. *Seiyūdamashī* [A voice artist's soul]. Tokyo: Seikasha Shinsho, 2015.

Parreñas, Rhacel. *Illicit Flirtations: Labor, Migration, and Sex Trafficking in Tokyo*. Stanford, CA: Stanford University Press, 2011.

Peele, Thomas, ed. *Queer Popular Culture: Literature, Media, Film, and Television*. New York: Palgrave Macmillan, 2007.

Peletz, Michael G. *Gender Pluralism: Southeast Asia since Early Modern Times*. New York: Routledge, 2009.

Pflugfelder, Gregory M. *Cartographies of Desire: Male-Male Sexuality in Japanese Discourse, 1600–1950*. Berkeley: University of California Press, 2007.

Pike, Kathleen M., and Amy Borovoy. "The Rise of Eating Disorders in Japan: Issues of Culture and Limitations of the Model of 'Westernization.'" *Culture, Medicine and Psychiatry* 28 (2004): 493–531.

Plourde, Lorraine. "Cat Cafes, Affective Labor, and the Healing Boom in Japan." *Japanese Studies* 34, no. 2 (2014): 115–33.

Podmore, Julia A. "Disaggregating Sexual Metronormativities: Looking Back at 'Lesbian' Urbanisms." In *The Routledge Research Companion to Geographies of Sex and Sexualities*, edited by Gavin Brown and Kath Browne, 21–28. London: Routledge, 2016.

Poitras, Gilles. "Contemporary Anime in Japanese Pop Culture." In *Japanese Visual Culture: Explorations in the World of Manga and Anime*, edited by Mark W. MacWilliams, 48–67. Armonk, NY: M. E. Sharpe, 2008.

Puar, Jasbir K. "Global Circuits: Transnational Sexualities and Trinidad." *Signs: Journal of Women in Culture and Society* 26, no. 4 (2001): 1039–65.

Puar, Jasbir K. *The Right to Maim: Debility, Capacity, Disability*. Durham, NC: Duke University Press, 2017.

Raha, Nat. "A Queer Marxist Transfeminism: Queer and Trans Social Reproduction." In *Transgender Marxism*, edited by Jules Joanne Gleeson and Elle O'Rourke, 85–115. London: Pluto, 2021.

Rainie, Lee, Sara Kiesler, Ruogu Kang, Mary Madden, Maeve Duggan, Stephanie Brown, and Laura Dabbish. *Anonymity, Privacy, and Security Online*.

Washington, DC: Pew Research Center, 2013. https://www.pewresearch.org /internet/2013/09/05/anonymity-privacy-and-security-online/.

Ramírez, Horacio N. Roque. "Gay Latino Cultural Citizenship: Predicaments of Identity and Visibility in San Francisco in the 1990s." In *Gay Latino Studies: A Critical Reader*, edited by Michael Hames-García and Ernesto Javier Martínez, 175–97. Durham, NC: Duke University Press, 2011.

Reddy-Best, Kelly L., and Elaine L. Pedersen. "Queer Women's Experiences Purchasing Clothing and Looking for Clothing Styles." *Clothing and Textiles Research Journal* 33, no. 4 (2015): 265–79.

Reddy-Best, Kelly L., and Elaine L. Pedersen. "The Relationship of Gender Expression, Sexual Identity, Distress, Appearance, and Clothing Choices for Queer Women." *International Journal of Fashion Design, Technology and Education* 8, no. 1 (2015): 54–65.

Reichert, Jim. *In the Company of Men: Representations of Male-Male Sexuality in Meiji Literature*. Stanford, CA: Stanford University Press, 2006.

Roberson, James E., and Nobue Suzuki. Introduction to *Men and Masculinities in Contemporary Japan: Dislocating the Salaryman Doxa*, edited by James E. Roberson and Nobue Suzuki, 1–19. New York: Routledge, 2003.

Robertson, Jennifer. *Takarazuka: Sexual Politics and Popular Culture in Modern Japan*. Berkeley: University of California Press, 1998.

Robinson, Amanda S. "Finding Healing through Animal Companionship in Japanese Animal Cafés." *Medical Humanities* 45, no. 2 (2019): 190–98.

Robinson, Amanda S. "Paid Companions: Human-Nonhuman Animal Relations in Japanese Animal Cafés." *Society and Animals* 3, no. 3 (2022): 340–56.

Ronald, Richard, and Allison Alexy, eds. *Home and Family in Japan: Continuity and Transformation*. New York: Routledge, 2011.

Roquet, Paul. *Ambient Media: Japanese Atmospheres of Self*. Minneapolis: University of Minnesota Press, 2016.

Rosenberg, Jordy, and Amy Villarejo. "Introduction: Queerness, Norms, Utopia." GLQ: *A Journal of Lesbian and Gay Studies* 18, no. 1 (2012): 1–18.

Saeki Junko. *Josō to dansō no bunkashi* [The cultural history of male-to-female and female-to-male crossdressing]. Tokyo: Kodansha Sensho Metier, 2009.

Sakurai, Tetsuo. "The Generation Gap in Japanese Society since the 1960s." In *Japan's Changing Generations: Are Young People Creating a New Society?*, edited by Gordon Mathews and Bruce White, 15–30. London: Routledge, 2004.

Salamon, Gayle. *The Life and Death of Latisha King: A Critical Phenomenology of Transphobia*. New York: New York University Press, 2018.

Salerno, John P., Natasha D. Williams, and Karina A. Gattamorta. "LGBTQ Populations: Psychologically Vulnerable Communities in the COVID-19 Pandemic." *Psychological Trauma: Theory, Research, Practice, and Policy* 12, no. 1 (2020): 239–42.

Schilt, Kristen. *Just One of the Guys? Transgender Men and the Persistence of Gender Inequality*. Chicago: University of Chicago Press, 2010.

Schilt, Kristen, and Laurel Westbrook. "Doing Gender, Doing Heteronormativity: 'Gender Normals,' Transgender People, and the Social Maintenance of Heterosexuality." *Gender and Society* 23, no. 4 (2009): 440–64.

Sears, Alan. "Queer Anti-Capitalism: What's Left of Lesbian and Gay Liberation?" *Science and Society* 69, no. 1 (2005): 92–112.

Sedgwick, Eve Kosofsky. *Tendencies*. New York: Routledge, 1994.

Sender, Katherine. *Business, Not Politics: The Making of the Gay Market*. New York: Columbia University Press, 2004.

Shah, Nayan. *Stranger Intimacy: Contesting Race, Sexuality and the Law in the North American West*. Berkeley: University of California Press, 2011.

Shamoon, Deborah. *Passionate Friendship: The Aesthetics of Girls' Culture in Japan*. Honolulu: University of Hawai'i Press, 2012.

Shigematsu, Setsu. *Scream from the Shadows: The Women's Liberation Movement in Japan*. Minneapolis: University of Minnesota Press, 2012.

Shilling, Chris. *The Body and Social Theory*. London: Sage, 2003.

Shilling, Chris. "Educating the Body: Physical Capital and the Production of Social Inequalities." *Sociology* 25, no. 4 (1991): 653–72.

Shimizu Akiko. "Yōkoso, gei furendorī na machi e" [Welcome to the gay-friendly city]. *Gendai Shisō* 43, no. 16 (2015): 144–55.

Slade, Toby. *Japanese Fashion: A Cultural History*. Oxford: Berg, 2009.

Slater, David H., and Patrick W. Galbraith. "Re-narrating Social Class and Masculinity in Neoliberal Japan: An Examination of the Media Coverage of the 'Akihabara Incident' of 2008." *electronic journal of contemporary japanese studies* 11, no. 3 (2011). https://japanesestudies.org.uk/articles/2011/SlaterGalbraith.html.

Smith, Dorothy E. *The Everyday World as Problematic: A Feminist Sociology*. Boston: Northeastern University Press, 1987.

Spade, Dean. "Compliance Is Gendered: Struggling for Gender Self-Determination in a Hostile Economy." In *Transgender Rights*, edited by Paisley Currah, Richard M. Juang, and Shannon Minter Price, 217–41. Minneapolis: University of Minnesota Press, 2006.

Stachowiak, Dana M. "Queering It Up, Strutting Our Threads, and Baring Our Souls: Genderqueer Individuals Negotiating Social and Felt Sense of Gender." *Journal of Gender Studies* 26, no. 5 (2017): 532–43.

Steele, Valerie. "A Queer History of Fashion: From the Closet to the Catwalk." In *A Queer History of Fashion: From the Closet to the Catwalk*, edited by Valerie Steele, 7–76. New Haven, CT: Yale University Press, 2013.

Steinfield, Jemimah. "Forced Out of the Closet: As People Live Out More of Their Lives Online Right Now, Our Report Highlights How LGBTQ Dating Apps Can Put People's Lives at Risk." *Index on Censorship* 49, no. 2 (2020): 101–4.

Stewart, Kathleen. *Ordinary Affects*. Durham, NC: Duke University Press, 2007.

Stickland, Leonie R. *Gender Gymnastics: Performing and Consuming Japan's Takarazuka Revue*. Melbourne: Trans Pacific Press, 2008.

Stryker, Susan. *Transgender History: The Roots of Today's Revolution*. 2nd ed. Berkeley, CA: Seal, 2017.

Stryker, Susan. "Transgender Studies: Queer Theory's Evil Twin." *GLQ: A Journal of Lesbian and Gay Studies* 10, no. 2 (2004): 212–15.

Stryker, Susan, and Aren Z. Aizura. "Introduction: Transgender Studies 2.0." In *The Transgender Studies Reader 2*, edited by Susan Stryker and Aren Z. Aizura, 1–12. New York: Routledge, 2013.

Suganuma, Katsuhiko. "Sexual Minority Studies on Japan." In *Routledge Handbook of Sexuality Studies in East Asia*, edited by Mark McLelland and Vera Mackie, 244–54. New York: Routledge, 2015.

Sugiura, Ikuko. "Increasing Lesbian Visibility." In *Transforming Japan: How Feminism and Diversity Are Making a Difference*, edited by Kumiko Fujimura-Fanselow, 164–76. New York: Feminist Press, 2011.

Sugiura, Ikuko. "Lesbian Discourses in Mainstream Magazines of Post-War Japan." *Journal of Lesbian Studies* 10, nos. 3–4 (2007): 127–44.

Sunagawa Hideki. "Kison no yokuatsu ni kajū sareru kon'nan: Shingata korona uirusu kansenshō to LGBT" [Difficulties compounded by existing oppression: New coronavirus infections and LGBT]. *Buraku Kaihō* 802 (2021): 30–44.

Sunagawa Hideki. *Shinjuku ni-chōme no bunka-jinruigaku: Gei komyuniti kara toshi wo manazasu* [A cultural anthropology of Shinjuku Ni-chōme: Looking at the city from the perspective of the gay community]. Tokyo: Tarōjirō Editāzu, 2015.

Sunagawa Hideki. "Tayō na shihai, tayō na teikō" [Diverse rule, diverse resistance]. *Gendai Shisō* 43, no. 16 (2015): 100–6.

Swarr, Amanda Lock. *Sex in Transition: Remaking Gender and Race in South Africa*. Albany: State University of New York Press, 2012.

Takeda, Hiroko. "Structural Reform of the Family and the Neoliberalisation of Everyday Life in Japan." *New Political Economy* 13, no. 2 (2008): 153–72.

Takeyama, Akiko. *Staged Seduction: Selling Dreams in a Tokyo Host Club*. Stanford, CA: Stanford University Press, 2016.

Tamagawa, Masami. *The Japanese LGBTQ+ Community in the World: The Covid-19 Pandemic, Challenges, and the Prospects for the Future*. London: Routledge, 2022.

Tanaka Ray. *Toransujendā feminizumu* [Transgender feminism]. Tokyo: Impact, 2006.

Taniguchi, Hiroyuki. "Japan's 2003 Gender Identity Disorder Act: The Sex Reassignment Surgery, No Marriage, and No Child Requirements as Perpetuations of Gender Norms in Japan." *Asian-Pacific Law and Policy Journal* 14, no. 2 (2013): 108–17.

Taylor, Emily. "Dating-Simulation Games: Leisure and Gaming of Japanese Youth Culture." *Southeast Review of Asian Studies* 29 (2007): 192–208.

Taylor, Jami K., Daniel C. Lewis, and Donald P. Haider-Markel. *The Remarkable Rise of Transgender Rights*. Ann Arbor: University of Michigan Press, 2018.

Teti, Michelle, Kristen Morris, L. A. Bauerband, Abigial Rolbiecki, and Cole Young. "An Exploration of Apparel and Well-Being among Transmasculine Young Adults." *Journal of LGBT Youth* 17, no. 1 (2020): 53–69.

Thornton, Sarah. *Club Cultures: Music, Media and Subcultural Capital.* Cambridge, UK: Polity, 1995.

Tokuhiro, Yoko. *Marriage in Contemporary Japan.* London: Routledge, 2010.

Tongson, Karen. *Relocations: Queer Suburban Imaginaries.* New York: New York University Press, 2011.

Torai Masae. *Kataritsugu toransujendā-shi* [Transgender history to be handed down]. Tokyo: Jūgatsusha, 2003.

Toyama, Hitomi. "The Era of Dandy Beauties." Translated by James Welker. In *Queer Voices from Japan: First-Person Narratives from Japan's Sexual Minorities*, edited by Mark McLelland, Katsuhiko Suganuma, and James Welker, 153–65. Lanham, MD: Lexington Books, 2007.

Toyama Hitomi. *Miss Dandy: Otoko to shite ikiru josei-tachi* [Miss Dandy: Women living as men]. Tokyo: Shinchōsha, 1999.

Tracy, Sarah J. *Qualitative Research Methods: Collecting Evidence, Crafting Analysis, Communicating Impact.* Hoboken, NJ: Wiley Blackwell, 2020.

Tsing, Anna Lowenhaupt. *The Mushroom at the End of the World: On the Possibility of Life in Capitalist Ruins.* Princeton, NJ: Princeton University Press, 2015.

Tsing, Anna Lowenhaupt. "Sorting Out Commodities: How Capitalist Value Is Made through Gifts." *Hau: Journal of Ethnographic Theory* 3, no. 1 (2013): 21–43.

Tsuruta Sachie. *Seidōitsuseishougai no esunogurafī* [An ethnography of gender identity disorder]. Tokyo: Harvest, 2009.

Udris, Reinis. "Cyberbullying among High School Students in Japan: Development and Validation of the Online Disinhibition Scale." *Computers in Human Behavior* 41 (2014): 253–61.

Uema Yoko. "Gendai joshi kōkōsei no aidentiti keisei" [The identity formation of present-day high school girls]. PhD diss., Tokyo Metropolitan University, 2002.

Ueno, Chizuko. *The Modern Family in Japan: Its Rise and Fall.* Melbourne: TransPacific Press, 2009.

Ueno, Chizuko. *Nationalism and Gender.* Translated by Beverley Yamamoto. Melbourne: Trans Pacific Press, 2004.

United Nations. *The World's Cities in 2018: Data Booklet.* New York: United Nations, 2018. https://digitallibrary.un.org/record/3799524?ln=en.

Uno, Kathleen S. "The Death of 'Good Wife, Wise Mother'?" In *Postwar Japan as History*, edited by Andrew Gordon, 293–322. Berkeley: University of California Press, 1993.

Valentine, David. *Imagining Transgender: An Ethnography of a Category.* Durham, NC: Duke University Press, 2007.

Valentine, David. "'I Went to Bed with My Own Kind Once': The Erasure of Desire in the Name of Identity." In *The Transgender Studies Reader*, edited by Susan Stryker and Stephen Whittle, 407–19. New York: Routledge, 2006.

Valentine, James. "Pots and Pans: Identification of Queer Japanese in Terms of Discrimination." In *Queerly Phrased: Language, Gender, and Sexuality*, edited by Anna Livia and Kira Hall, 95–114. Oxford: Oxford University Press, 1997.

Vijlbrief, Afiah, Sawitri Saharso, and Halleh Ghorashi. "Transcending the Gender Binary: Gender Nonbinary Young Adults in Amsterdam." *Journal of LGBT Youth* 17, no. 1 (2020): 89–106.

Wacquant, Loïc J. D. "Pugs at Work: Bodily Capital and Bodily Labour among Professional Boxers." *Body and Society* 1, no. 1 (1995): 65–93.

Wakatabe, Masazumi. "Is There Any Cultural Difference in Economics? Keynesianism and Monetarism in Japan." In *The Development of Economics*, edited by Tochiro Asada, 134–54. London: Routledge, 2014.

Wallace, Jane. "Stepping-Up: 'Urban' and 'Queer' Cultural Capital in LGBT and Queer Communities in Kansai, Japan." *Sexualities* 23, no. 4 (2020): 666–82.

Ward, Jane. "Gender Labor: Transmen, Femmes, and Collective Work of Transgression." *Sexualities* 13, no. 2 (2010): 236–54.

Weber, Brenda R. *Makeover TV: Selfhood, Citizenship, and Celebrity*. Durham, NC: Duke University Press, 2009.

Weeks, Jeffrey. *Sexuality and Its Discontents: Meanings, Myths, and Modern Sexualities*. London: Routledge, 2002.

Wei, John. *Queer Chinese Cultures and Mobilities: Kinship, Migration, and Middle Classes*. Hong Kong: Hong Kong University Press, 2020.

Welker, James. "Beautiful, Borrowed, and Bent: 'Boys' Love' as Girls' Love in Shōjo Manga." *Signs* 31, no. 3 (2006): 841–70.

Welker, James. "Lilies of the Margin: Beautiful Boys and Queer Female Identities in Japan." In *AsiaPacifiQueer: Rethinking Genders and Sexualities*, edited by Peter A. Jackson, Fran Martin, Mark McLelland, and Audrey Yue, 46–66. Urbana: University of Illinois Press, 2008.

Welker, James. "Telling Her Story: Narrating a Japanese Lesbian Community." *Journal of Lesbian Studies* 14, no. 4 (2010): 359–80.

Welker, James. "Toward a History of 'Lesbian History' in Japan." *Culture, Theory and Critique* 58, no. 2 (2017): 147–65.

Westbrook, Laurel, and Kristen Schilt. "Doing Gender, Determining Gender: Transgender People, Gender Panics, and the Maintenance of the Sex/Gender/Sexuality System." *Gender and Society* 28, no. 1 (2014): 32–57.

Whittle, Stephen. "Where Did We Go Wrong? Feminism and Trans Theory—Two Teams on the Same Side." In *The Transgender Studies Reader*, edited by Susan Stryker and Stephen Whittle, 194–202. New York: Routledge, 2006.

Williams, Raymond. *Marxism and Literature*. Oxford: Oxford University Press, 1977.

Wilson, Ara. *The Intimate Economies of Bangkok: Tomboys, Tycoons, and Avon Ladies in the Global City*. Berkeley: University of California Press, 2004.

Wilson, Ara. "Queering Asia." *Intersections: Gender and Sexuality in Asia and the Pacific*, no. 14 (2006). http://intersections.anu.edu.au/issue14/wilson.html.

Wilson, Elizabeth. *Adorned in Dreams: Fashion and Modernity*. London: I. B. Tauris, 2003.

Winge, Therèsa M. "Tokyo Subcultural Street Styles: Japanese Subcultural Street Style as a Uniform." *East Asian Journal of Popular Culture* 3, no. 1 (2017): 7–21.

Winge, Therèsa M. "Undressing and Dressing Loli: A Search for the Identity of the Japanese Lolita." *Mechademia: Second Arc* 3 (2008): 47–63.

Wolkowitz, Carol. *Bodies at Work*. London: Sage, 2006.

Wood, Andrea. "Boys' Love Anime and Queer Desires in Convergence Culture: Transnational Fandom, Censorship and Resistance." *Journal of Graphic Novels and Comics* 4, no. 1 (2013): 44–63.

Wood, Andrea. "'Straight' Women, Queer Texts: Boy-Love Manga and the Rise of a Global Counterpublic." *Women's Studies Quarterly* 34, nos. 1–2 (2006): 394–414.

Xie, Tianyi Vespera. "Ikemen Dansō Girls: How Cross-Dressing Girls Portray the Ideal Gender in Contemporary Japan." In *Beyond Kawaii: Studying Japanese Femininities at Cambridge*, edited by Brigitte Steger, Angelika Koch, and Christopher Tso, 193–226. Zurich: Deutsche Nationalbibliothek, 2020.

Yagi, Yoko. *Tokyo Street Style*. New York: Abrams, 2018.

Yamada Masahiro. *Parasaito shinguru no jidai* [The era of parasite singles]. Tokyo: Chikuma Shinsho, 1999.

Yamada, Toshio. "Japanese Capitalism and the Companyist Compromise." In *Japanese Capitalism in Crisis: A Regulationist Interpretation*, edited by Robert Boyer and Toshio Yamada, 19–31. New York: Routledge, 2000.

Yamagishi, Reiko. "A Promised Land for Men: The Rising Popularity of Hosts in Contemporary Japanese Society." PhD diss., National University of Singapore, 2009.

Yano, Christine R. *Pink Globalization: Hello Kitty's Trek across the Pacific*. Durham, NC: Duke University Press, 2013.

Yonezawa Izumi. "Media to toranjendā" [Media and transgender]. In *Toransujendarizumu sengen: Seibetsu no jikoketteiken to tayō na sei no kōtei* [Transgenderism declaration: Sex/gender rights and affirmation of diverse genders/sexualities], edited by Izumi Yonezawa, 77–83. Tokyo: Shakaihihyōsha, 2003.

Yoshimi, Shunya. "'Made in Japan': The Cultural Politics of 'Home Electrification' in Postwar Japan." *Media, Culture and Society* 21, no. 2 (1999): 149–71.

Yoshimoto, Mitsuhiro. "The Postmodern and Mass Images in Japan." *Public Culture* 1, no. 2 (1989): 8–25.

Yoshimoto Taimatsu. "Shota josōshōnen otoko no ko: Nijigenhyōgen niokeru 'otoko no ko' no hensen" [Shota crossdressing boys otoko no ko: Transition of two-dimensional "otoko no ko"]. *Eureka* 667, no. 47-13 (2015): 210–24.

Yue, Audrey. "Trans-Singapore: Some Notes towards Queer Asia as Method." *Inter-Asia Cultural Studies* 18, no. 1 (2017): 10–24.

Yuen, Shu Min. "Cultural Citizenship: Secret Guyz." In Japanese Media and Popular Culture: An Open-Access Digital Initiative of the University of Tokyo, edited by Patrick W. Galbraith, Jason G. Karlin, and Shunsuke Nozawa. University of Tokyo, 2020. Article published April 27, 2020. https://jmpc-utokyo.com/keyword/cultural-citizenship/.

Zahlten, Alexander. *The End of Japanese Cinema: Industrial Genres, National Times, and Media Ecologies.* Durham, NC: Duke University Press, 2017.

Zelizer, Viviana A. *The Purchase of Intimacy.* Princeton, NJ: Princeton University Press, 2005.

European homoerotic cultures, 11.
See also Chitty, Christopher
Evangelion (anime), 198n59

fabulousness (moore), 141, 142, 154, 155.
See also fashion
family registry (koseki), 55, 131, 193n76,
195n9; changing gender in, 41–42;
and GID, 42
fan. See also fandom; idol (aidoru);
moe; oshi (pushing for)
fandom: of anime, manga, games, 82,
96; as characterizing second wave of
contemporary dansō/josō cultures,
91, 144; as connected to subjectivity,
120; defined, 104; of fudanshi (rotten boys), 194n96; of fujoshi (rotten
girls), 194n96; Garçon as place for,
107; and moe (fan affect), 186n93;
related to adana (nicknames) 97;
Akihabara known as place of, 1.
See also Boys Love (BL) media;
fudanshi (rotten boys); fujoshi
(rotten girls); moe (fan affect)
Fanasca, Marta, 101; and dansō escorts,
116–17
fashion: defined, 212n3; during Edo period, 139–40; as enabling resistance
to commonsense constructions of
gender, 170; and gender, 142–44;
genders emerging from, 139; influence of on the gender binary in,
160; during Meiji period, 139–140;
as a productive site from which
genders and sexualities emerge,
148; as proliferating emergent genders, 168; queer styles as giving rise
to various genders and sexualities,
158; as a tool of survival, 9, 26, 157.
See also ganguro (black face); kogyaru (high school girl); queer style
female-to-male crossing-dressing individuals. See dansō joshi
feminine abilities. See joshi ryoku
femininity: at Paradise, 152, 156
Filipina hostess clubs, 110, 115
Fingertip Milk Tea (Yubisaki miruku tī)
(anime), 89

flexible work, 14; rise of, 15. See also
lifetime employment
Foucault, Michel, 11; and biopolitics,
114; and biopower, 42, 206n15; and
genealogical approach, 30; and
technologies of the self, 154
freeter, 37–38, 56, 76, 102–104, 118–19;
defined, 192n60
FTM Nihon (alternative media), 41.
FTM, 20, 34, 41,147, 191n37. See also FTX;
MTX; MTF; XTX
FTX, 19, 133, 138, 140, 147, 167. See also
FTM; MTX; MTF; XTX
Fudanjuku (dansō unit), 90, 104, 146,
151. See also The Hoopers (dansō
idol group)
fudanshi (rotten boys): defined,
194n96
Fujimoto Yukari, 85
fujoshi (rotten girls), 73, 81, 88, 151,
194n96, 201n6; and dansō, 82.
See also Boys Love (BL) media
fun'iki (atmosphere): at Garçon, 70,
72, 102
fureai (contact), 48, 122, 135, 137, 164;
and kakawaru (to interact with),
122. See also tsunagari (social
connectedness)
Fushimi Noriaki, 19
Fūzoku Kitan (magazine): as example
of "perverse magazine," 34; and
josō column, 34; limited dansō
stories, 34

G-Front Kansai (LGBT organization),
43. See also Poco a poco (journal)
Gaish (Shinjuku Boys), 27–30, 39–41,
56–59, 117; as popular, 112–14; as
considering working at Marilyn an
occupation, 113; as resisting categorization, 50. See also Kazuki; Marilyn
(bar); Shinjuku Boys; Tatsu
Galbraith, Patrick, 84, 117
ganguro (black face), 143; defined,
213n22, 216n80; as subcultural
street fashion, 143; together with
kogyaru and Lolita. See also
kogyaru (high school girl)

Garçon (*dansō* café-and-bar): as affirming employees' sense of self, 111; in Akihabara, 2–3, 66, 81; as alternative home, 72–74, 131; as benefiting from contemporary *dansō* culture, 151; birth of, 63–64, 82, 89; casual speech at, 70–71, 109, 134–35; categorial innovation at, 31, 82; closing of, 173, 174, 175–76; and customers attachments to employees at, 58, 99, 105, 142; description of, 2–4, 91–92; dress at, 121; employees at, 120–121, 123–24; employees motivation for working at, 111, 131–37, 119–23, 136; forbidding relationships at, 69–70, 105, 125; ownership of, 65; pink economies at, 63, 78; as potentially exploitative, 109–10, 137; as profit motivated, 54, 109; as reinforcing the status quo, 54, 58; as space for emergent genders, 6–7; salaries at, 124, 125, 126, 209n60, 209n61; special events at, 64, 71–72, 134; spending at, 71–72, 92. *See also* Akihabara; *dansō*; Garçon customers; Garçon employees; Paradise

Garçon customers: intimate bonds as survival for, 15; Hikaru, 102–5, 126, 150; Ken 65, 72–73, 78, 98; Tanaka, 99–102. *See also* Saito; Sakura

Garçon employees: Yu, 49–50, 102–3, 105, 153, 155–56, 167; Yuka (owner) 4, 7, 63–64, 65–66, 150–51, 198n61, 214n45. *See also* Hiyori; Ikki; Oban; Yuta

*Garçon Girls* (*dansō* magazine), 145; promoting *dansō* as a way of life, 147 48

gay bars, 10, 35, 78, 128, 177, 219n23; as homosexual-style, 62–63; as *josō*-style, 62–63, 81. *See also* gay boom; *gei*

gay boom, 16, 35, 38, 62, 86–87. *See also* gay bars; *gei*

gay boy boom, 16. *See also* gay boy; *gei*

gay boy (*gei bōi*), 16, 62, 185n85; Betty as, 34. *See also* Betty (singer); gay boy boom; *gei* (gay)

gay. *See gei*

*gei* (gay): defined, 16, 185n85, 192n62; *gei* politics, 38. *See also* gay boy; gender and sexual minorities (*seitekishōsūsha*); Organization for Lesbian and Gay Movement (OCCUR); *rezubian* (lesbian); other gender categories

Genda Yuji, 56

gender and sexual minorities (*seitekishōsūsha*), 10; as having cross-cultural dimensions, 38; scholarship not focused on economy, 11; as reinforcing status quo, 114; as threatening productivity, 114; as vulnerable during COVID-19, 172, 175; and digital technologies, 175–76; and discrimination, 184n61; discrimination against, 171; and the queer movement, 38. *See also* individual gender categories; Organization for Lesbian and Gay Movement (OCCUR)

gender identity disorder (GID) (*seidōitsuseishōgai*), 19; activism for, 42; discourse of, 38–39, 41–42, 187n106, 193n69; GID Act, 41, 42, 186n105; *onabe* work as resisting, 112, 114; as prescriptive, 43; rejection of, 29, 31, 42–43, 45. *See also* Act on Special Cases in Handling Gender Status for Persons with Gender Identity Disorder (*seidōitsuseishōgai-sha no seibetsu no toriatsukai no tokirei ni kansuru hōritsu*)

gender presentation: Garçon/Paradise as empowering space for, 121, 136–37

gender: and capitalism, 5, 7, 54–56; defying existing gender/sexuality categories, 7, 8, 9, 28, 43, 51, 110, 145; emerging categories of, 13, 18, 31, 51, 106, 110, 116, 165; and family registry (*koseki*), 41–42; and fashion, 139–40, 142–44, 160; identity and sexual orientation as not aligned, 21, 33, 38–39, 49, 86, 165–166; innovations, 5, 7, 13, 17, 25–26, 27, 30, 86, 88, 95, 106, 140,

gender (continued)
144; innovation at Garçon/Paradise, 82, 136, 155; innovation during recession, 37–38, 43, 116, 170; gender binary, 39, 40, 43–45, 48, 51, 62, 112, 116, 131, 132, 133, 143, 160, 187n110, 190n24; gender discrimination, 130; gender division of labor, 55, 72, 76, 84; gender experimentation, 8, 85; gender order in crisis, 77; gender pluralism, 6, 181n23; gender policing, 160; gender subjectivities, 26; and passing, 129; public embrace of gender crossing, 30, 32, 82, 144; and sexuality not tied to religious condemnation, 21; as socially constructed, 6, 143. *See also* gender and sexual minorities (*seitekishōsūsha*); gender identity disorder (GID) (*seidōitsuseishōgai*); gender presentation; individual gender categories

genderless styles: defined, 143–144; as distinct from *josō/dansō*, 144

Gibson-Graham, J. K., 5, 9, 12, 180n13, 181n39, 184n69, 185n78; and "(re) subjectivation," 139, 189n136

Gimlin, Debra, 152, 158

girls bars (*gāruzubā*), 126, 127, 129, 209n64

girls (*shōjo*) manga, 34, 83. *See also* anime, manga, games; *bishōjo* (beautiful girl); *bishōnen* (beautiful boy)

Golden Gai, 3, 179n5

good wife, wise mother, 83, 201n15

Great East Japan Earthquake, 122–23

Grewal, Inderpal, 132

*hako-oshi* (a fan of the place), 107; defined, 80–81, 102; Tanaka as, 101. See also *oshi* (pushing for)

Halberstam, Jack, 28, 116; and "female masculinity," 117, 158; and vernacular innovations, 180n14; and "in-between spaces," 92; and "queer subject," 120

Hall, Stuart: and "double-stake," 106

handsome girls boom, 151. See also *ikemen joshi*

handsome girls. See *ikemen joshi*

Hayashi (Paradise owner), 1–2, 4, 6, 7, 66–69, 124–25, 128; as a celebrity, 148; as founder of Paradise, 89; image on signboard, 93. *See also* Paradise employees; Paradise customers

healing (*iyashi*), 103, 115, 205n84; healing boom, 73, 100; healing labor, 81, 115; "healing style" (*iyashi-kei*), 100; as recuperating people to contribute to capitalist economy, 100

Hebdige, Dick, 16

Hello Kitty, 83

Hibari-tei (*otoko no ko* maid café), 89; beginnings of, 199n68; closing of, 151; as first *josō/otoko no ko* maid café in Akihabara, 67–68; relocating from Akihabara to Shinjuku, 148

high school girl cafés, 2, 81, 179n4. *See also* concept cafés; other examples of concept cafés

high school girl style. See *kogyaru* (high school girl)

*hikkikomori* (social withdrawal), 122, 208n56

*himote* (young men who are unpopular with women), 122, 208n56

Hiyori (Garçon employee), 3–4, 14, 21, 108–10, 121, 122; as adopting masculine speech, 121; and *dansō*, 21; as inspired by K-pop, 3–4, 108, 133; as non-binary, 4, 7, 14, 108; as paying the cost of body work, 156; as not aligned with LGBT, 206n1; as resisting categorization, 50; valued connection with customers, 135, 137. *See also* Garçon employees

hobby/taste. See *shumi*

Hochschild, Arlie, 116, 117

home/belonging: alternative forms of belonging, 13, 59, 78, 97; at-home space, 131, 134, 136; as critique of cis-heteronormative world, 59, 72, 76; at Garçon/Paradise, 54, 70–72; *ibasho* (homey), 56, 72; and *josō/dansō/otoko no ko* café-and-bars, 54,

parasite single (Yamada), 56, 156n18

Parreñas, Rhacel, 110, 153

passing (O'Shea), 129; defined, 210n74; failing to pass and violence, 166–67

Pedersen, Elaine, 160

pericapitalism, 9, 14, 18, 24, 25, 44, 46, 54, 171; and masculinity, 74–78; dynamics of within Garçon/Paradise, 109–10, 121; allowing emergent genders to flourish, 110, 132, 136–37; as employees' motivation for working at Garçon/Paradise, 111; 114, 119; and fan-idol relations, 104; and nonmonetary benefits, 110, 121; queer subjects within, 121; as reconfiguring productivity, 77; and relations of production, 73. *See also* capitalism

*Pia kyarotto e yōkoso* (*Welcome to Pia Carrot!!*; game), 87

pink economies 25, 171; in Akihabara, 82–88, 90, 107; defined, 35, 54, 59, 188n134; and emergent genders, 51; as encapsulated by *moe*, 83, 96; Garçon and Paradise within, 63, 70, 78, 151, 171; in Japan, 59–63; and labor, 115; as not limited to otaku, 83; located within transnational economies, 60–61; and pink capitalism and rainbow capitalism, 10; and pink yen, 59; *pinku*, 60. *See also* capitalism; Japanese economy; neoliberalism

pink films (*pinku eiga*), 60, 196n34, 196n35

*Pink Mood Show* (TV show), 60

pink salons, 60, 61, 196n33, 196n35

*Poco a poco* (journal), 43. *See also* G-Front Kansai (LGBT organization)

Polaroids (*cheki*): of/with employees, 104–5, 173, 174

popular culture: as having encouraged a (re)turn to *josō/dansō*, 106; nonnormative potential of, 85; as productive for generating gender categories, 106; reimagining to innovate genders, 85; as reworked by new gender categories, 106. *See* anime, manga, games; Akihabara

postfeminism, 152, 163, defined 216n77

postwar era/period, 16, 25, 30, 51, 55, 59, 60, 63, 72, 82; in Britain, 16; and Cool Japan, 203n45; economic growth in, 6, 59; gender division of labor in, 76, 83, 84; mass consumption in, 87, 106; and modern capitalism in Japan, 10; perverse publications in, 34; pink economies in, 60; *salaryman* in, 56; in Tokyo, 51; and the waning of women's domestic roles 83–84. *See also* Cool Japan; Japan; World War II

*Precarious Japan* (Allison), 14

precarity: of *dansō* employees 142; of *dansō/josō* café-and-bars, 174; of employees at Garçon/Paradise, 125; of gender and clothing in Japan, 142; of Japan/Japanese people, 6, 7, 14, 56, 70, 72, 170, 178; of *josō* employees, 119, 130. *See also* discrimination; Garçon; Paradise

Pretty Rhythm (multimedia franchise), 72. *See also King of Prism* (anime film spinoff)

*Princess Knight* (manga), 34

*Princess Princess* (game, anime, girls' manga), 47

Propaganda (*josō* event): closing of, 151–52, 215n47; and "Japan's largest *josō* event, 67–69. *See also* Diffusion (*josō* club party)

prostitution ban: on cis-heteronormative prostitution, 61–62; closure of brothels, 62; Prostitution Prevention Law, 60, 61

Prostitution Prevention Law (*Baishun bōshi hō*), 60, 61

proto-capitalist economies, 11

purple-collar labor (David), 127

*Puru Moenjeru Aidoru Aiko* (game), 47

quasi-heterosexual relations, 116–17

queen personalities. *See onē-tarento*

queer and trans materialist approaches, 8–13, 39, 110, 111–14; critiques from, 8

queer anti-urbanism, 116

queer Asia, 21

www.ingramcontent.com/pod-product-compliance
Lightning Source LLC
Chambersburg PA
CBHW020843270326
41928CB00006B/526